# THE AMERICAN CIVIL WAR
## 1863–1865

American History Archives™

The American Civil War
1863–1865

3 4 5 6 7 8 9 10 / 16 15 14 13 12 11
ISBN 978 1 58159 309 9

The History Channel Club
c/o North American Membership Group
12301 Whitewater Drive
Minnetonka, MN 55343
www.thehistorychannelclub.com

Published by North American Membership Group under license
from Osprey Publishing Ltd.

Previously published as Essential Histories 5: *The American
Civil War (3) The war in the East 1863–1865* and Essential
Histories 11: *The American Civil War (1) The war in the West
1863–1865* by Osprey Publishing, Midland House, West Way,
Botley, Oxford OX2 0PH, United Kingdom

© 2006 Osprey Publishing Ltd.  OSPREY
PUBLISHING

Editor: Rebecca Cullen
Design: Ken Vail Graphic Design, Cambridge, UK
Cartography by The Map Studio
Picture research by Image Select International
Index by Sandra Shotter
Originated by PPS Grasmere Ltd., Leeds, UK
Printed in China through World Print Ltd.

FRONT COVER
**Courtesy of the National Archives and Records Administration**

East (Part 1) author ROBERT K. KRICK was born in
California, and has been responsible for the preservation of
several battlefields in Virginia for more than 30 years. He is
the author of a dozen books and more than one hundred
published articles. His Stonewall Jackson at Cedar Mountain
won the Douglas Southall Freeman Award for Best Book in
Southern History.

West (Part 2) author JOSEPH T. GLATTHAAR is currently
Professor of History at the University of Houston. Among his
publications are *The March to the Sea and Beyond: Sherman's
Troops in the Savannah and Carolinas Campaign*; *Forged in Battle:
The Civil War Alliance of Black Soldiers and White Officers*; and
*Partnerships in Command: The Relationships between Leaders in
the Civil War*.

Professor ROBERT O'NEILL, AO D.Phil. (Oxon), Hon D. Litt.
(ANU), FASSA, is the Series Editor of the Essential Histories.
His wealth of knowledge and expertise shapes the series
content and provides up-to-the-minute research and theory.
Born in 1936 an Australian citizen, he served in the Australian
Army (1955–68) and has held a number of eminent positions
in history circles, including the Chichele Professorship of the
History of War at All Souls College, University of Oxford,
1987–2001, and the Chairmanship of the Board of the Imperial
War Museum and the Council of the International Institute
for Strategic Studies, London. He is the author of many books
including works on the German Army and the Nazi party, and
the Korean and Vietnam wars. Now based in Australia on his
retirement from Oxford, he is the Director of the Lowy
Institute for International Policy and Planning Director of
the US Studies Centre at the University of Sydney.

# Contents

# The United States in 1860

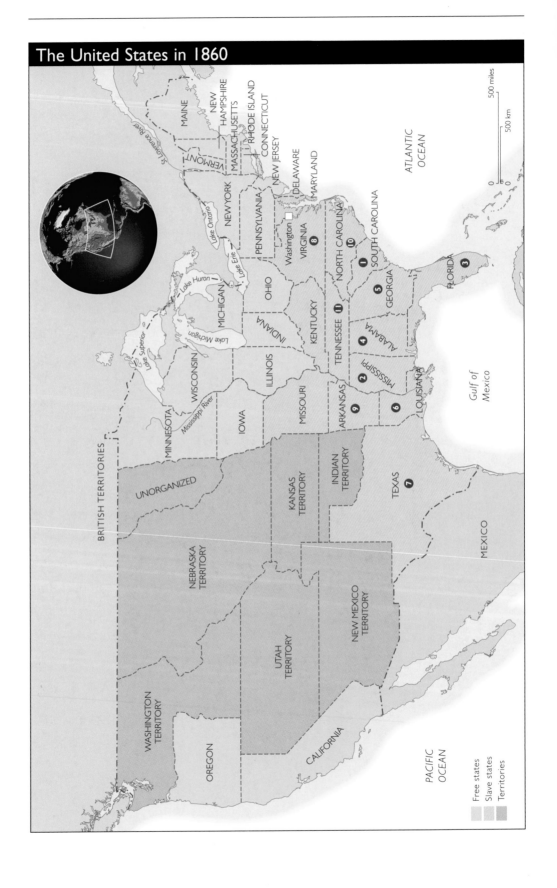

ATLANTIC OCEAN

500 miles

500 km

MAINE

NEW HAMPSHIRE

VERMONT

MASSACHUSETTS

RHODE ISLAND

CONNECTICUT

NEW JERSEY

DELAWARE

MARYLAND

NEW YORK

PENNSYLVANIA

Washington

VIRGINIA ❽

NORTH CAROLINA ❿

SOUTH CAROLINA ❶

GEORGIA ❺

FLORIDA ❸

St. Lawrence River

Lake Ontario

Lake Erie

Lake Huron

Lake Superior

Lake Michigan

Mississippi River

OHIO

MICHIGAN

INDIANA

KENTUCKY

TENNESSEE ⓫

ALABAMA ❹

MISSISSIPPI ❷

WISCONSIN

ILLINOIS

MISSOURI

ARKANSAS ❾

LOUISIANA ❻

Gulf of Mexico

MINNESOTA

IOWA

BRITISH TERRITORIES

UNORGANIZED

KANSAS TERRITORY

INDIAN TERRITORY

TEXAS ❼

NEBRASKA TERRITORY

UTAH TERRITORY

NEW MEXICO TERRITORY

MEXICO

WASHINGTON TERRITORY

OREGON

CALIFORNIA

PACIFIC OCEAN

Free states

Slave states

Territories

# Introduction

Robert Penn Warren, Pulitzer Prize winner and American Southerner, has suggested that the Civil War rivets the attention of readers because of the striking human images it offers for contemplation – 'a dazzling array of figures, noble in proportion yet human, caught out of Time as in a frieze, in stances so profoundly touching or powerfully mythic that they move us in a way no mere consideration of "historical importance" ever could.' Most of those towering figures who carry a special aura functioned in the war's Eastern Theater, which is the focus of this volume. Lee, Jackson, Grant, and others of the American soldiers who fought that war continue to fascinate modern students.

We have divided the story of the American Civil War into two volumes. The rupture of the United States into two nations in 1861, detailed in *The American Civil War: 1861–1863*, led to a vast internecine war. Hundreds of thousands of young men eagerly embraced the adventure of war. They joined volunteer units near their homes and cheerfully, innocently, headed away to what seemed surely to be a short, clean conflict. It would end, they felt certain, in victory for whichever of the contending sides they embraced. The frolicsome aspect of war dissipated in the intense mayhem along Bull Run, on the plains of Manassas, in July 1861. For months thereafter, thousands of boys in both armies died of disease. Many of the rustic youngsters-turned-soldiers had never been far from rural homes and they fell prey in droves to common childhood diseases such as measles.

After a relatively quiet first year of the war, the spring of 1862 ushered in months of steady campaigning in Virginia and Maryland, across the narrow swath of country between the contending capital cities of Washington, DC, and Richmond,

Virginia. General Robert E. Lee assumed command of the Confederate Army of Northern Virginia on 1 June 1862, and with it drove the besieging Federal Army of the Potomac away from Richmond. During the 11 succeeding months, Lee steadily defeated an array of opposing generals: George B. McClellan, John Pope, Ambrose E. Burnside, and Joseph Hooker. The arenas in which Lee conquered that succession of enemies are among the most famous in American military history: the Seven Days' Campaign, Second Manassas (or Bull Run), Antietam, Fredericksburg, and Chancellorsville.

This second volume covers the war in the Eastern and Western Theaters from June 1863 to the surrender at Appomattox in April 1865. Part 1 covers the war in the East. In the aftermath of Chancellorsville, the war in Virginia was about to undergo a fundamental change in tenor. The enormous Northern advantages in industrial might and population numbers would affect operations. With his invaluable lieutenant, 'Stonewall' Jackson, dead, Lee would find his options narrowed. Hoping to retain the initiative, Lee grasped the momentum offered by Chancellorsville and surged northward into enemy territory. When he returned after Gettysburg, the nature of the war in Virginia would trend steadily away from Confederate opportunities, and toward eventual Unionist victory.

The great Battle of Gettysburg opened this second phase of the story. From Wilderness and Spotsylvania Court House the next spring, the contending armies moved to an extended siege of Petersburg, and eventually to the Confederate surrender at Appomattox. The Confederate Army of Northern Virginia followed General Robert E. Lee through the entire period. That army's sturdy, if ill-led,

ON  THE  CONFEDERATE  LINE  OF  BAT

FROM  THE  PAINTING

/ITH FATE AGAINST THEM."

(Public domain)

RT GAUL.

counterpart was the Union Army of the Potomac. General George G. Meade took over the Army of the Potomac just a few hours before its great victory at Gettysburg, and retained that command to the end of the war. The arrival of the commander of all Union armies, General U. S. Grant, in the field near the Army of the Potomac in the spring of 1864 overshadowed Meade and he never has received the immense credit that he deserves for winning the war.

Part 2 focuses on the war in the West, where Ulysses S. Grant rose to prominence and where Union armies developed an unstoppable momentum. This part of the book opens with the conclusion of the Vicksburg campaign, perhaps the most masterly of the entire war. It focuses on the burgeoning partnership between Grant and Sherman and their rise to power and influence over the Union war effort. Ultimately, the war in the west came under Sherman's direction, and he left his distinct mark on the way Federal armies would conduct their campaigns.

Here, the Federals also witness the decline of a slow yet capable commander, Major-General William Rosecrans, who committed a blunder based on faulty information, and the rise of a talented replacement, Major-General George H. Thomas, whose stellar service saved the army that day.

On the Confederate side in the Western Theater, no Robert E. Lee emerged. Neither Braxton Bragg, Joseph E. Johnston, nor John Bell Hood proved themselves even pale imitations.

*The American Civil War 1863–1865* shows that wars invariably generate momentum of their own, leading to results that neither side envisioned, or would have tolerated, at the outset. By 1864 the old-fashioned war of 1861–63, caparisoned with the trappings of antique chivalry, had given way to what aptly has been called 'the first modern war.' Railroads for the first time played an essential role. Industrial and mechanical might weighed in as heavily as tactical prowess and strategic skill. Troops who had been scornful of earthworks in 1861 frantically dug dirt in 1864 at every opportunity, to protect themselves. Perhaps most significantly, most in the modern vein, civilians and their property became the targets of military power.

As have most attempts to win independence and freedom over the centuries, the efforts to create a Confederate nation had to rely upon wearing down the will of their foe. Southerners had nothing remotely like the means to (or any interest in) subjugate their opponents as a vassal state; they merely longed to be let alone. Perhaps the most important day in the second half of the war, therefore, was 8 November 1864, when the Northern populace voted a second term for President Abraham Lincoln – who had been certain a few weeks earlier that he would lose. With the aggressive war party still in power in the North, determined to win the war, Confederates had no hope of beating an enemy with thrice the military population and virtually all of the continent's industrial capacity.

The surrender at Appomattox followed inevitably, leaving behind legendary battles and leaders who remain among the most-studied military topics in the English language. The war also left a ghastly harvest of more than 620,000 dead men in its wake, by far the largest proportional loss in American history; freed several million black men and women from slavery; and created an unmistakable watershed in United States history.

From June 1862 to May 1863, Confederate General Robert E. Lee had steadily defeated an array of opposing Federal generals. (Author's collection)

# Chronology

**1863  1 January** Lincoln issues final Emancipation Proclamation

**2 January** Second day of fighting at Stone's River

**11 January** Federal gunboats capture Fort Hindman, Arkansas

**25 January** Joseph Hooker replaces Burnside as commander of the Army of the Potomac

**30 January** Ulysses S Grant assumes command of the expedition against Vicksburg, Mississippi

**25 February** US Congress passes the National Banking Act

**3 March** US Congress passes the Enrollment Act

**7 March** Nathaniel Banks; Federal force moves to Baton Rouge to cooperate with Grant's Vicksburg expedition

**2 April** Women take to the streets in Richmond 'bread riot' to protest against food shortages

**16 April** Porter's flotilla runs past Vicksburg batteries

**17 April** Confederate Benjamin Grierson launches a raid into Mississippi to draw attention from Grant's expedition

**24 April** Confederate Congress enacts the Tax-in-Kind Law, an unpopular measure requiring a portion of various crops to be given to the government

**30 April** Porter ferries part of Grant's army across the Mississippi River

**1 May** Battle of Port Gibson, Mississippi

**2 May** Grierson's raiders reach Baton Rouge, Louisiana

**1–4 May** Battle of Chancellorsville

**10 May** 'Stonewall' Jackson dies

**12 May** Grant defeats Confederates at Raymond, Mississippi

**14 May** Engagement at Jackson, Mississippi, Grant defeats Confederates

**16 May** Battle of Champion's Hill, Mississippi, Grant defeats Pemberton

**17 May** Battle of Big Black River, Grant defeats Pemberton

**18 May–4 July** Siege of Vicksburg, Mississippi

**27 May** Banks attacks, besieges Port Hudson; first major engagement for black soldiers

**9 June** Cavalry battle at Brandy Station

**11 June** Banks's attack repulsed at Port Hudson

**14–15 June** Second Battle of Winchester

**14 June** Banks's attack repulsed for third time at Port Hudson

**23 June** Rosecrans advances on Tullahoma, Tennessee

**28 June** General George G Meade replaces Hooker in command of the Army of the Potomac

**1–3 July** Battle of Gettysburg

**3 July** Bragg retreats to Chattanooga, Tennessee

**4 July** Pemberton surrenders Vicksburg to Grant

**9 July** The fall of Port Hudson

**13–14 July** Lee's Confederates recross the Potomac River into Virginia, ending the main phase of the Gettysburg campaign. Frenzied mobs in New York City riot in opposition to conscription, killing or wounding hundreds of victims, many of them black citizens resented as a visible cause of the war and the draft

**8–14 September** Lee detaches General Longstreet to go west and reinforce Confederate operations in Georgia and Tennessee. Meade moves south against Lee, but only heavy skirmishing results.

**19 July** Union attack on Fort Wagner led by 54th Massachusetts (Colored) Infantry

**15 August** Burnside begins campaign for Knoxville, Tennessee

**16 August** Rosecrans beings campaign for Chattanooga

**21 August** Quantrill's raid on Lawrence, Kansas

**2 September** Burnside occupies Knoxville

**9 September** Rosecrans occupies Chattanooga

**18 September** Longstreet's men being to reinforce Bragg's army

**19 September** Battle of Chickamauga begins

**20 September** Longstreet breaks Rosecrans's line

**23 September** Bragg lays siege to Chattanooga

**24 September** Hooker leaves for Chattanooga with XI and XII Corps

**14 October** Battle of Bristoe Station

**17 October** Grant made commander of all the Union forces in the West

**19 October** Thomas replaces Rosecrans

**23 October** Grant arrives at Chattanooga

**4 November** Longstreet detached to attack Burnside at Knoxville

**7 November** Battle of Rappahannock Station
**19 November** President Lincoln delivers the
Gettysburg Address
**20 November** Sherman arrives at Chattanooga
with reinforcements
**23 November** Thomas seizes Orchard Knob
**24 November** Hooker drives Confederates off
Lookout Mountain
**25 November** Sherman's attack stalls; Thomas's
men storm Missionary Ridge
**26 November–2 December** Battle of Mine Run
**28 November** President Lincoln offers pardons
to any Confederate willing to take an oath
of allegiance
**29 November** Longstreet repulsed by Burnside
at Knoxville
**1 December** Bragg resigns as Army of the
Tennessee commander
**27 December** Johnston assumes command
of Army of the Tennessee

**1864** **3 March** Sherman leaves Vicksburg on
Meridian campaign
**4 March** Sherman completes Vicksburg
campaign
**12 March** Grant is commissioned lieutenant-
general, to command all Federal armies
**18 March** Sherman assumes command of
Union forces in the west
**25 March** Banks begins Red River campaign
**8 April** Banks defeated by Richard Taylor at
Sabine Crossroads, Louisiana
**12 April** Forrest's massacre of black soldiers at
Fort Pillow, Tennessee
**4–6 May** Battle of the Wilderness
**6 May** Sherman opens Atlanta campaign
**8–21 May** Battle of Spotsylvania Court House
**9 May** McPherson's flanking movement stalls
**11 May** Battle of Yellow Tavern; General J E B
Stuart is mortally wounded
**13–16 May** Battle of Resaca
**15 May** Battle of New Market
**18 May** Battle of Yellow Bayou, Lousiana,
the last battle of the Red River campaign
**19 May** Johnston's attack at Cassville
never develops
**23–27 May** Battle of the North Anna River;
Sherman outflanks Johnston's position at
Allatoona, Georgia
**25–27 May** Battle around Dallas, Georgia

**1–3 June** Battle of Cold Harbor
**5 June** Battle of Piedmont
**8 June** Lincoln re-nominated for president
**12 June** Army of the Potomac starts to cross
James River
**14 June** Lieutenat-General Leonidas Polk killed
at Pine Mountain
**15–18 June** Opening engagements around
Petersburg, while Confederate General Jubal
Early arrives near Lynchburg to launch
Shenandoah valley campaign
**22–23 June** Battle for the Weldon Railroad
near Petersburg
**27 June** Sherman's assault on Kennesaw
mountain repulsed
**4–9 July** Sherman maneuvers across
Chattahoochee River
**9 July** Battle of Monocracy
**11–12 July** Early's Confederate stand on the
outskirts of Washington
**17 July** Hood replaces Johnston as commander
of Army of the Tennessee
**20 July** Hood repulsed at Peachtree Creek
**22 July** Hood fails to turn Sherman's army
at Battle of Atlanta; Major-General James
B McPherson is killed
**24 July** Second Battle of Kernstown
**28 July** Hood's attack at Ezra Church repulsed
**30 July** Explosion of mine at Petersburg turns
into the Battle of the Crater
**5 August** Farragut wins Battle of Mobile Bay
**18–25 August** Battles of the Weldon Railroad
and Reams' Station
**23 August** Lincoln submits to his cabinet a
sealed memo stating that 'it seems extremely
probable that this Administration will not
be re-elected.'
**29 August** McClellan nominated for president
**31 August** Battle of Jonesboro, Georgia
**1 September** Battle of Jonesboro concluded;
Hood evacuates Atlanta
**2 September** Sherman occupies Atlanta
**14–17 September** The Beefsteak Raid
**19 September** Third Battle of Winchester;
Price crosses into Missouri
**22 September** Battle of Fisher's Hill
**27 September** Anderson's attack on Centralia,
Missouri
**28 September** Hood moves to strike at
Sherman's supply line

**29 September–7 October** Fighting around Richmond and Petersburg at Fort Harrison, Chaffin's Bluff, New Market Heights, Darbytown Road, and Boydton Plank Road
**October** Hood fails to capture Allatoona; Sherman in pursuit
**9 October** Cavalry fights at Tom's Brook
**18 October** Hood crosses into Alabama
**19 October** Battle of Cedar Creek
**23 October** Price defeated at Westport; begins retreat
**27 October** Battle of Burgess' Mill
**30 October** Sherman shifts Schofield's troops to support Thomas in Middle Tennessee
**8 November** President Lincoln re-elected
**15 November** Sherman's troops burn Atlanta; begin March to the Sea
**19 November** Hood opens push into Middle Tennessee
**23 November** Milledgville, capital of Georgia, falls to Sherman
**29 November** Schofield escapes at Spring Hill, Tennessee
**30 November** Schofield repulses Hood at Franklin; Lieutenant-General Patrick Cleburne killed
**2 December** Hood besieges Nashville
**13 December** Sherman captures Fort McAllister
**15–16 December** Thomas routs Hood's army
**21 December** Sherman occupies Savannah
**25 December** Butler repulsed at Fort Fisher, North Carolina

**1865** **15 January** Fort Fisher falls to Porter and Terry; Hood relieved of command of Army of the Tennessee
**31 January** Thirteenth Amendment abolishing slavery passes in Congress
**1 February** Sherman begins Carolinas campaign
**5–7 February** Battle of Hatcher's Run
**6 February** Lee appointed Commander-in-Chief of all Confederate armies
**17 February** Columbia falls to Sherman, burns
**18 February** Charleston seized by Union troops
**22 February** Wilmington surrenders to Schofield; Johnston recalled to command Confederate forces against Sherman
**2 March** Early's last remnant destroyed at the Battle of Waynesboro

**4 March** Lincoln's Second Inaugural Address, 'With malice toward none…'
**13 March** Confederate Congress approves raising of black troops
**16 March** Sherman pushes back Hardee at Averasborough, North Carolina
**17 March** Major-General E R S Canby attacks Mobile, Alabama
**19–21 March** Sherman repulses Johnston's attack at Bentonville, North Carolina
**24 March** Sherman occupies Goldsboro, North Carolina, ending the Carolinas campaign
**25 March** Attack on Fort Stedman near Petersburg
**28 March** Lincoln, Grant, Sherman and Porter confer on peace terms
**29–31 March** The final campaign in Virginia begins with fighting around the Dinwiddie Court House
**1 April** Battle of Five Forks
**3 April** Richmond falls
**8 April** Sherman resumes march on Johnston
**9 April** Lee surrenders to Grant at Appomattox Court House
**12 April** Mobile falls to Canby; Johnston tells President Jefferson Davis resistance is hopeless
**13 April** Raleigh falls to Sherman
**14 April** Lincoln assassinated
**18 April** Sherman and Johnston sign broad surrender agreement
**21 April** Sherman's terms rejected
**26 April** Johnston accepts same terms as Grant gives Lee
**10 May** President Davis is captured at Irwinsville, Georgia
**12 May** Last battle of the war, at Palmito Ranch, Texas
**23–24 May** Grand Review in Washington, DC
**26 May** General Kirby Smith surrenders Confederate forces west of the Mississippi

**1866** **2 April** State governments having been installed to meet Unionist directives, President Andrew Johnson officially proclaims 'that the insurrection … is at an end'; Confederate government evacuates Richmond

**1877** The last enforced military government is removed and home rule is restored at the state level

# Part I

## The war in the East

# From innocents to warriors

No American war, and few of any other sort, has ever been fought with a lower proportion of trained soldiers than the American Civil War. The United States had from its origins suffered from a deep mistrust of standing armies and professional military men. The nation also wallowed in a nostalgic, but misguided, fondness for the notion of an untrained but devoted citizen-militia. At the outbreak of war in 1861, the United States Army included fewer than 15,000 officers and men; a few months later there would be more than one hundred times that many men under arms – far too many troops for the regular army to serve as an effective cadre.

A computerized index of official service records of both the Union and Confederate armies has for the first time made available hard data about the number of men mustered into service during the war. This is a subject about which arguments have raged among partisans of each side, and of various states, since the war years without any means of clear resolution. We now know that 1,231,006 Confederate service records exist, and 2,918, 862 Federal records. Virginia supplied the largest Confederate increment, followed by Georgia and Tennessee. New York (456,720) led Federal recruitment, followed by Pennsylvania and Ohio. Those three Northern states, in fact, among them supplied almost as many troops as the entire Confederacy could muster. It should be recognized that the number of records does not indicate a precise number of men. Some Northern troops re-enlisted in different units at the expiration of a term of enlistment, and many Southern soldiers changed organizations in the spring of 1862 under the working of the new conscription law. Even so, the newly established totals

of service records constitute the first unmistakable benchmark on the subject.

Civil War soldiers almost without exception had been civilians in 1860. The census that year revealed the overwhelming advantages the Union enjoyed in numbers.

The seceded states had a population of 9.1 million, 5.4 million of them white and therefore directly available for military

Confederate volunteers head off for war in 1861. (Public domain)

service. The other states counted 22.3 million inhabitants, and more than 800,000 alien passengers arrived at Northern ports during the war. The agrarian Confederacy faced even greater challenges in materiel. The 1860 census showed the South with only 7 percent of the nation's industrial output, 8 percent of its shipping, and one-fourth of its railroad mileage.

The capacities of the warring sides, described in detail in *The American Civil War: 1861–1863*, had begun by 1863 to play a steadily more important role in the progress of the conflict. The United States navy held unmistakable sway over all navigable waters, without any notable opposition. As a result, the portion of the Virginia Theater viable for Confederate operations extended no farther east than the fall lines of the several rivers flowing nominally eastward through the state: the Potomac, the Rappahannock, the James, and the Appomattox. Federal weaponry outmatched Southern equipment in every way. Union infantry carried rifles almost exclusively, while a substantial proportion of Confederates still had to make do with smoothbores (with one-tenth the range). As the conflict wore on, Northern cavalry would enjoy the advantage of breech-loading carbines, and eventually of repeating weapons. Union artillery fired farther and more accurately than Southern

cannon, and Northern ordnance usually exploded on cue, whereas a Confederate battalion commander at Chancellorsville reported that only one in every 15 of his shells detonated.

By the spring of 1863, the organization and command of the main armies of the Virginia Theater had taken on distinctive characteristics. The Union Army of the Potomac had been tempered into a strong, resolute, military implement, patient in the face of steadily inept leadership. If President Abraham Lincoln would ever place a capable commander over the army, and support him, the veteran organization stood ready to be the bulwark of the national cause. The Confederate Army of Northern Virginia had long enjoyed superb direction from Lee, but without Stonewall Jackson to execute Lee's daring initiatives, a new mode of fighting would now be necessary.

As the contending armies in the Virginia Theater moved north in the late spring of 1863, away from Chancellorsville, they were pursuing a long and tortuous road that would lead them eventually to Gettysburg. They also were launching a new phase of the American Civil War.

Tredegar Iron Works in Richmond provided invaluable war materials, but the Confederacy had relatively few such industrial facilities. (Public domain)

# The war without Jackson to Lee's last stand

## The spring of 1863

A great, mournful cry went up all across the Confederacy as news spread in May 1863 of the death of General Thomas J. 'Stonewall' Jackson, of wounds received at the Battle of Chancellorsville. A Georgia Confederate wrote dolefully on 15 May that 'all hopes of Peace and Independence have forever vanished.' Another Confederate told his wife back in Alabama, with more earnestness than literary precision: 'Stonewall Jackson was kild ... I think this will have a gradeal to due with this war. I think the north will whip us soon.' General Robert E. Lee faced the daunting task of reorganizing his army in Jackson's absence, and filling it with a sturdy spirit that could keep the 'whip us soon' forecast from becoming a self-fulfilling prophecy.

Lee's stunning victory at Chancellorsville on 1–6 May, against daunting odds, had generated enough momentum to carry the Confederate Army of Northern Virginia northward on a new campaign. (For Chancellorsville, see Gallagher, *The American Civil War*.) Before he could launch such an effort, though, Lee had to reorganize his army to fill the yawning chasm left by Jackson's demise. He decided to go from the two-corps system that had worked so long and well for managing his infantry to an organization in three corps. The veteran General James Longstreet, reliable if contentious, kept command of the First Corps. General Richard S. Ewell, returning after nine months of convalescing from a wound, assumed command in late May of Jackson's old Second Corps. General A. P. Hill won promotion to command a new Third Corps composed of pieces extracted from the other two, combined with a few new units drawn to Virginia from service elsewhere in the Confederacy. General J. E. B. Stuart remained in command of the army's capable cavalry arm. Lee's artillery benefited from an excellent new organization into battalions, and from an officer corps that included many brilliant young men; but at the same time it suffered from inferior weaponry and at times from woefully inadequate ammunition.

Across the lines, General Joseph Hooker's Army of the Potomac loomed in Lee's way. The seasoned Northerners in that army by now knew their business thoroughly well and stood ready to continue their role as bulwark of the Federal Union. What they wanted and needed was a competent commander. At Chancellorsville, Hooker had demonstrated beyond serious contention that he was not such a man. The Army of the Potomac would finally receive a leader who matched its mettle in late June, but as the 1863 campaign unfolded, Hooker's palsied hand remained at the helm. His veteran corps commanders offered reliable leadership at the next level below Hooker.

After two consecutive battles along the line of the Rappahannock river, both armies knew the countryside intimately. Lee had won both battles in resounding fashion, but had not been able to exploit the victories into overwhelming triumphs that destroyed his enemy. Now he proposed to move north across the Potomac and carry the war into the enemy's country. Political hyperbole (including President Lincoln's famous 'Gettysburg Address') always insisted that the Confederates hoped to conquer the North and subjugate that much larger portion of the continent to some sort of serfdom. Such rodomontade, of course, reflected nothing of actual Southern aims.

Lee's move north must be recognized as a raid, not an invasion designed to conquer Pennsylvania or any other territory. He sought

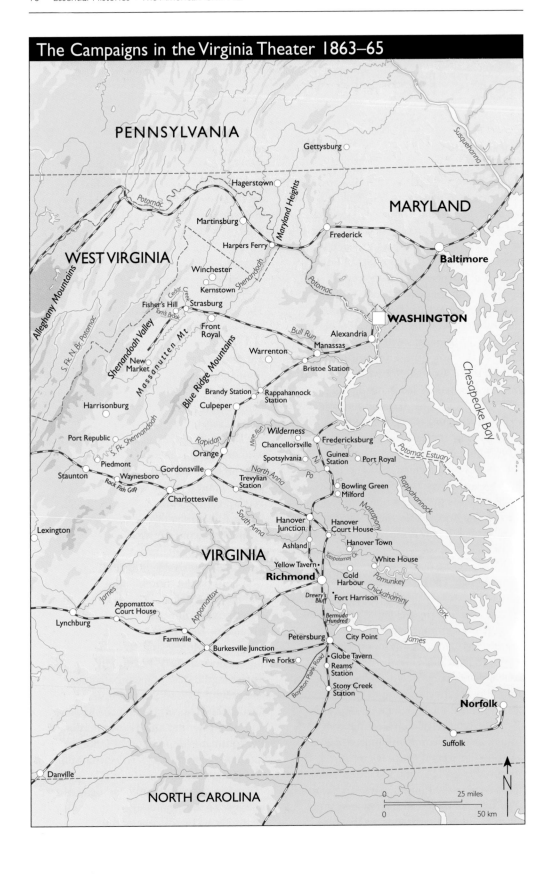

# The Campaigns in the Virginia Theater 1863–65

**PENNSYLVANIA**

Gettysburg

Hagerstown

**MARYLAND**

Maryland Heights

Martinsburg

Frederick

Harpers Ferry

**WEST VIRGINIA**

**Baltimore**

Potomac

Winchester

Kernstown

Alleghany Mountains

Fisher's Hill  Strasburg

Cedar Creek

Tom's Brook

S. Fk. N. Br. Potomac

Front Royal

Bull Run

Alexandria

**WASHINGTON**

New Market

Warrenton

Manassas

Shenandoah Valley

Massanutten Mt.

Bristoe Station

Harrisonburg

Brandy Station

Rappahannock Station

Blue Ridge Mountains

Culpeper

Chesapeake Bay

Port Republic

Wilderness

Chancellorsville

Fredericksburg

Potomac Estuary

S. Fk. Shennandoah

Rapidan

Spotsylvania

Guinea Station

Port Royal

Orange

Mine Run

Po

Ni

Piedmont

North Anna

Staunton

Gordonsville

Trevylian Station

Bowling Green

Milford

Waynesboro

Rock Fish Gap

Charlottesville

Rappahannock

South Anna

Mattapony

Lexington

Hanover Junction

Hanover Court House

Hanover Town

White House

Ashland

**VIRGINIA**

Yellow Tavern

Pamunkey

Totopotomoy Cr.

**Richmond**

Cold Harbour

Chickahominy

Drewry's Bluff

Fort Harrison

York

Appomattox Court House

Bermuda Hundred

James

Appomattox

Lynchburg

Petersburg

City Point

James

Farmville

Burkesville Junction

Five Forks

Globe Tavern

Reams' Station

Boydton Plank Road

Stony Creek Station

**Norfolk**

Suffolk

Danville

N

**NORTH CAROLINA**

| | |
|---|---|
| 0 | 25 miles |
| 0 | 50 km |

The Confederates counterattack at Brandy Station.
(Painting by Don Troiani, www.historicalartprints.com)

to lift the heel of war from Virginia, not only for humanitarian reasons, but also to allow that home country to recover from hostile occupation so that it could sustain Lee's army in future months. The country north of the Potomac also offered a much wider field for

The Confederate high tide at Chancellorsville propelled Lee's army into a new campaign that swept north past Winchester into Maryland and then Pennsylvania, where the Federal Army of the Potomac repulsed it in the war's largest battle. During the fall of 1863, the two armies clashed again in Virginia at Bristoe Station, Rappahannock Station, and Mine Run, but none of those engagements developed into a major battle. The next spring, with Commander-in-Chief U. S. Grant accompanying it, the Army of the Potomac crossed the Rapidan river and fought at Wilderness and Spotsylvania. Although they could not defeat Lee, the Federals determinedly pushed on to the North Anna River, Cold Harbor, and the outskirts of Richmond and Petersburg. After 10 months attempting to break into the Confederate capital, Grant finally succeeded in April 1865 and Lee was forced to surrender at Appomattox Court House on the 9th.

maneuver, a military element in which Lee excelled. An ostensible threat to the Federal political capital in Washington also held out potential advantages: knowing that his enemy *must* keep the city covered foreshadowed in mirror image the 1864 campaign in which Richmond served as a similar focus and pivot for Lee on the defensive.

Lee moved away from Fredericksburg and the Rappahannock river line early in June 1863, and headed northwestward through piedmont Virginia toward the Shenandoah valley. On 9 June his cavalry force fought one of the largest all-mounted engagements of the war around Brandy Station. Hooker had sent his own cavalry out with orders to 'disperse and destroy' the Confederates they found, and the Northern troopers came close to doing that. They completely surprised the

General Joseph Hooker. (Public domain)

usually vigilant Southern mounted men early in the morning and drove them some distance. A rally on the low, rounded eminence of Fleetwood Hill saved the day for General Stuart's men. They inflicted about 1,000 casualties on the Northern attackers and suffered half that many themselves.

Brandy Station ended as a tactical draw, but Union troopers who had been battered relentlessly for two years had finally stood up to their adversaries and now had a positive experience upon which to build.

General J. E. B. ('Jeb') Stuart led most of the Confederate cavalry on a long ride around the Federal army en route to Pennsylvania, thus depriving Lee of his 'eyes and ears' as he maneuvered toward Gettysburg. (Public domain)

## The Battle of Gettysburg

'Jeb' Stuart's Southern cavalry again occupied center stage as the armies sidled northward and crossed the Potomac – or, more accurately, Stuart's cavalry exited stage right and became conspicuous by their absence. While Lee pushed north, into and through the Shenandoah valley, Stuart embraced the chance to ride a raid entirely around the Union army. He had done just that twice before, in June and October 1862. This time the dashing maneuver backfired in deadly fashion. The cavalry detachment accompanying the main force in Stuart's absence had neither the men nor the leadership necessary to perform the essential function of screening Lee from enemy view, while simultaneously finding the enemy and tracking his progress and intentions. When Stuart finally rejoined Lee very tardily at Gettysburg, the commanding general said quietly, but in clear rebuke, 'Well ... you are here at last,' and 'I had hoped to see you before this.' Stuart's ride became one of the most-disputed subjects among postwar

Above. General George Gordon Meade took command of the Federal Army of the Potomac scant hours before the Battle of Gettysburg, but still won a great victory there. He has never received the credit he deserves for his achievement, largely because he scorned journalists and belonged to the wrong political party. (Public domain)

Left. Confederate General James Longstreet's behavior on 2 July remains the most controversial aspect of the Battle of Gettysburg. (Public domain)

Right. The war's largest battle engulfed the farms and hillsides around Gettysburg, Pennsylvania, on the first three days of July 1863. The Confederate army won a tremendous victory northwest of town on 1 July and swept through the streets in triumph. The Federals made a stand on a fishhook-shaped line south of Gettysburg, taking advantage of the slopes of Cemetery Ridge and anchored on the formidable heights of Culp's Hill and Little Round Top. Lee's efforts against the Federal right on 2–3 July met with very little success, but near the Round Tops the Confederates came close to a major success. On 3 July, with his options dwindling, and loath to return to Virginia, Lee flung his center across open fields toward Cemetery Ridge. This attack, usually known as 'Pickett's Charge,' unfolded with immense drama and elicited tremendous courage from its participants, but yielded nothing for Lee but daunting casualties. He now had no choice but to retreat south toward Virginia.

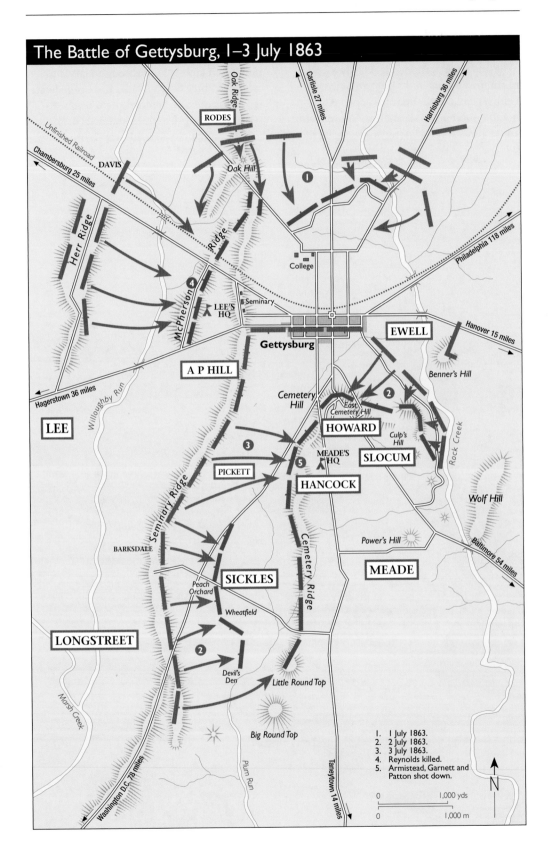

# The Battle of Gettysburg, 1–3 July 1863

RODES

Oak Ridge

Carlisle 27 miles

Harrisburg 36 miles

Unfinished Railroad

Chambersburg 25 miles

DAVIS

Oak Hill

①

②

Herr Ridge

McPherson Ridge

College

Philadelphia 118 miles

④

Seminary

LEE'S HQ

Hanover 15 miles

EWELL

Gettysburg

Benner's Hill

A P HILL

Hagerstown 36 miles

Willoughby Run

LEE

Cemetery Hill

East Cemetery Hill

HOWARD

②

Culp's Hill

Rock Creek

③

MEADE'S HQ

⑤

SLOCUM

PICKETT

HANCOCK

Wolf Hill

BARKSDALE

Seminary Ridge

Power's Hill

Baltimore 54 miles

MEADE

Cemetery Ridge

SICKLES

Peach Orchard

Wheatfield

LONGSTREET

②

Devil's Den

Little Round Top

Marsh Creek

Big Round Top

1.  1 July 1863.
2.  2 July 1863.
3.  3 July 1863.
4.  Reynolds killed.
5.  Armistead, Garnett and Patton shot down.

Washington D.C. 78 miles

Plum Run

Taneytown 14 miles

N

| 0 | | 1,000 yds |
| 0 | | 1,000 m |

Confederates, and remains controversial to this day.

While Stuart galloped fecklessly across northern Virginia and Maryland and Pennsylvania, Lee's infantry achieved notable success at Winchester, Virginia, on 14–15 June. Ewell's energy and success there prompted Southerners to hope that he would emerge as a sort of reincarnation of Stonewall Jackson. On through Maryland and deep into Pennsylvania the Confederate columns pressed. Some of them reached Carlisle and York and the outskirts of the state's capital city, Harrisburg. Fighting

at the crossroads town of Gettysburg that began on 1 July would draw all of them back south into the maw of the war's greatest battle. The long columns of blue-clad Union troops marching north through an arc surrounding Washington also wound up adjusting their route of march for that place. Gettysburg was a 'meeting engagement' in every sense. No one picked the battle site. Roads drew small contending

A nineteenth-century view looking northwest from the crest of Little Round Top across the scenes of the heaviest fighting in the history of North America. (Public domain)

Looking across the valley of death, from little Round-Top.

formations together and soon everyone
else pitched in.

The battle of 1 July 1863, considered
alone, must be adjudged one of the Army of
Northern Virginia's greatest victories. Fighting
opened that morning west of Gettysburg, a
farming community of about 2,400 souls.

Confederate skirmishers ran into Northern
cavalry commanded by salty, unflappable
General John Buford. A brigade of Southern
infantry under President Jefferson Davis's
nephew, General Joseph Davis, drove forward
with marked success, but then the green
brigadier clumsily allowed his men to be

from the superb timing – the result of luck, not prescience – with which the fresh Southern division of General Robert E. Rodes dropped squarely onto the north flank of the Federal position. Intense fighting ensued on both sides of the road leading from Chambersburg to Gettysburg, with success perching first upon one banner then another, but the arrival of Rodes's division and other associated troops at a fortuitous point doomed Federal resistance. Eventually the whole Union line west of town collapsed and the Confederates enjoyed a field day chasing their fleeing foe into Gettysburg. Alexander Schimmelfennig, a Prussian-born general, eluded capture by hiding in a pigsty. Thousands of other men in blue became prisoners of war.

One of the battle's most-discussed turning points came as Confederates converged on Gettysburg from the north and west, and contemplated riding the crest of the tidal wave of momentum they had created. Lee characteristically left to the discretion of his new corps commander, General Ewell, the responsibility for continuing the advance. Possession of the crest of a long ridge that curled around Gettysburg and ran east to East Cemetery Hill and Culp's Hill would guarantee control of the military terrain for a considerable distance. Ewell equivocated, consulted, temporized – and never attacked. For the next two days, his troops would suffer mightily against the same two hills, by then strongly occupied, attacking again and again where he had not chosen to fight under far better terms. On the evening of 1 July, Ewell did nothing. His inaction remains highly controversial today. The counter-factual question, 'What would Jackson have done had he been there?' is, of course, unanswerable. A North Carolina soldier who fought there thought he knew. 'We missed the genius of Jackson,' he wrote a few days later. 'The simplest soldier in the ranks felt it.'

trapped in a deep cut of an unfinished railroad and lost most of them.

Confederate fortunes were abetted when a bullet killed Union General John F. Reynolds, a soldierly and much-admired officer commanding everything Federal on the field at that early hour. They benefited even more

Federals scrambling to get to Gettysburg to blunt Lee's burgeoning success faced far better prospects than they would have a few days earlier. A Federal turning point in the campaign, indeed in the entire war in Virginia, had come on 27 June when General Hooker submitted his resignation in a fit of pique over having his wishes ignored. President Lincoln delightedly accepted the resignation and on 28 June General George Gordon Meade reluctantly took command of the Army of the Potomac.

Three days later Meade was fighting the war's largest battle. No American officer, in any war or era, has ever had so much crucial responsibility thrust upon him with such short notice. Meade met the challenge masterfully, beyond any imaginable degree that could have been expected, and far more ably than Hooker could have done. He confronted Lee's army at the high tide of Southern success, positioned deep in Federal country, and with Confederate numerical strength at a peak. At Gettysburg, Meade reached the battlefield as Lee swept everything before him late on 1 July. Against those odds the brand-new Federal commander won a pivotal battle.

Meade's challenge early on 2 July was to restore confidence in his army and place it carefully on the powerful position available to him. The Federal line around Gettysburg resembled a fishhook. The shank of the fishhook ran straight south from town along Cemetery Ridge and ended on the massive anchor of two commanding hills, Big Round Top and Little Round Top. The hook curled around Gettysburg, turning east to another superb anchor at Culp's Hill. Meade's line enjoyed the obvious tactical advantage of high ground. Its hook also ensured the ability to exploit interior lines, with the invaluable privilege of reinforcing from one point to another directly and under cover. The sole tactical defect of the line was its vulnerability to artillery rounds pouring in from across a wide arc – the 'converging fire' that is an artillerist's ideal. That defect never came into play. Confederate artillery, out-gunned and

As a member of the US Congress before the war, Daniel E. Sickles had murdered his wife's lover and got away with the crime. At Gettysburg, he aggressively advanced his division on 2 July and became the target of a savage Confederate attack. (Public domain)

tacitly commanded by an ineffectual preacher-general, never levied converging fire against Meade's fishhook.

Although the great Confederate charge of 3 July garners the most attention, Gettysburg came to its decisive juncture on 2 July as Lee tried to exploit the advantages gained on the 1st. Meade resisted stoutly and to good effect, aided to some degree by Confederate failings. On the Federal right, Southern assaults against Culp's Hill faltered after much desperate bravery on both sides. The attack never came close to substantial success. At dusk, two brigades of Rebels pressed determinedly up the steep face of East Cemetery Hill – precisely where Ewell had feared to go the previous day under far more advantageous circumstances. Despite canister flung into their flanks, and Federal

musketry in front, the Confederates reached
the crest and held there for some time before
Northern reinforcements flocked to the site
in enough numbers to expel them.
Meanwhile, the most portentous
Confederate initiative during the Battle of
Gettysburg had faltered far down on the
Federal left, near the Round Tops.

At Chancellorsville, Lee had won a great
victory by deploying to the point of decision a
flanking column led by his most trusted
subordinate, Stonewall Jackson. With Jackson
dead, James Longstreet was clearly Lee's
primary military asset. Longstreet did not want
to fight on the offensive, however, and
apparently spent 1–3 July sulking over Lee's
variant view of things. Such defensive
triumphs as the Battle of Fredericksburg
appealed to Longstreet (and every other
Confederate), but how often would one find a
pliant Ambrose Burnside willing to slaughter
his own army? Longstreet did not wish to take
the initiative at all, so only grudgingly – and
very tardily – moved away with Lee's
maneuver element. The army commander
remained near his other corps commanders,
both of them brand new. After a sluggish
march, marked by confusion and backtracking,
Longstreet's column arrived opposite the
Federal left in front of the two Round Tops.

The nature of the violent combat that
swept across the fields and hills south of
Gettysburg on 2 July was affected in a
fundamental way by the impulsive actions
of Federal General Daniel E. Sickles. The
General came not from a military
background but from the political realm,
having been a powerful Congressman from
New York. Sickles' legacy includes not just
his Civil War service, but also a series of
bumptious endeavors: he killed his wife's
lover before the war, and escaped on a plea
of temporary insanity; as postwar US
ambassador to Spain, he had an affair with
that country's queen; and he played the
central role in preserving Gettysburg
battlefield early in the twentieth century. In
July 1863, Sickles always insisted, he had
saved the battle itself for the Union, by
pushing forward in front of the main line

General George E. Pickett, a foppish fellow of starkly
limited capacity, became one of the most famous names
in American military history because of the mighty
charge on 3 July 1863. He and his division did little else
during the war. (Public domain)

without Meade's permission. As Longstreet
slowly approached action, Sickles moved
forward into his path.

The assault by Longstreet's Confederates
drove Sickles off his new position, and cost
the Federal general his leg (after the war, a
Congressman once again, Sickles took
visiting constituents to the medical museum
in Washington to show them his leg bones,
donated as an exhibit). General William
Barksdale of Mississippi, as fiery an *ante
bellum* politician as Sickles had been, led
a dramatic charge into Sickles' line.
Southerners swept east and northeast in
a wide arc that resulted in bitter fighting
across a landscape that became forever
famous: The Peach Orchard; The Wheatfield;
Devil's Den; Little Round Top. The latter
position held the key to that sector of the
battlefield, looking down on the others and
also commanding Cemetery Ridge to the
north. After a desperate struggle,
Confederates from Texas and Alabama
receded from the crest of the hill, leaving a
ghastly harvest of prostrate comrades behind
them. As darkness fell, the Federals held the

key ground and Lee's great opportunity had passed. Controversy still rages over the efficacy of Sickles' relocation, and about Longstreet's lassitude in moving to battle.

Impeccable hindsight shows convincingly that Lee's decision to attack the next day,

Depiction of one segment of the fighting on July 3, from the immense 19th-century cyclorama painting by Philippoleaux, the largest piece of Gettysburg art and probably the most famous. (Ann Ronan Picture Library)

Confederate Colonel Waller T. Patton fell dreadfully wounded at the height of 'Pickett's Charge.' He died 18 days later as a prisoner of war.

3 July, against Meade's center, was his worst of the war. He doubtless undertook the forlorn hope because it seemed the only remaining option he had to get at his enemy. The Army of Northern Virginia had

reached the end of a very long supply limb, about 120 miles (190km) from the nearest railroad-served depot back in the Shenandoah valley. Stocks of commissary, quartermaster, and ordnance stores (particularly artillery ammunition) had dwindled and could not be renewed. Overwhelming tactical success on 1 July had yielded the opportunity for an even greater triumph on 2 July, but that opportunity dissolved under frustrating circumstances. Lee's infantry had never failed to do what he asked of them. Might not a full fresh division of them, just arrived on the field, with support from other units and massed artillery, break the Federal center?

In the event, they could not. About 12,000 Confederates tried, in the most renowned attack in all of American military history. 'Pickett's Charge' actually included about as many men from other units as from General George E. Pickett's division, which prompted postwar quarrels about the event's famous name. Confederate Colonel E. Porter Alexander massed artillery for a thunderous advance barrage, which used up much of the tenuous supply of shells. The barrage also fired too high against a target obscured by smoke and dust. When the infantry stepped out, they faced a maelstrom of shell-fire, then canister at closer range, and finally musketry in sheets as they charged past the humble farmhouse of the Codori family. A Virginian in Pickett's command wrote: 'On swept the column over ground covered with dead and dying men, where the earth seemed to be on fire, the smoke dense and suffocating, the sun shut out, flames blazing on every side, friend could hardly be distinguished from foe.'

Generals Lewis A. Armistead and Richard B. Garnett suffered mortal wounds at the front of the attack. Garnett's body was never recovered from the carnage, although his sword turned up in a pawn shop years later. Fully one-half of their men went down as well (Northern losses reached perhaps 1,500). A handful of brave Confederates broke into the Federal line for a time and hand-to-hand fighting raged around a battery near an angle

in a stone fence. A Northern major marveled at how 'the rebels ... stood there, against the fence, until they were nearly all shot down.' They had reached what often has been called 'the high-water mark of the Confederacy.'

When the survivors turned back in sullen retreat, they suffered as dreadfully as on the way in. Among the Southern officers mangled was Colonel Waller Tazewell Patton, one of six brothers in the army and a great-uncle of the General Patton famous during the Second World War. The Colonel had grasped a cousin's hand, said 'it is our turn next,' and leaped over the stone wall at the attack's high-water mark, then went down with his lower jaw shot away. As he lay dying in a Federal hospital, unable to talk, 'Taz' scribbled a note to his mother: 'my only regret is that there are no more brothers left to defend our country.'

Fighting continued on 3 July in lesser volume on the far Federal right at Culp's Hill, and Jeb Stuart's cavalry engaged mounted foe well behind the main Union line, but Pickett's Charge proved to be the final major engagement of the Battle of Gettysburg. Each army had lost about 25,000 men. During the night of 4–5 July, Lee's army began to retreat toward the Potomac river through a violent rainstorm. The miles-long column of wagons bearing suffering and dying men became a train of utter misery. Meade pursued with some energy. Skirmishing flared along the route each day, but by 14 July Lee had managed to cross the rain-swollen river back into Virginia across a set of precarious pontoon bridges.

General Meade came in for more calumny than praise. President Lincoln was disgusted that he had not captured the entire Confederate force, which looked far easier on a Washington map than on a muddy Maryland ridgeline. George Meade had won the war's largest battle, scant hours after taking command, and had done so against an enemy army that had been inevitably triumphant theretofore; but politicians and press, followed eventually by many historical writers, grumbled that he should have done more.

Meade commanded the Army of the Potomac for the rest of the war as by far its most successful leader. In a very real sense, he saved the Union – yet he has never received much recognition for his achievement. That is probably because General U. S. Grant subsequently came east at a convenient moment, when numbers and materiel made it possible to end the war by simply shooting down many tens of thousands of men on both sides until arithmetic held sway.

## The fall and winter of 1863–64

The perspective of years seems to suggest that Gettysburg turned the war onto a new axis, especially when taken with Federal conquest of the Mississippi river through the fall of Vicksburg on 4 July. History is, of course, lived forward but written backward. Americans struggling to further their opposite causes in 1863 saw little of what is now said to have been obvious. Confederates who fought at Gettysburg, and their families writing from home, rued the reverse they had suffered, but almost never displayed any notion of impending doom. When the Yankees came back across the Potomac, they believed, the invaders would be as susceptible to defeat as they always had been – and the veteran Confederate army set about to prove it.

Back on Virginian soil, Lee resumed his adroit maneuvering to counter each Unionist initiative, and proved to be almost uniformly successful in foiling his enemy. The armies edged southward and eastward, out of the Shenandoah valley and into piedmont country, finally fetching up about 40 miles (64km) of latitude south of the Potomac. Through the late summer and fall of 1863, operations centered on a corridor between Warrenton and Culpeper and Orange. None of the sallies and probes evolved into a major engagement. Lee dispatched Longstreet in early September with one-third of the army's infantry to the Western Theater, where the reinforcements would arrive just in time to play a crucial role in

General Ambrose Powell Hill had been one of Lee's most capable division leaders, but at Bristoe Station and elsewhere he failed to perform up to his commander's expectations. (Public domain)

the Battle of Chickamauga. Two Federal corps followed Longstreet west, where they spent the rest of the war. Longstreet returned to Virginia in the following spring.

Lee's reduced strength threw him squarely on the defensive. Meade promptly pushed his foe south of the Rapidan river in mid-September, but on 9 October Lee grasped the initiative again, as he so much preferred to do. The Confederates advanced columns around both of Meade's flanks, forcing the Federal army to fall back north beyond Warrenton toward Manassas. A. P. Hill's troops took the lead. Hill had been almost invisible at Gettysburg during his first battle at the helm of the Third Corps. Now he had the advance at a portentous moment on 14 October.

Unfortunately, Hill displayed more dash than judgment. Without reconnoitering the position, he threw two brigades of North Carolinians at a Union force ensconced behind a railroad embankment at Bristoe Station. The Northerners proved to be the entire Federal II Corps, veteran and unmovable. The Carolinians fell in windrows without any hope of success, losing about 1,400 men in a short interval. The Federal II Corps then withdrew unmolested. Lee conveyed his sad reaction to Hill in a typically restrained rebuke. As the two generals rode across the scene and Hill sought to explain how the disaster unfolded, Lee said quietly: 'Well, well, General, bury these poor men and let us say no more about it.'

Three weeks after Bristoe Station, the Federals inflicted another minor disaster on Lee's army. Confederates in Virginia were accustomed to achieving most of their goals, and had never been driven from a fixed, well-defended position. When Lee fell back across the Rappahannock river in the aftermath of Bristoe Station, he incautiously left a *tête-de-pont* on the river's north bank at Rappahannock Station. A reliable brigade of Louisiana infantry occupied strong entrenchments north of the river, and artillery posted on the south bank offered supporting fire. When General Jubal A. Early, commanding the Confederates in the vicinity, noticed enemy strength concentrating nearby, he sent another brigade of infantry across to support the Louisianians.

Both brigades were doomed. Union General John Sedgwick closed in on the position with his VI Corps on 7 November 1864. A bright young West Point graduate (he had just turned 24), Colonel Emory Upton, led the advance with determination and swept over the works. Outflanked Confederates raced for safety across the pontoon bridges that connected the bridgehead with the southern bank. Only by means of a daring exploit were the Southerners able to cut loose the pontoon

The youthful Emory Upton had much to do with the striking Federal success at Rappahannock Station. He would be heard from again at Spotsylvania Court House and Cold Harbor, and after the war would play a central role in the reorganization of the United States Army. (Public domain)

bridges and put the river between themselves and the victorious enemy. The Federals had inflicted about 2,000 casualties, most of them in the form of prisoners. The youthful Upton would be heard from again with another daring attack the following May, and then as a leader in reorganizing the United States Army after the war.

With the Rappahannock line breached, Meade could move into the excellent bivouac country south of that river and north of the Rapidan. For the next six months, the Rapidan river would constitute the military frontier in Virginia. (The river

Modern aerial view of Wilderness Battlefield, looking east down the Orange Turnpike. The open space is Saunders Field, where the heaviest fighting raged on 5–6 May 1864. General Grant's headquarters were situated on the north (left) of the main road, where it bends left near the top of the photo.

had been named in colonial times for British Queen Anne. Its rapid flow prompted settlers to call the stream the 'Rapid Anne,' subsequently shortened to Rapidan.) Skirmishing through the fall of 1863 and the following winter only threatened major operations once, at the end of November. On the 26th, Confederates who had been easing into what they thought would be winter quarters learned that Meade was moving in strength toward crossings lower on the Rapidan, not far west of the familiar ground around Chancellorsville.

Elements of the contending armies collided on 27 November at Payne's Farm and a hot, confused fight blossomed. Much of it raged in densely wooded country. Captain John C. Johnson of the 50th Virginia, 'a large and stout man of about fifty years of age,' who towered over most of his men at 6'7" of height, decided that his men 'were not doing as well as they ought.' To shame them into maintaining a steadier fire, Johnson stalked to the crest of the position, lay down on the ground, 'broadside to the enemy,' and told his men that 'if they were afraid … they could use him as a breastwork.' Undaunted and pragmatic, several infantrymen did just that, resting their rifles on Johnson and firing 'steadily from that position until the fight was over.' Johnson survived the gesture, and also a chest wound he suffered in 1864 and two periods as a prisoner of war, to return home in 1865.

Once both sides had tested their opponents around Payne's Farm, the engagement there became the nexus upon which a long set of parallel lines spread across the countryside just south of the Rapidan. During the last three days of November and the first day of December, men in uniforms of both colors spent more time digging than shooting. A weather front brought in bitter cold and whistling wind on the heels of a long downpour, making everyone miserable at the same time that it reduced the potential for major military movements on the region's few and poor roads.

Meade's lines ran north–south, facing west toward Lee's position. Between the two ran Mine Run, which gave its name to the week-long action. Meade prepared a major turning movement around the Confederate right (southern) flank for the morning of 30 November, but when the time came he recognized that his foe was ready to repulse the attack from strong works. The Pennsylvanian courageously cancelled the attack and two days later recrossed the Rapidan, having lost about 1,500 men south of the river. Lee and most of his soldiers were bitterly disappointed. 'We should never have permitted those people to get away,' Lee seethed.

Meade recognized that sending the vain assault forward would have been popular with President Lincoln and elsewhere in Washington, but he wrote officially, 'I cannot be a party to a wanton slaughter of my troops for any mere personal end.' To his wife, Meade admitted, 'I would rather be ignominiously dismissed, and suffer anything, than knowingly and wilfully have thousands of brave men slaughtered for nothing.' His estimate doubtless was correct: had he thrown in attacks that cost 10,000 (or even 15,000) more men, he surely would have enjoyed, and retain to this day, a glossier image. He might have retained independent control of the Army of the Potomac and emerged as the war's great hero in the North.

As the armies filed away from the Mine Run earthworks, they were ending a year of campaigning that had taken them on broad sweeps across Virginia, Maryland, and Pennsylvania. Only twice during 1863, however, had they fought full-scale, pitched engagements. Chancellorsville was the largest battle ever fought in Virginia, and Gettysburg the costliest of the entire war; but 1863 had produced far less intense combat than the armies had experienced in 1862. The soldiers who settled into winter camps in December 1863 faced, unawares, a new year that would bring far more fighting than the year just past, and under far different circumstances.

## Into the Wilderness

In May 1864, the Federal army advanced
across the Rapidan river and ended a period
of six months during which that stream had,
almost without interruption, constituted the
military frontier between the United States
and the Confederate States. General Robert
E. Lee's Army of Northern Virginia had spent
the winter spread across the rolling fields
beyond the right bank of the river in Orange
County, around Orange Court House and
Gordonsville and Verdiersville. General
George G. Meade's Federal Army of the
Potomac wintered in the piedmont
countryside north of the Rapidan, centered
on Culpeper Court House.

Southern troops by this time had begun
to suffer markedly for want of rations, both
in volume and in quality, at least in part
because the president of the key rail line in
central Virginia was an *ante bellum*
immigrant from the North who secretly
accepted pay from the Federal Secretary of
War. Northern troops enjoyed infinitely
better supplies. Their army also underwent a
profound change during this winter. Meade
remained its nominal commander, and
would occupy that role to the war's end. The
newly minted Commander-in-Chief of all
Federal armies, however, established his
headquarters next to Meade, leaving the
army commander consigned to a secondary
profile. Ulysses S. Grant had come east as the
hero of benchmark Federal triumphs at
Vicksburg and Chattanooga to be
commissioned into the newly created rank of
lieutenant-general. For the rest of the war,
Meade's army commonly appeared in the
press as 'Grant's army' because the
Commander-in-Chief was with it. Writing on
the war still uses that locution, and in fact it
will appear this way in most instances
through the rest of this book.

As spring hardened the roads in 1864,
'Grant's army' prepared to take the offensive
with a new-found determination imparted
by Grant himself. A reorganization
consolidated some of the familiar old corps
out of existence, leaving only the II, V, and

VI Corps. General Ambrose E. Burnside's
IX Corps also marched with the army. The
once-disgraced Burnside had enough
political currency to have landed back in
corps command, and to be immune to
Meade's orders. He would report directly to
Grant, in awkward contravention of the
most basic principles of unity of command.

The combined Federal force that crossed
the Rapidan at the beginning of May
numbered about 120,000 men. Lee could
counter with only a few more than half as
many troops, including Longstreet's infantry,
newly returned from their adventures (and
mis-adventures) in Tennessee and Georgia.
Grant could – and did – draw on
innumerable reinforcements through the
coming campaign; the Confederate
manpower cupboard by this time had
become close to bare.

Grant intended to move south across the
Rapidan east of Lee's army and slice straight
through 'the Wilderness' to get between his
enemy and Richmond. That would force Lee
to react rapidly under circumstances in
which his enemy could choose the terms of
engagement. Much late-twentieth-century
writing has professed to recognize the
striking wisdom that places did not matter,
only the enemy's army. Lee and his
government knew better. Richmond must be
held for an array of fundamental reasons,
industrial, logistical, military, political, and
spiritual. When it in fact fell in April 1865,
the war in Virginia ended almost
concurrently. Grant's attempt to force Lee's
small army to defend the approaches to
Richmond in the spring of 1864 was
precisely the right formula.

Getting through the Wilderness proved to
be far more difficult than Grant had hoped.
The dense second-growth thickets that gave
the region its name covered about 70 square
miles (180km$^2$) on the south bank of the
Rapidan–Rappahannock line, about
12 miles (19km) wide and six miles (9.5km)
deep. When Lee received word that his
adversary had crossed the Rapidan into the
Wilderness, he hurled his troops eastward
and they struck the Federal right flank like a

## The Battle of the Wilderness, 5–6 May 1864

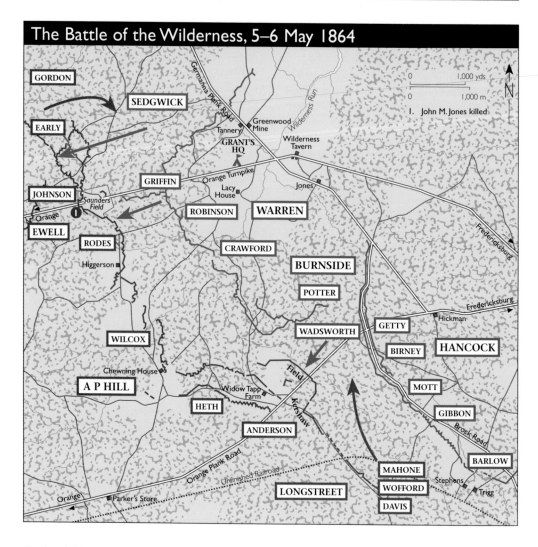

The first clash between the war's two most famous leaders, Robert E. Lee and U. S. Grant, unfolded in the dense thickets of 'the Wilderness' on 5–6 May 1864. Grant's plan to slip across Lee's front and get between him and the Confederate capital at Richmond crumbled when the Confederates came in from the west and struck him a violent blow. For two days the fighting raged in woods and the few clearings, notably Saunders Field and the Widow Tapp Farm, and along the corridors of the Orange Turnpike and the Orange Plank Road. The Federals came close to success in each of the sectors, which were fought in virtual isolation from each other because of the underbrush; but on 6 May Confederate attacks turned and shattered both Federal flanks. On 7 May, Grant moved southeast away from the Wilderness, toward Spotsylvania Court House.

thunderbolt. The Brock Road offered Grant and Meade the only practicable route

southward through the Wilderness. Two east–west roads served Lee as corridors of advance and attack. The old Orange Turnpike ran 2.5 miles (4km) north of the parallel Orange Plank Road. Densely scrubby country separated them. The intersections of the two Orange roads with the Brock Road network became the focus of the strivings of both armies for two days, 5–6 May 1864.

The Battle of the Wilderness erupted on the Orange Turnpike on the morning of the 5th when Federal detachments in that quarter saw Confederates of General Richard S. Ewell's corps threatening from the west. Grant directed Meade to attack. Meade sent General Gouverneur K. Warren's V Corps. The Confederates had begun to build earthworks along the crest of a ridge at the western edge of a 40-acre (16-ha) open space known locally as Saunders Field. When Warren's men marched in determined ranks into the field and started up the other side, they were inaugurating a pattern that defined much of the subsequent two days of fighting on the Turnpike. Confederate firepower pouring down the slope into Saunders Field, from behind defensive works, proved more than flesh and blood could stand – both at the first attack and through many others that followed. An early Unionist surge did attain the western crest, killing Southern General John M. Jones and breaking the line. However, Confederates pounding rapidly eastward on the Turnpike soon ejected the interlopers and restored the position.

Much of General John Sedgwick's Federal V Corps went to Warren's aid. Throughout 5 May men on both sides, particularly the blue-clad attackers, died in the struggle for Saunders Field. A section of guns stranded between the lines served as a magnet for repeated hand-to-hand strife. At day's end, the initial situation around the field remained unchanged despite a daunting expenditure of blood: Federals held the eastern edge, Confederates the western.

The thickets of the Wilderness, broken by only a few rude paths and desolate farmsteads, made maneuvering and fighting on a large scale impracticable between the Turnpike and the Plank Road. Both armies recognized the potential advantage of using the unoccupied middle ground as a means of threatening an exposed enemy rear; both made gestures toward exploiting the opportunity; neither ever managed to effect a serious lodgment.

Meanwhile, a separate battle raged on the Orange Plank Road, nearly in isolation from

The Texans turn Lee back on the Widow Tapp Farm, Wilderness Battlefield. (Painting by Don Troiani, www.historicalartprints.com)

events a few miles to the north. General
A. P. Hill's Confederate Third Corps moved
eastward on the Plank Road. The sturdy
Federal II Corps, commanded by the
indomitable General Winfield Scott Hancock,
interposed an obstacle between Hill and the
crucial intersection. General George W.
Getty's division, extracted from VI Corps up
on the Turnpike, hurried south to help
Hancock hold the Brock–Plank crossroads.
Bitter fighting seethed through the confusing
thickets. Men died by the hundreds and fell
maimed by the thousands.

Federal strength threatened to overwhelm
Hill, but at the end of 5 May he had held.
One-third of Lee's infantry, the First Corps
under General James Longstreet, did not
reach the battlefield at all on 5 May.
Hill's troops, weary and decimated and
ill-organized, lay in the brush of the
Wilderness that night with the desolate
awareness that they could not withstand a
serious attack in the morning.

The arrival of Longstreet's first troops early
on 6 May salvaged a desperate situation for
Lee and resulted in a moment of high
personal drama for the Southern leader.
Hancock had carefully arranged for a broad
attack on both sides of the Plank Road. Soon
after dawn, he launched his assault with
characteristic vigor. It rolled steadily forward,
scattering Hill's regiments and threatening to
rupture Lee's entire front. Artillery had been
of little use in the thickets, but a battalion of
a dozen Confederate guns lined the woods at
the western edge of the Tapp field, a
30-acre clearing around the rude cabin and
modest farm of a widow named Tapp – the
only sizable open space anywhere in the
battle zone along the Plank Road. The
cannon flung canister across the Tapp Farm
space in double-shotted doses, making the
ground untenable for Union infantry.
Northern troops filtered around the edge of
the clearing to get in behind the guns and
complete the victory. Then, without any time

whatsoever to spare, the van of Longstreet's
column reached the point of crisis.

Among the first units up was the famed
Texas Brigade, perhaps Lee's best shock
troops. The battles that had won the Texans
their well-deserved renown had cost them
enormous casualties: fewer than 800 of them
remained to carry muskets into the
Wilderness that morning. As the brigade
moved resolutely through the hard-pressed
artillery, Lee rode quietly beside them. The
General recognized his army's peril, and had
determined to take a personal role in
repairing the rupture. When the Texans
noticed him, and recognized his intention,

The final Confederate attack on 6 May swept
all the way to the Brock Road, but could not
hold the position. (Public domain)

'a yell rent the air that must have been heard for miles around.' The Texans urged Lee to go back, shouting that they would not go forward until he did so. A soldier (there would later be dozens of claimants for the honor) grasped Lee's bridle and turned him back.

A participant in the event, writing soon thereafter, noted that Lee had not said much, but it was 'his tone and look, which each one of us knew were born of the dangers of the hour' that 'so infused and excited the men.' A Texan next to the observer, 'with tears coursing down his cheeks and yells issuing from his throat

exclaimed, "I would charge hell itself for that old man."'

Lee went back. The Texans went forward and redeemed their pledge. Federal bullets hit nearly three-fourths of them within a few minutes, but they stabilized the situation and saved the day. The 'Lee-to-the-Rear' episode immediately became an integral part of army lore. A monument at the spot today says simply, 'Lee to the rear, cried the Texans, May 6, 1864.'

Once Longstreet's reinforcements had stabilized the situation, the Confederate commanders looked for a means to regain the initiative. They found it in an unfinished

Hundreds of helpless wounded men of both sides burned to death when muzzle flashes light the thickets of the Wilderness on fire. (Public domain)

railroad – graded and filled, but not yet tracked – that ran south of and parallel to the Plank Road. A mixed force of four brigades pulled from various divisions got astride the rail corridor, moved east until opposite the dangling Federal left flank, then turned north and completely routed Hancock's troops. In Hancock's words, the Confederates rolled up his line 'like a wet blanket.' Most of the attackers pushed as far north as the Plank Road. Some of them actually went into the woods north of the road.

In the ensuing chaos, a mistaken 'friendly' volley tore into a cavalcade of Confederate officers reconnoitering on the road. It killed General Micah Jenkins and inflicted a dreadful wound on Longstreet. Lee's most capable surviving subordinate eventually recovered, but he would be out of service until long after the war had settled into a siege at Petersburg. The fatal volley, reminiscent of the mistaken fire that had mortally wounded Stonewall Jackson nearby exactly one year earlier, extracted all the

energy from the Confederate success. An attack later in the day pressed all the way to the heart of the enemy line on the Brock Road, but in the end it produced nothing but more losses.

While Lee inspired the Texans and then regained the initiative on the Plank Road, General Ewell's Confederates continued to hold firm control of their crucial wood line up on the Turnpike. General John B. Gordon – a non-professional soldier who would bloom late in the conflict into a remarkable warrior – spent much of 6 May attempting to secure permission for an attack in the woods on the far left, where Grant had failed to protect his right flank. Timidity ruled Ewell's behavior by this time in the war (he had lost a leg and gained an extremely strong-willed wife, with deleterious impact upon his élan and *amour-propre*). By the time Gordon extracted authority to attack, daylight was dwindling. Even so, the surprise assault captured two Yankee generals and hundreds of men, and thoroughly shattered Grant's flank. In a ghastly aftermath to the Wilderness fighting, leaves and brush caught fire from muzzle flashes and hundreds of helpless wounded men of both sides burned to death.

For two weeks, Lee's Confederates stubbornly resisted the Federal army under Grant and Meade in the woods and fields around Spotsylvania Court House. After Confederates won the race for the key intersection on 8 May, both armies entrenched on a steadily widening front. On 10 May, a Federal assault broke into the Doles' salient and two days later about 25,000 Northern troops crushed the nose of the Mule Shoe. Lee hurriedly constructed a new final line across the base of the Mule Shoe, and easily repulsed an attack against the position on 18 May. The next day, a brisk fight at the Harris Farm, northeast of the main battlefield, ended major action at Spotsylvania. On the 21st, Grant moved southeast in a new attempt to interpose between Lee and Richmond.

# The Battle of Spotsylvania Court House

After two days of intense combat in the Wilderness, Grant had lost about 18,000 men, Lee perhaps 8,000 (Confederate casualties for the last year of the war are difficult to ascertain with any precision). Wilderness was the only major battle in the Virginia Theater in which an army had both of its flanks shattered. Grant had vivid, immediate proof that fighting Lee would be nothing at all like toying with Generals Bragg and Johnston and Pemberton in the west. Nothing daunted, the Federal Commander-in-Chief calmly determined

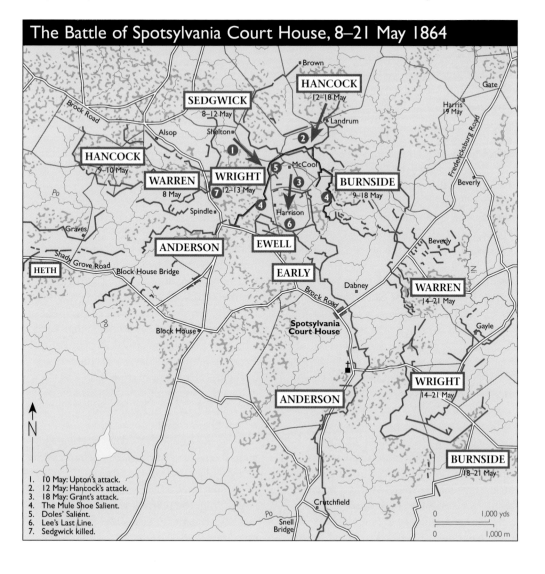

**The Battle of Spotsylvania Court House, 8–21 May 1864**

1. 10 May: Upton's attack.
2. 12 May: Hancock's attack.
3. 18 May: Grant's attack.
4. The Mule Shoe Salient.
5. Doles' Salient.
6. Lee's Last Line.
7. Sedgwick killed.

to press southward again, keeping the pressure on Lee.

Early on 7 May, Grant issued orders to leave the Wilderness and head southeast toward Spotsylvania Court House, where the regional road net afforded a chance to slip between Lee and Richmond. When Grant turned south, despite having suffered as grievous losses as had prompted other commanders to return north, he put the war in Virginia onto a new track. Soldiers sensed the new resolve when they divined the direction of the move, and cheered boisterously. Tens of thousands of them would be shot in the next four weeks, but the army would continue to press steadily southward.

The march toward Spotsylvania Court House turned into a dramatic race fraught with mighty consequences. In a remarkable bout of prescience, Lee had ordered months before the improvement of a set of woods roads that paralleled the Brock Road, leading toward Spotsylvania. He selected General Richard H. Anderson, a phlegmatic officer, to replace temporarily the wounded Longstreet at the head of the First Corps. Anderson put his troops on the road to Spotsylvania, and found no good place to stop because of burning woods and narrow byways – so he kept marching all night long.

Federal progress on the far better Brock Road faltered in the face of scattered, but determined, resistance from Confederate cavalry. General Philip H. Sheridan, a Grant crony from the west, was new to command of the Federal cavalry, which should have shouldered the gray-clad skirmishers out of the way with ease. Sheridan was scheming this night, however, about getting out from under Meade's orders and instead reporting directly to his friend Grant. As a result, the Confederate resistance held on at one sketchy position after another all night.

Early on 8 May the race to Spotsylvania ended with Confederates controlling the key intersection on the Spindle Farm a matter of moments before Meade's advance arrived there. The consequence of Sheridan's indifference and Anderson's inability to stop

Confederates used felled trees covered with earth to fabricate an intricate set of field fortifications unlike anything that had been used earlier in the war. This view is in the vicinity of the nose of the Mule Shoe, near what became 'the Bloody Angle.' (Public domain)

was a very narrow margin of success for the Confederates. All day long, Federals trudged across an open field into Southern rifle fire, hoping to gain the intersection that they had lost in the race. They never succeeded, on 8 May or on several subsequent days. Thousands of them fell killed or wounded in the forlorn attempts.

The Battle of Spotsylvania Court House churned across a broad stretch of country for two weeks, from the meeting engagement on 8 May until 21 May. Never before had field armies in Virginia remained in close contact for more than a few days. Now the war was changing, edging away from dash and maneuver toward mighty defensive works and, eventually, positional warfare resembling a siege.

Most of General Lee's defensive line at Spotsylvania took advantage of good ground along a ridge that covered four miles (6.4km) of farming country between the Po and Ni rivers. From the point at which the 8 May race ended, units of both sides spread in both directions, entrenching as they went.

Federal reinforcements pressed southwest toward the Po, hoping to get beyond Lee's flank; Confederates arrived to counter them. When both armies' flanks reached the Po, Federals began to push in the opposite direction, northeast from the Brock Road. Confederates countered that initiative too, but in the process created an unfortunate anomaly in their position.

General Edward 'Allegheny' Johnson (the nickname came from an early war victory at a place called Allegheny) led his Confederate division northeast from the Brock Road long after sundown. In the inky darkness, Johnson's staff and the van of the division emerged from thick woods into the edge of a clearing. They could see Federal campfires in the distance at what seemed to be a lower elevation, so they stopped and began to erect defensive works. By morning, the Confederate line they had fortified and extended stretched far north of the generally east-to-west axis of the troops nearer the Brock Road. This 'salient' swung up and back through a broad arc that prompted some of the farm lads who fought there to bestow upon it the name 'Mule Shoe.'

The Mule Shoe salient, about one mile (1.6km) deep north-to-south and half that wide, became the paramount military feature through most of the Battle of Spotsylvania. The location of the line did take advantage of high ground, and it did afford protection for Confederate supply routes farther south; but it proved to be fatally vulnerable in a tactical sense. Southern infantry erected a vast, complex array of defenses of dirt and felled trees to strengthen the salient. They also constructed traverses – interior defensive walls perpendicular to the main line – to protect against fire coming in from hostile country opposite their flanks. No fortifications, however, could extinguish the elemental defect of a salient: an enemy who broke through at any point across the entire arc immediately had at his mercy the rear of every defending unit.

General Grant's strength in numbers and materiel gave him the luxury of dictating the action. For two weeks he intermittently

General John Sedgwick, commander of the Federal VI Corps, declared 'they couldn't hit an elephant at that range' just moments before a sharpshooter's bullet killed him. (Public domain)

probed at Lee's line, occasionally bludgeoning it with a massive attack. On 9 May the Army of the Potomac lost the reliable veteran commander of its VI Corps, General John Sedgwick. The corps commander's troops had been building breastworks next to the Brock Road when long-range Confederate rifle fire, from about 650yds (600m) away, drove them from their jobs. Sedgwick sought to inspire them to do their duty by standing tall. 'They couldn't hit an elephant at that range,' he said. A dull whistle announced the passage of another well-aimed bullet which whistled past. The one after that hit Sedgwick beneath his left eye and killed him instantly. He was the highest-ranking Federal officer killed during the war.

Federals probed west of the Po, where Confederates blocked them successfully, but the heaviest fighting surged back and forth across the entrenched positions in the Mule Shoe salient. On 10 May, General Emory Upton, the bright young New Yorker in command of a Federal brigade, sold army headquarters on the notion of attacking a vulnerable segment of Lee's line. Upton led a dozen regiments to the edge of a wood that looked across 150yds (135m) of open field toward the northwest corner of the Mule Shoe. There a salient on the salient – a small bulge on the corner of the larger projection – offered an attractive target. The Federals waiting to attack dreaded the deadly fire they would face the moment they emerged from cover. 'I felt my gorge rise,' one of them wrote, 'and my stomach and intestines shrink together in a knot … I fully realized the terrible peril I was to encounter. I looked about in the faces of the boys around me, and they told the tale of expected death. Pulling my cap down over my eyes, I stepped out.'

Upton's direct assault surprised the Confederates – Georgians under General George Doles. It burst over the works, captured several hundred Southerners, and seemed poised to rupture the whole Mule Shoe position; but Confederate reinforcements hurriedly sealed the shoulder of the breach, some of them led by Lee himself. Federal supports did not come forward with the same élan Upton and his men had shown. When the fighting waned at dark, the breakthrough had been repulsed.

General Grant apparently considered Upton's success as admonitory. In the Wilderness, all of Grant's efforts to maneuver against Lee had been less than successful, and he wound up with both of the Union flanks turned and shattered. Now Upton had gone straight ahead. Perhaps the solution was simply to overwhelm the outnumbered Confederates? On 12 May, Grant launched an immense assault intended to do just that. The immediate result was the heaviest day of fighting at Spotsylvania and one of the most intense hand-to-hand combats of the war. In the longer term, Grant's preliminary success on the 12th probably convinced him to adopt the notion of full-scale, head-on frontal assaults that led to vast and futile effusions of blood over the next few weeks.

Through the night of 11–12 May, Federal troops marshaled opposite the northeast face of the Mule Shoe. Relentless rain and a

pitch-black night complicated their preparations (one general called the result an 'exquisitely ludicrous scene'), but by 4.30 am a force of about 25,000 men had consolidated into a dense mass, ready to attack. General Winfield Scott Hancock sent them forward in what would prove to be the most successful assault of its kind by Federals during the entire war in Virginia. Hancock's leadership and the men's bravery contributed to the attack's initial success, but it also benefited from two bits of happenstance: in

a dreadful stroke of bad timing, the
Confederate artillery had been withdrawn
from the Mule Shoe to be ready in case
Grant moved eastward; and the rain and
humidity had rendered most of the
Confederate infantry's weapons inoperative.

The noise of the gathering enemy had
been audible all night to Confederates
(McHenry Howard said it sounded 'like
distant falling water or machinery'), and
they had scrambled to get the artillery back
in position. When the attackers approached,

Modern aerial view of Spotsylvania Court House
Battlefield, looking southeast from above the Federal lines
toward the Bloody Angle. The Confederate position stood
at the edge of the trees beyond the field. The modern
road winds down the shoulders of the Mule Shoe salient.

they made an incomparable target for
canister or other artillery rounds – rolling
forward in a wide, deep formation,
impossible to miss. Most of the Confederate
guns scurrying back toward the nose of the
Mule Shoe, however, arrived just in time to

For hours the combatants struggled at hand-to-hand range, separated only by fortifications made of earth and wood. (Public domain)

be captured without firing a round. When the Southern infantry leveled muskets and pulled triggers, the commander of the famous old 'Stonewall Brigade' expected the results he had seen many times before: volleys that knocked down the enemy in windrows and halted the assailants' momentum. But 'instead of the leaping line of fire and the sharp crack of the muskets,' General James A. Walker wrote in dismay, 'came the pop! pop! pop! of exploding caps as the hammer fell upon them. Their powder was damp!' The military rubric, 'Keep your powder dry,' belonged to earlier wars fought with flintlock muskets. This affair on 12 May 1864 was the only major instance in which damp powder affected tactical events during the Civil War.

The Federal tide swept over the strong works at the nose of the Mule Shoe and roared on southward for several hundred yards. Then the chaos and disorientation, often as incumbent upon military success as upon military failure, dissolved the

momentum. Desperate Confederates, some led by General Lee in person (as on 6 May and 10 May), knit together new lines across the Mule Shoe and up its sides. By dint of intense, costly fighting they pushed Hancock's Federals back to the outer edge of the northern tip of the works. By then both sides had exhausted their initiative and the swirling fighting dissolved into a deadly, bloody, close encounter across the entrenchments. For 20 hours the contending forces occupied either side of a gentle bend in the works that stretched for about 160yds (145m), making it forever famous as 'the Bloody Angle' – a *nom de guerre* christened with the blood of hundreds of soldiers.

The Bloody Angle was made possible by the tall, thick earthworks, new to the war in this campaign. No one could have fought for more than a few minutes over the kind of primitive trenches in use only a few months before. The nose of the Mule Shoe featured embattlements made of tree trunks laid lengthwise, sometimes two parallel rows with dirt between. Dirt piled over the bulk of the fortification made it impenetrable by either bullets or shells. The ditch behind the works was deep enough to require a firing step for defenders to see to fire, through a space between the main wall and a head log perched above it.

About 2,000 men from South Carolina and Mississippi clung to the south face of the works. Far more Federals from the VI and II Corps threatened the Bloody Angle from the north, but numbers mattered little in that narrow front. Most Union troops went to ground behind the lip of a draw about 40yds (37m) north of the works; others lay directly behind the north edge of the contested line. Brave men of both sides leaped atop the works to fire a round then drop back, if they survived. Others threw bayoneted rifles across like harpoons. A steady rain added misery to terror. The trenches filled with water 'as bloody as if it flowed from an abattoir.'

A Confederate called the scene 'a perfect picture of gloom, destruction and death – a very Golgotha of horrors.' A Federal general who visited the scene described the results of a fire so intense and long-continued 'that the brush and logs were cut to pieces and whipped into basket-stuff … men's flesh was torn from the bones and the bones shattered.' Toward midnight of 12–13 May, an oak tree 22 inches (56cm) thick fell. It had been hit not by a cannonball, but by countless thousands of bullets, which gradually nibbled their way through its dense bole.

Just before dawn on 13 May, the Confederate survivors finally received orders to abandon the Bloody Angle and fall back to a new line drawn across the base of the Mule Shoe – where Lee's position probably should have been formed from the outset. A Northerner who visited the newly won position at the nose of the salient left a graphic description of the place's horrors: 'Horses and men chopped into hash by the bullets … appearing … like piles of jelly … The logs in the breastworks were shattered into splinters … We had not only shot down an army, but also a forest.' In the aftermath of 'this most desperate struggle of the war,' one Mississippian who survived admitted that the tension and dread of the ordeal had shattered their nervous systems. Once they

reached safe ground, the weary veterans simply 'sat down on the wet ground and wept. Not silently, but vociferously and long.'

Through the period 13–17 May, the Federal army slipped steadily eastward, then southeastward, extending toward and around the Confederate right. This tactical measure foreshadowed Grant's strategic agenda for the next month, during which a crablike sliding movement to the southeast sought always to get closer to Richmond than Lee's army. Already he had unleashed Sheridan's cavalry to raid toward the Southern capital. The raiders did not get into Richmond, but they did kill the Confederacy's incomparable cavalry leader, General J. E. B. Stuart, in fighting around Yellow Tavern. Stuart had said 'I had rather die than be whipped.' Lee would miss his skill in screening and reconnaissance functions.

Although fighting flared all across the lines with regularity, the next major Federal attempt did not come until 18 May. On that morning, Grant launched another massive frontal assault against Lee's troops in their strongly entrenched new lines across the base of the Mule Shoe – a position that came to be called 'Lee's Last Line.' Upton's head-on attack on 10 May had worked; so had the Hancock onslaught on 12 May; perhaps what was needed was simply to bludgeon Lee. This time, though, Confederate cannon stood ready. Without needing much help from supporting infantry, they slaughtered Grant's attackers without the least difficulty or danger.

The Army of the Potomac recoiled after heavy losses, never having come close to their enemies. As General Meade wrote wearily to his wife the next day, after the thorough repulse 'even Grant thought it useless to [continue to] knock our heads against a brick wall.' Most Southern infantry hardly mentioned the event in their letters and diaries, the repulse having been so easy that it required 'but little participation of our infantry.' A Confederate artillery colonel wrote regretfully that the Yankee infantry 'wouldn't charge with any spirit.' In the words of a boy from Richmond, 'the Union troops broke and fled.'

## To the North Anna and the James

Fighting on 19 May at the Harris Farm, northeast of the old salient position and beyond the Ni river, brought to a close two weeks of steady combat. Grant moved southeast in his continuing efforts to intrude between Lee and Richmond and force battle on his own terms. The two armies clashed across and around the North Anna river, midway between Spotsylvania and Richmond, on 23–27 May. They waged no pitched engagement during that time, but jockeyed steadily for position.

The river, running roughly perpendicular to the Federal line of advance, offered only three usable crossings. The left (northern) bank of the stream at the fords on the eastern and western edges of the battlefield commanded the right bank, making it

possible for Grant to force troops across. At Ox Ford in the middle, ground made the Confederates masters of the locale. Nonchalantly, almost indifferently, Grant pushed his columns across on each flank, giving Lee a golden opportunity to defeat either side in detail. The river and its difficult fords markedly complicated Federal options, to Lee's advantage.

In 1862 or early 1863, such circumstances would have yielded a thorough thrashing for Grant. In May 1864, however, Lee did not have the means to gather in the toothsome prize. All three of his corps commanders were out of action, and a temporary illness had almost prostrated Lee himself. He could only seethe from his cot: 'We must strike them a blow – we must never let them pass us again – we must strike them a blow.'

Grant steered his army southeast once more, from the North Anna river toward Totopotomoy Creek, ever closer to Richmond. Lee's customary interposition kept nudging the Federals eastward even as

Union engineer troops at work on the banks of the North Anna river, where Lee stymied Grant for four days in late May 1864. (Public domain)

General Evander M. Law's Alabama troops slaughtered attacking Federals at Cold Harbor. 'It was not war,' Law wrote, 'it was murder.' (Public domain)

they pressed south. Steady but desultory fighting at Totopotomoy led Grant toward scenes familiar from the earlier campaigns around Richmond.

By 2 June the armies were concentrating around Cold Harbor, where Lee's first great victory had been won on 27 June 1862 in the Battle of Gaines' Mill. The Confederate line that was hurriedly entrenched at the beginning of June 1864 ran right through the old battlefield; some of the 1864 fighting of greatest intensity would rage where the same armies had jousted two years before. A Northern newspaperman described the Southern entrenchments as 'intricate, zig-zagged lines within lines, lines protecting flanks of lines … a maze and labyrinth of works within works and works without works.'

On 3 June, weary of being blocked at every turn and always inclined toward brutally direct action, Grant simply sent forward tens of thousands of men right into that formidable warren of defenses, and into the muzzles of rifles wielded by toughened veterans. The young Northerners obliged to

participate in this disaster at Cold Harbor knew what the result would be. A member of General Grant's staff noticed them pinning to their uniforms pieces of paper bearing their names and home places, so that their bodies would not go unidentified. In very short order on that late-spring morning, 7,000 Union soldiers fell to Confederate musketry without any hope of success.

A Federal from New Hampshire wrote bluntly: 'It was undoubtedly the greatest and most inexcusable slaughter of the whole war … It seemed more like a volcanic blast than a battle … The men went down in rows, just as they marched in the ranks, and so many at a time that those in rear of them thought they were lying down.' General Emory Upton, who had been so successful at Rappahannock Station and Spotsylvania with carefully planned attacks, wrote on 4 June that he was 'disgusted' with the generalship displayed. 'Our men have … been foolishly and wantonly sacrificed,' he wrote bitterly; 'thousands of lives might have been spared by the exercise of a little skill.'

Some Southerners dealing out death from behind their entrenchments around Cold Harbor blanched at the carnage, but a boy from Alabama reflected on what was being inflicted upon his country and admitted that 'an indescribable feeling of pleasure courses through my veins upon surveying these heaps of the slain.' A pronouncement by that Alabamian's brigade commander, General Evander M. Law, has been the most often-cited summary of Cold Harbor. 'It was not war,' Law mused, 'it was murder.'

The bloodshed northeast of Richmond settled into steady, but deadly, trench warfare for the week after 3 June. Rotting corpses from the hopeless assault spread a suffocating stench across both lines; flies and other insects bedeviled the front-line troops; sniping between the lines inflicted steady casualties and made life difficult. Troops who had been scornful of digging earthworks earlier in the war now entrenched eagerly. Soon they had constructed elaborate lines and forts that stretched for miles across the countryside.

By the time of the slaughter at Cold Harbor, troops in both armies had become convinced of the value of field fortifications. They soon constructed elaborate lines that stretched for many miles. This view depicts a fort on the line around Petersburg. (Public domain)

Much of the 10 months of war that remained to be fought in Virginia would feature such horrors, but the site of most of those operations would be south of the James river. On 12 June, Grant began carefully to extract substantial components of his army from the trenches and move them southward toward a crossing of the river. In managing that successful maneuver, Grant skilfully and thoroughly stole a march on General Lee, and achieved his most dramatic large-scale coup of 1864. Soldiers would continue to battle in the outskirts of Richmond for the rest of the war, but the focus of operations henceforth would move below the James to the environs of Petersburg.

## Petersburg besieged

For 10 months, the primary armies in the Virginia Theater of war struggled for control of Petersburg, Virginia. They fought pitched battles for possession of key roads and rail lines; they covered the surrounding countryside with massive forts and entrenchments; and Federals fired artillery into the city. The war came to Petersburg initially, however, not with a mighty roar, but in a slowly building rhythm.

General Benjamin F. Butler's 35,000-man Army of the James posed the earliest threat to the city when it landed at Bermuda Hundred on 4 May 1864. Because the omnipotent Federal navy could land Butler's troops with impunity, they found themselves unopposed and only eight miles (13km) northeast of Petersburg. Confederate General P. G. T. Beauregard inherited the difficult task of knitting together the sparse and disparate units in the vicinity to keep Butler in check.

The Federal general's paramount goal was Richmond, but he turned first toward Petersburg. Although steadily outnumbered by odds of three-to-one, Beauregard managed to thwart Butler in four actions between 9 May and 22 May at Port Walthall Junction, Swift Creek, Chester Station, and Drewry's Bluff. The Confederates benefited immeasurably from Butler's ineptitude, timidity, and contentiousness with his own subordinates. By 22 May, Butler had given up and begun to entrench the neck of the Bermuda Hundred peninsula. In the memorable phrase of a disgusted General U. S. Grant, this left Butler's force 'as completely shut off from further operations ... as if it had been in a bottle strongly corked.'

On 9 June, Butler tried again. He sent 6,500 men from inside the corked bottle to capture Petersburg, which lay almost entirely unprotected and apparently within easy reach. The Federal cavalry swung around to come in from the south while their infantry mates went at the town from the northeast. They were repulsed in a desperate fight that became famous as 'The Battle of Old Men and Young Boys.' An array of citizens beyond the outer limits of military age (ranging in age from at least 14 to 61), ill-armed and untrained, threw themselves in the path of the invaders – and turned them back. One veteran battery arrived in time to play a crucial role in the narrow margin of victory. Nearly a hundred of the civilians became casualties as they saved their hometown. Anne Banister was standing on the porch of her home with her mother and sister when a wagon brought up 'my father's lifeless body shot through the head, his gray hair dabbled in blood.' On the evening of 9 June, 'universal mourning was over the town, for the young and old were lying dead in many homes.'

By the time the rag-tag civilian assemblage had held Petersburg, U. S. Grant had decided to devote his main army to the task of capturing the city. The incredibly costly repulse of his troops at Cold Harbor on 3 June had eroded even Grant's oblivious determination. Taking Petersburg would sever most of the roads and railroads heading to Richmond, thus cutting the Confederate capital off from the rest of the Confederacy. On 12 June, Grant began deftly to disengage major units of the Army of the Potomac from its trenches and move it by stages to the James river. On the 14th the crossing began, in part on transports and in part by way of an enormous pontoon bridge, more than 2,000ft (600m) in length, that was one of the engineering wonders of the war.

General Robert E. Lee's remarkable ability to divine his enemy's intentions stood him in good stead in many a campaign, but it deserted him in early June. Grant slipped

away from Lee's presence without the Confederate chieftain learning of the move. When Beauregard reported the arrival south of the James of portions of the main enemy army, Lee discounted the news. Beauregard's tendency to concoct visionary schemes and embrace implausible notions contributed to Lee's uncertainty, but Grant thoroughly and unmistakably stole a march on his adversary. The result was a three-day span during which Petersburg stood almost defenseless against a Northern horde.

One of the war's great marvels is that Grant's men did not simply march into Petersburg during 15–18 June. They surely would have done so had they not been enervated by the bloodletting of the previous month. On the 15th, more than 15,000 Northerners faced barely 2,000 Southerners. The defenders spread themselves in thin, widely separated clusters among works begun in 1862 to protect the city. Late on the 15th, a portion of that line fell to attacking Federals. 'Petersburg,'

Southerners called General Benjamin F. Butler 'Beast Butler' for his attitudes toward civilians in occupied New Orleans in 1862. In 1864, Butler fumbled hopelessly in his operations around Petersburg. (Public domain)

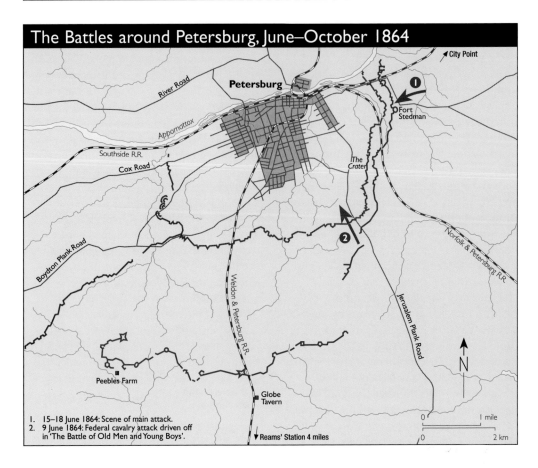

**The Battles around Petersburg, June–October 1864**

1.  15–18 June 1864: Scene of main attack.
2.  9 June 1864: Federal cavalry attack driven off
    in 'The Battle of Old Men and Young Boys'.

Beauregard wrote, 'was clearly at the mercy of the Federal commander.'

For two more days, Grant's troops swarmed around Petersburg without making a decisive move. Early on 18 June, the first men from Lee's Army of Northern Virginia finally arrived, and Lee himself reached the town before noon. The Confederates bought time by abandoning their outer works on the 18th, leaving the first Federal attack to dissipate in a confusing complex of empty trenches.

When the blue-clad legions reformed and moved forward again, they attacked without concert – and without success. The First Maine Heavy Artillery, which Grant had extracted from a cozy post in the quiet forts around Washington and sent into the line with muskets, was butchered. More than 630 of the Maine men fell in an utterly hopeless assault. During the entire Civil War, no regiment suffered as many losses in one

For 10 months beginning in mid-June 1864, the war in Virginia swung around the pivot of Petersburg. The roads and railroads leading through Petersburg to Richmond became the Confederate capital's final lifeline. For weeks in early June the city lay virtually undefended, but the first Federal raiders suffered a repulse at the hands of old men and youngsters beyond the age limits for regular army service. During 15–18 June, uncoordinated attacks failed to break into Petersburg despite being opposed by only a tiny handful of Southern troops. Thereafter the fighting became a deadly struggle for the railroads. Grant pushed columns west, gradually closing off Confederate use of the Jerusalem Plank Road, then the Weldon Railroad, and eventually the Boydton Plank Road. If he could reach the South Side Railroad, Petersburg and Richmond would be strangled. The winter of 1864–65 closed in before Grant could accomplish that final measure.

engagement. One of the minority who survived unscathed described the experience: 'The earth was literally torn up with iron and lead. The field became a burning, seething, crashing, hissing hell, in which human courage, flesh, and bone were struggling with

The brave but hopeless charge of the 1st Maine Heavy Artillery at Petersburg, 18 June 1864. The Maine unit lost more men here in a single battle than any other regiment on either side during the entire war. (Painting by Don Troiani, www.historicalartprints.com)

an impossibility … In ten minutes those who were not slaughtered had returned.' The next morning a dense fog lifted to reveal a 'field of slaughter, strewn thick with the blue-coated bodies … decomposing in the fierce rays of a Southern sun.'

While the bitter Maine veteran gazed across a field covered with his friends' bodies, major elements of Lee's Army of Northern Virginia were filing steadily into the defenses. Those sturdy troops would not be routed from their entrenchments by any kind of frontal assault. Petersburg had been saved, and for more than nine months would stand, with Richmond, as the last major Confederate citadel in Virginia.

## The Crater

When the wretchedly managed Federal assaults of 15–18 June ended in an ineffectual welter of blood, Grant faced the necessity to begin a siege. He had lost more than 10,000 men in the awkward attempt to batter his way into Petersburg, as against appreciably fewer than half as many Confederate casualties. With characteristic determination, Grant quickly arranged to extend his lines southwestward across Lee's front. His purpose in this and several subsequent initiatives was to snap Southern railroads and other lines of communication and supply. At the same time, his almost limitless resources in men and materiel would benefit from ever-longer front lines. Eventually the limited Confederate strength would be stretched to the breaking point. Execution of those two initiatives constituted the story of the next nine months.

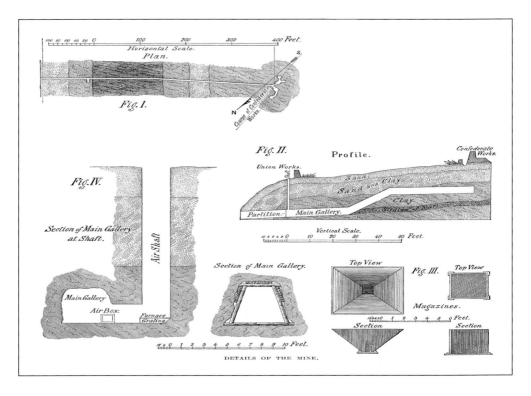

The sturdy coal miners who dug the tunnel between the lines faced considerable danger and discomfort even before it was packed with 8,000lbs (3, 629kg) of powder. Their ingenious system for drawing fresh air into the tunnel made the project possible. (Public domain)

Grant's first move of his left beyond Lee's right came on 21 June. The reliable II Corps, under the magnificent leadership of General Winfield Scott Hancock, moved across the Jerusalem Plank Road, permanently denying that artery to the Confederates, and on toward the Weldon Railroad. Lee could not surrender the vital rail link without a fight. He sent two divisions out to intercept Hancock's force. The tactical result was stunning. The glorious old Federal II Corps folded and ran in the face of a smaller force, losing 2,500 men, the vast majority of them as prisoners of war.

This embarrassing result, which could not have been imagined under any circumstances from that seasoned formation a few months earlier, highlighted the condition of Grant's army. It had been bled so thoroughly, and enervated so completely, that it had lost its

hard-won and long-held prowess. Most of the army's field-grade officers, company officers, and non-commissioned officers lay moldering in graves between the Rapidan and James rivers, or languishing wounded in facilities along the east coast.

Conventional historical wisdom has long credited Grant with a sort of quiet genius that recognized the necessity of slaughtering troops of both sides in endless hecatombs until arithmetic won the war. The unmistakable historical record shows that accepting about 200,000 combined casualties in getting to Richmond did end the war in a year of bloodshed. A minority opinion suggests that the immutable advantages of terrain and strategic imperatives available to the Federal cause around Petersburg would have set a far more desirable stage upon which to invoke elements of the military art. By the time the Army of the Potomac reached that advantageous ground in 1864, however, the army retained only a barely recognizable shadow of its former might. The months to come would feature operations in the image of the Weldon Railroad.

General Winfield Scott Hancock's superb leadership had made the Federal II Corps into a redoubtable force. (Public domain)

Through the summer of 1864, Grant intermittently pushed his left farther west, and Lee countered on his right. Most of the soldiers' energies, however, went into work with shovels rather than with rifles. A warren of forts and redoubts and trenches sprang up and ambled across the Virginia countryside. Men fought from behind works of wood and dirt, and lived in 'bombproofs,' as they called their rude homes hollowed out in the earth and reinforced with timber.

One of the war's most remarkable episodes, the product of an amazing engineering feat, grew out of the stalemate imposed by impregnable fortifications. Attacking a deeply entrenched enemy afforded little hope of success, against a guarantee of staggering casualties. A regiment recruited in coal-mining country, the 48th Pennsylvania Infantry, conceived the notion of digging a tunnel far beneath the earth's surface that would lead under the Confederate line, which then could be blown to smithereens. The Pennsylvanians undertook the novel project with a great deal of energy and ingenuity. They modified ration boxes to use for removing the dirt. They sent parties out to cut timber to shore up the excavation. They fabricated a complex but clever means to exhaust bad air from the lengthening tunnel and bring in

The fight for control of the Crater developed into a savage hand-to-hand struggle. (Public domain)

fresh air through a wooden conduit. After three weeks of labor, the miners had completed a tunnel that ran 511ft (156m) and ended squarely beneath the main enemy line. For 10 days they dug a lateral chamber and then packed it full of gunpowder – four tons of it. They planned to blow up the massive charge at dawn on 30 July.

The Pennsylvanian soldier-miners had achieved an incredible success, but the Federal military hierarchy had not done nearly as well preparing to capitalize on the fruits of their labor. General Ambrose E. Burnside, who had failed so egregiously at Fredericksburg in 1862, was back with the army in command of the Federal IX Corps and responsible for the sector where the 48th had dug so diligently. He decided to assign his well-trained but untested all-black division to exploit the gap to be made by the explosion. General Meade refused to let Burnside use the black troops as the first wave because he knew that, if they took heavy losses, he would be pilloried by politicians and journalists. Burnside chose (by the mindless expedient of drawing straws) to substitute the least effective of his white divisions, commanded by the inept – and perhaps drunken – General James H. Ledlie.

Exploding the mine involved moments of high drama. An officer of the 48th lit the long, long fuse at 3.00 am and thousands of men in blue waited in breathless silence for the explosion. Thousands of Confederates in deadly danger dozed in innocence. Nothing happened. By 4.15 am it had become apparent that nothing was going to happen without intervention. Two brave Pennsylvanians, Lieutenant Jacob Douty (a doughty fellow indeed) and Sergeant Harry Reese, crawled into the long, dark mine to investigate. They found that the fuse had failed at one of its several splices, relit it, and scurried to safety. Finally, at 4.45 am the 'earth trembled for miles around,' as a Virginia soldier put it, under the echoes of a mighty explosion. The blast killed or wounded nearly 300 South Carolinians.

When Smith Lipscomb, who survived, tumbled out of the air and landed on his feet, his 'thies [thighs] felt like they were almost shivered.' Lipscomb thought that he must have been badly crippled, but a Federal volley 'convinced me I was not as badly hurt as I thought I was,' he recalled later. The injured man staggered back under cover and began rubbing his painful legs. Before long he had found a rifle and began shooting at the enemy. The carnage continued until

HEADQUARTERS OF GENERAL GRANT AND BASE OF SUPPLIES, CITY POINT, ON

Smith 'saw the blood run down [a] little drain ditch several feet.'

Ledlie's troops dashed forward toward the breach and gazed in awe at a chasm about 170ft long, 80ft wide, and 30 ft deep (50m × 25m × 10m). While they stared at the place known ever since as 'the Crater,' Confederates behind the gap and on either side began to rally. Federal reinforcements pushed into the Crater and beyond, but fire from either flank limited their penetration. General Lee pulled Southern reinforcements from points all around his front to use in re-establishing his line. For several hours, an opening blown in the Confederate position beckoned Federals to lunge through and capture the city just beyond. Eventually Burnside received permission to commit the black division to the fight, but long after the crucial moment for which those troops had been trained. The black soldiers simply added to the chaos in the muddy, bloody Crater.

As Confederate units closed in, Federals in the Crater became defenders instead of attackers. Artillery shells, some of them from newly deployed high-angle mortars, exploded above the Crater and flung shards into its corners. The Confederate charge that retook the position erupted over the lip of the Crater and surged through its midst in hand-to-hand combat that turned the pit into 'one seething cauldron of struggling, dying men.' General J. C. C. Sanders of Alabama, who commanded a brigade at the scene, wrote that Southern guns 'literally mowed down the enemy piling up Yankees and Negroes on each other.' Confederate artillerist Frank Huger used similar language: 'our men literally butchered them.' A Massachusetts officer described the crowded situation inside the Crater as so tight that 'many of those killed were held in a standing position until jostled to the ground.'

The performance of the black troops generated considerable controversy. Some Northerners applauded their efforts; others damned them. A private from Massachusetts, writing the next day, called the black soldiers 'cowardly rascals' and declared that they 'didn't get far before they broke and skedaddled … one might as well try to stop the wind.' The Yankee lad expressed a wish that the newspapermen so fond of extolling black troops should go into battle with them. General Sanders, watching from across the lines, admitted that the black troops 'fight much better than I expected but … many of them were shot down by the [Yankees].' Southerners who had never fought against freed slaves before relentlessly fired into the Crater and killed men under circumstances that would usually have resulted in captures. 'This day was the jubilee of fiends in human shape,' a Southerner wrote, 'and without souls.' A conflict in which slavery had become a steadily more significant issue had now reached a point where former slaves fought directly on the front line for their freedom and that of their brothers.

When the last Federal survivor dashed back to the lines beyond the Crater, an unusually dramatic battle ended and a dazzling opportunity had disappeared. The Union army lost 4,000 men on 30 July; the Confederates about 1,500. General Grant removed Burnside and Ledlie from their commands, and summarized the Crater in regretful benediction: 'It was the saddest

:IVER.  FROM AN OIL-PAINTING.          (Public domain)

affair I have witnessed in the war.' There would be no other chance to go straight at Petersburg until the war's final week. For Grant, it was back to striking westward toward the railroads.

## The struggle for the railroads

Ten days after the fight for the Crater, another gigantic explosion rocked the region. In the war's most dramatic incident of espionage and sabotage, Confederate agent John Maxwell blew up a time bomb on a barge full of explosives at Grant's headquarters complex at City Point, a few miles below Petersburg. The result, a colonel wrote to his wife, was 'terrible – awful – terrific.' The blast and secondary explosions killed 50 Federals, destroyed several structures, and did millions of dollars' worth of damage. The North's seemingly bottomless industrial capacity easily replaced the losses, but Southerners had occasion to cheer a daring and dramatic act.

Supplies and their transportation took center stage through the summer and fall of 1864. Railroads and wagon roads leading into Petersburg from the west and southwest sustained Lee's army around the city and also supplied sustenance for both troops and civilians around the national capital, 30 miles (48km) northward. Lee had to fight to keep those lines open. Grant welcomed the chance to close them, and to meet Lee's dwindling strength in the open, away from the powerful fortifications that neutralized the armies' differences in strength.

In mid-August, Grant moved again toward the Weldon Railroad. This time he stuck there. On the 18th, Warren's Federal V Corps effected a lodgment near Globe Tavern on the railroad. Two Confederate brigades hurried to the site and routed an isolated Union detachment, but did not have nearly enough strength to drive Warren away. The next day a further Confederate effort, this time in more strength, again achieved localized success. A Virginian fighting near Globe Tavern called it 'the warmest place'

General Gouverneur K. Warren led his Federal V Corps in several sweeps south and west from Petersburg, steadily extending the lines and stretching Lee's Confederates toward breaking point. (Public domain)

that he ever had been in, 'subjected to fire from the front, right flank, & rear all at the same time.'

In fact, it was Warren's right flank that came under the greatest pressure. He lost most of two seasoned regiments as prisoners, and the situation seemed desperate for a brief interval. Reinforcements enabled Warren to hold fast on 19 August, and on 21 August he handily repulsed a series of Southern attacks. In one of them, a bullet tore through both of General John C. C. Sanders' thighs and he bled to death. He had reached his twenty-fourth birthday four months before. A few days later his sister back in Alabama wrote to a surviving brother of her wrenching loss. Fannie Sanders described dreaming of John every night, then awakening to the living nightmare of the truth. 'Why! Oh why, was not my worthless life taken instead of that useful one!' Fannie cried. 'I have been blinded with tears.' Families on both sides of the Potomac had abundant cause for grief.

The fight for Globe Tavern and the railroad cost some 4,300 Union casualties, and 2,300 Confederate.

With a new anchor on the Weldon Railroad, Grant's lines stretched farther westward, requiring Lee to match the expansion, despite the direly thinning Southern resources. Grant immediately sent his once-powerful II Corps right down the Weldon line to destroy it as far south as possible. He could not permanently occupy that zone south of Globe Tavern, but he welcomed the chance to destroy more Southern transportation. The II Corps had been eviscerated in May, though, and repeated its poor showing of June in the Battle of Reams' Station on 24–25 August.

Confederate General A. P. Hill led out a mixed reaction force of eight infantry brigades drawn from various portions of the line, forming what in later wars would be called a 'battle group,' brought together for a specific mission. The infantry joined with General Wade Hampton's Southern cavalry to surround and batter the Federals, who put up only a feeble resistance. General Hancock, the superb commander of the Union corps, rode among his men, waving his hat and his sword, shouting 'For God's sake do not run!' His bravery accomplished little. Hill inflicted about 2,700 casualties, many of them captured, and lost only 700 men himself. The new Union bulwark at Globe Tavern, however, remained intact.

During 14–17 September, Hampton's mounted troops executed one of the most successful raids of the war – 'the Beefsteak Raid.' About 4,000 Confederate horsemen dashed far behind the Union army and rustled a huge herd of beef cattle from under their enemies' noses. Hungry Southern troopers found most of the cattle guard 'cozily sleeping in their tents.' Hampton lost only a few dozen men and returned with 300 human prisoners and 2,500 cattle. The hunger rampant in the South by this time made the beef a tantalizing prize of war.

Elsewhere, September was a bad month for Confederate arms in Georgia, where Atlanta fell to General William T. Sherman,

On 29 September, a determined Federal assault captured Fort Harrison on Lee's main defensive line outside Richmond. (Public domain)

and in Virginia's Shenandoah valley. Late in the month Federal initiatives also brought on some of the heaviest fighting of the year along the Richmond–Petersburg lines. Between 29 September and 7 October 1864, intense action erupted below Richmond and north of the James, and also around Petersburg west of the new Union establishment at Globe Tavern. Grant had attacked unsuccessfully north of the James twice before near Deep Bottom, in coordination with his offensives around Petersburg. This new effort fell with impressive might on the Confederate

General U. S. Grant's dogged determination dictated the nature of the 10-month-long investment of Richmond and Petersburg. (Author's collection)

defensive line around Chaffin's Bluff and New Market Heights. Federal attackers ran headlong into a linchpin of the defensive complex at Fort Harrison, and captured it at the climax of a bloody assault. A New Hampshire soldier described the deadly work: 'Our men fall riddled with bullets; great gaps are rent in our ranks as the shells cut their way through us, or burst in our midst; a solid shot or a shell … will bore straight through ten or twenty men; here are some men literally cut in two, others yonder are blown to pieces.'

The cost of the success, which included the death of General Hiram Burnham, commander of an attacking brigade, drained away momentum in the Union ranks. Once again a temporary advantage wilted for lack of immediate exploitation. Lee directed a counterattack in person the next day, hoping to retake Fort Harrison, but it failed. The Southern leader faced the necessity of carving out a new position closer to Richmond. Fighting in the area continued intermittently for a week, killing General John Gregg of the famous Texas Confederate brigade on Darbytown Road on 7 October, but no decision resulted. Confederate territory on the Richmond–Petersburg lines continued to shrink.

While Lee struggled to maintain his position outside Richmond, Grant simultaneously renewed his pressure south and west of Petersburg. General Warren again commanded a mixed force vectored toward that sensitive Confederate flank. His target this time was the Boydton Plank Road, west of Globe Tavern. Beyond that road ran a truly significant target – the South Side Railroad, Lee's last rail link into Petersburg. Warren found early success, but Confederate counter-measures directed by General A. P. Hill yielded results by now familiar: tactical victories for the Confederates against dispirited Yankees; but strategic success for Grant in the form of farther extension of his lines to the west. On 30 September and 1 October, the troops fought fiercely on the Peebles Farm and the Jones Farm. Hill's men held Warren away from the Boydton Plank Road, and far short of the South Side Railroad, inflicting about 3,000 losses as against 1,300 Confederate casualties. When the smoke cleared, however, Unionist forts and earthworks had begun to sprout in this new sector.

In late October, the final major Federal effort to westward in 1864 moved toward the same target that had eluded Warren at Peebles Farm. While the customary diversionary demonstrations unfolded near Richmond, a mighty force composed of troops from three infantry corps, supported by a strong cavalry detachment, would push once again to the Boydton Plank Road and then beyond toward the much-coveted South Side Railroad.

On 27 October, General Hancock and his II Corps succeeded in brushing aside Confederate cavalry and reaching the Boydton road, breaking across it near Burgess' Mill on Hatcher's Run. In that vicinity the victorious Yankees came up against infantry and artillery in a good position. Warren's Federal V Corps floundered through tangled brush in a vain attempt to help. Meanwhile, the customary Confederate reinforcements pounded rapidly down the roads from Petersburg. Late on the 27th, those new troops attacked Hancock's

men with vigor. Although they did not break the Union line, the Southerners hammered it so hard that Hancock retreated overnight and left his wounded behind. Burgess' Mill had cost him 1,800 casualties, the Confederates 1,300.

As winter spread its grip across Virginia, and major operations became impracticable, Lee's line stretched far wider than the Southern leader would have preferred. When next the weather would allow Grant to move farther west, Lee would have little chance of resisting effectually. The armies retired into watchful winter quiet in their heavily entrenched lines. Desertion increased on both sides. War-weary Confederates slipped away steadily. Even the ever-more-powerful Union armies suffered more than 7,300 desertions nationwide per month on average during 1864.

## The Shenandoah Valley Campaign of 1864

In the spring of 1862, General Thomas J. 'Stonewall' Jackson catapulted to lasting fame by waging a campaign in Virginia's fertile and lovely Shenandoah valley that captured the imagination of the South and transformed the nature of the war. By turns careful and then dazzling in his maneuvers, Jackson utilized the valley's features to his own advantage. The two forks of the Shenandoah river served as moats, being crossed at only three places in 100 miles (160km) by bridges. The Massanutten Mountain massif ran down the heart of the valley for 50 miles (80km) as an immense bulwark and shield. The northeastern end of the valley reached a latitude north of Washington, and looked like a shotgun pointed at the Northern capital. A Unionist who fought in the region described its military character: 'The Shenandoah Valley is a queer place, and it will not submit to the ordinary rules of military tactics. Operations are carried on here that Caesar or Napoleon never dreamed of. Either army can surround the other, and I believe that both can do it at the same time.'

The irascible but able General Jubal A. Early fought against heavy odds in the Shenandoah valley. General Lee called him 'my bad old man.' (Public domain)

As Confederate options near Richmond and Petersburg narrowed in 1864, General Lee determined to take advantage of the valley again. He sent his trusted and able lieutenant, General Jubal A. Early, to raise Jackson-like hell in that vulnerable sector.

Significant operations had been under way in the valley for several weeks by the time Early arrived. General Grant's comprehensive plan to keep pressure up all across the Confederacy's frontiers included the dispatch of two tentacles toward the valley. General William W. Averell led an expedition in southwestern Virginia against the Virginia and Tennessee Railroad. He was successful in a stubbornly contested action at Cloyd's Mountain on 9 May 1864, but Averell's mission did not have a major direct impact on the war's main theater.

At the same time, General Franz Sigel pushed a force of some 10,000 men south up the valley (the rivers run nominally northward, so south is 'up' the valley) toward the vital Confederate depot and rail

junction at Staunton. The German-born Sigel offered Grant and President Lincoln more political energy than military prowess, appealing as he did to the large population of German-born immigrants living in the North. A non-German in Sigel's army described the men's 'most supreme contempt for General Sigel and his crowd of foreign adventurers.' Even Grant admitted that he could not 'calculate on very great results' in western Virginia.

Against Sigel the Confederates mustered an army about half the size of their adversary's, led by General John C. Breckinridge, a former Vice-President of the United States and a future Confederate Secretary of War. The disparate fragments that made up Breckinridge's army included a detachment of boys who would become famous in the impending fighting, the teenaged cadets of the Virginia Military Institute (VMI). On 15 May 1864 the two small armies clashed at the crossroads village of New Market, with control of the valley at stake. A steady rain complicated the brutal business of firing muskets and cannon, holding the acrid gunsmoke close to the ground and making the battlefield an eerie stage. Men from Massachusetts, Pennsylvania, Ohio, and Connecticut peered down from a commanding crest on the Virginians pressing toward them. Colonel George S. Patton I commanded a key Southern brigade; his grandson and namesake would win fame 80 years later in a very different war.

In the midst of the Confederate line marched the 250 young cadets. Several had just turned 15 years of age. 'They are only children,' Breckinridge said worriedly to an aide, 'and I cannot expose them to such fire.' The exigencies of the moment left him no choice, and the youngsters dashed forward through sheets of lead so 'withering,' their commander wrote, that 'it seemed impossible that any living creature could escape.' The boys charged in a torrential thunderstorm across a fire-swept field so muddy that it sucked some of their shoes from their feet, then dashed into the midst of the Federal cannon. Regular troops on either side of them had played an important role, but the VMI cadets had behaved like veterans. Their youthful assault fostered a legend. Fifty-seven of them (21 percent) fell as casualties, 10 of those mortal. Among the dead lads was a grandson of Thomas Jefferson.

Breckinridge and his men chased Sigel north for miles, but the victory proved to be temporary. Breckinridge hurried across the Blue Ridge Mountains to help General Lee around Richmond. Sigel's military debits had finally outweighed his political assets and President Lincoln shelved him. General David Hunter reorganized Sigel's command and led it south again. On 5 June he destroyed a small, hurriedly assembled force led by Confederate General William E. 'Grumble' Jones (the nickname being well earned on the basis of Jones's personality) in the Battle of Piedmont. Ill-disciplined Confederate cavalry failed to perform at the crisis. When Jones fell dead his rag-tag army dissolved, and for the first time during the war, a Northern force gained control of the invaluable railroad junction and warehouses of Staunton. Hunter then moved south to Lexington, burning homes as he went – some of them belonging to his own kin, who seemed to receive especially harsh treatment. Soldiers torched the home in Lexington of Virginia's former governor, John Letcher, denying the family's women and children the chance to remove even clothing from the house before it became engulfed by the flames.

When Hunter crossed the mountains and closed in on Lynchburg, another vital railhead and supply depot, General Lee determined that he must be checked. To that end, he ordered Early to lead the Second Corps of the Army of Northern Virginia westward. The corps made an obvious choice: it had been in the famed 1862 Valley Campaign under Stonewall Jackson, and many of the men lived in or near the valley. Early was an equally good choice because of his energy and determination. The fiery Virginian stood up in his stirrups while scouting the lines around Lynchburg, shook a fist at the Yankees, and bellowed his scorn

General Thomas L. Rosser commanded Confederate cavalry in the valley. Early called him 'a consummate ass' and compared him – unfavorably – to Judas Iscariot. (Public domain)

for both his enemy and the irregular Southern troops he was replacing: 'No buttermilk rangers after you now, you God-damned Blue Butts!' Early used the derisive term 'buttermilk rangers' to refer to stragglers, especially cavalry, ranging to the rear for refreshments instead of doing their duty. His difficulties with poor cavalry would bedevil operations for the next five months.

Early's seasoned troops chased the Federals away from Lynchburg on 17–19 June 1864. Hunter's men straggled through the trackless mountains in West Virginia on a weary march that took them out of operations for weeks. Early promptly turned north and moved steadily down the entire length of the valley and into the very outskirts of Washington, DC. En route he fought an engagement on 9 July near Frederick, Maryland, on the banks of the Monocacy river. A blocking force under Federal General Lew Wallace (who would write the classic novel *Ben Hur* after the war) fought all day to retard Early's advance

The victorious charge of the youthful cadets of the Virginia Military Institute at New Market, as painted by Benjamin West Clinedinst, a postwar graduate of the Institute. (Virginia Military Institute Museum)

toward Washington. Wallace's troops eventually recoiled, but they had achieved their purpose.

President Lincoln worriedly wired to General Grant at Petersburg, urging him to come in person. Grant instead sent most of two corps of infantry to reinforce Washington – precisely the sort of result Lee had desired when he unleashed Early. Lincoln went to the forts on the

Although Federals outnumbered him by three-to-one, Confederate General Jubal A. Early put up a stout resistance in the northern Shenandoah valley in the autumn of 1864. In the Battles of Third Winchester (19 September), Fisher's Hill (22 September) and Cedar Creek (19 October), the Federals suffered considerably more casualties than they inflicted on their Southern foes – but they could afford the losses and Early could not. After Cedar Creek, Confederate presence in the once-fertile valley consisted of little more than a nuisance force of cavalry and irregular troops.

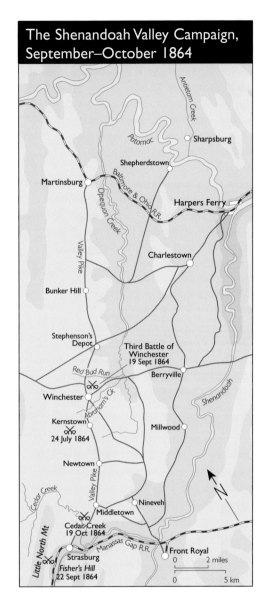

**The Shenandoah Valley Campaign, September–October 1864**

line outside Washington and came under desultory long-range fire. The Confederates did not get into the capital city proper, and could not have held it had they done so. As Jubal Early commented in summary: 'We haven't taken Washington, but we've scared Abe Lincoln like hell!'

Union forces pursued Early to the Potomac river as he retired, then to the slopes of the Blue Ridge, and then beyond to the Shenandoah river. Early's rearguard repulsed them along the way, then savagely turned on the Federals at Kernstown on 24 July, just south of Winchester. There the Confederates inflicted one of the most unmitigated thrashings of the war on their enemies, who suffered more than 1,200 casualties as against fewer than 250 Confederates lost. A few days later, General Grant sent a new commander to the Shenandoah valley, with strong reinforcements. His instructions to General Philip H. Sheridan were to whip Early, and then to turn the beautiful valley into 'a barren waste.'

Despite an enormous preponderance in numbers, Sheridan had a far easier time accomplishing the 'barren waste' element of his orders than he did in whipping Early. In the decisive battles of September and October, Sheridan was able to deploy more cavalry than Early had troops of all arms combined. Those cavalry, furthermore, enjoyed wide mobility on good horses, and carried weapons that dramatically out-performed the equipment available to the Southern horsemen. Early did not trust his cavalry. He had more than ample cause for queasiness, but his fractious relationship with the mounted arm only exacerbated a

deadly situation. In postwar quarreling with General Thomas L. Rosser, his chief cavalry subordinate during the campaign, Early referred to Rosser as 'a consummate ass,' compared him to Judas Iscariot, and suggested that if Rosser were to emulate Judas and hang himself, it would be 'the most creditable act' he could perform.

For more than six weeks, Sheridan followed Early's detachments hither and yon through the northern valley as the Confederates tore up the Baltimore and Ohio Railroad – a vital Federal artery – and feinted at supply depots as far north as the Potomac river. Early's energetic deployments convinced Sheridan that he faced far more enemy strength than actually existed. Finally, on 19 September, Sheridan hurled two corps through a narrow canyon east of Winchester and brought Early to pitched battle.

In bitter fighting that swirled across fields and woodlots between Red Bud Run and Abraham's Creek, exploding shells took a steep toll among ranking officers. Federal General David A. Russell, an accomplished brigade commander who had graduated from West Point and served in the *ante bellum* army, fell instantly dead when a shell fragment went through his heart. A piece of shell hit Confederate General Archibald C. Godwin in the head and killed him instantly. The highest-ranking casualty on either side was Confederate General Robert E. Rodes, perhaps the best division commander in the Virginia Theater, who also died from a shell fragment in the head.

Despite being direly outnumbered, the Southern infantry east of Winchester held their ground and inflicted staggering casualties on Sheridan's attackers. The moment of decision came from behind the sturdy defenders, northwest of the scene of the heavy fighting. A wall of Union cavalry swept into the northern outskirts of Winchester and simply overwhelmed the Confederate horsemen in front of them. Early had no choice but to collapse his outflanked main line and fight for time to get away before the enemy's mounted troops could deploy entirely behind his army. He succeeded in that effort, aided by the onset of darkness, falling back 20 miles (32km) to a strong position at Fisher's Hill.

George S. Patton, who had done so well at New Market, fell mortally wounded by another exploding shell during the retreat. Artillery fragments reaped an especially deadly harvest of braided officers on this

*Early's Confederates fought Sheridan's Federals to a standstill east of Winchester on 19 September 1864, but Northern cavalry eventually overran Early's left and decided the day. (Public domain)*

day. The Third Battle of Winchester extracted more than 5,000 casualties from Sheridan's attackers. Early lost 1,700 men killed and wounded. He reported 1,800 men missing, but declared that many of them were 'stragglers and skulkers,' not prisoners.

Twice more in the next month Early would fight Sheridan. Each time the formula would resemble that of Winchester: Early's indomitable infantry would attack successfully or bloodily repulse their enemies, then Confederate cavalry on Early's left flank would collapse and unravel the entire line.

Sheridan pressed briskly forward toward Fisher's Hill on 20 September and on the 21st he skirmished as necessary to secure the ridges opposite Early's new position. Keeping steady pressure on his outnumbered and reeling opponent made good sense. General

George Crook, who would later achieve notable success in the Indian Wars in the southwestern United States, conceived a bold plan to unhinge Early's line. Crook proposed taking his entire corps up onto the slopes of Little North Mountain, which anchored the Confederate left, then moving south until he was in a position to turn the enemy line. Sheridan cavalierly, and characteristically, claimed for himself all of the credit for this battle plan, although his own preliminary proposal had been to launch an utterly impractical frontal assault on the opposite end of the line.

On 22 September, while the rest of Sheridan's army demonstrated straight ahead toward Fisher's Hill, Crook put his plan into action. It worked fabulously well, in part because Early had again positioned his unreliable cavalry at the most vulnerable segment of his position. The Confederates reeled southward again in total disarray, losing prisoners and cannon as they went. Early's defeated fragments did not stop until they had scampered more than 50 miles (80km). An onlooker heard a weary Confederate chanting a home-spun ditty that began, 'Old Jube Early's gone up the spout.' Early blamed his army for the rout. When a passing soldier yelled irreverently at the army commander, Early spat back, 'Fisher's Hill, god damn you,' believing that the very name of that embarrassment was opprobrium enough.

Sheridan had cause to believe that he had forever removed Early's little army from serious consideration, and set about destroying the valley systematically. His men killed thousands of animals, burned countless barns and mills, and destroyed

Colonel George S. Patton I, grandfather of the Second World War general, commanded a brigade at Winchester until a shell mortally wounded him. (Public domain)

crops everywhere. The vandalism loosened or destroyed the reins of discipline in some instances, and Unionists went beyond warfare on agriculture to burn houses and savage civilian women in what Virginians called 'The Burning.' Ironically, the region most heavily affected included one of the largest concentrations of unflinching pacifists on the continent, most of them Mennonites or Dunkards; their buildings burned as briskly as anyone else's.

Southern cavalrymen, many of them watching their own homes aflame, could not stem the onslaught, but they took the chance to execute groups of enemy arsonists when they cornered them. War never treads gently, especially civil war, but the American strife in the 1860s had been amazingly civilized – until the fall of 1864. Rosser's enraged Confederate cavalry eventually stretched too far from infantry support and suffered a resounding beating on 9 October at Tom's Brook by Union cavalry under Generals George A. Custer, Wesley Merritt, and Alfred T. A. Torbert.

Incredibly, Early pushed back northward once more soon after Tom's Brook, a phoenix risen from the ashes, and by mid-October had again reached the vicinity of Fisher's Hill. Sheridan had concluded that his foe had been permanently vanquished, but the

Starting on 6 October, Sheridan's Federals systematically burned out the Shenandoah valley. (Public domain)

small Southern force launched against him one of the most amazing surprise assaults of the war. Lee had sent Early reinforcements from Richmond, among them some of the army's most dependable units. Confederate generals reconnoitered Sheridan's camps from a towering aerie atop Massanutten Mountain and discovered that the Federals were strewn randomly across a wide stretch of rolling country north of Strasburg and Cedar Creek, with scant attention to tactical considerations. They hatched a daring plan.

General John B. Gordon led a long, stealthy, circuitous march along a trail so primitive that he called it 'a pig's path.' Gordon's column crossed the North Fork of the Shenandoah, crept across the nose of a mountain, and came back to the river opposite the unsuspecting left flank of Sheridan's force. At dawn on 19 October, they splashed into the stream and dashed up the opposite slope into camps full of sleeping Yankees, screaming the chilling 'Rebel Yell' as they ran. The onslaught routed the entire Federal VIII Corps. The Federal XIX Corps

fought bravely for a time, but the momentum of the Southern surprise attack overwhelmed them too, and swept north to the vicinity of the village of Middletown.

Only the Federal VI Corps remained unassailed and unbroken. Together with the unhurt Northern cavalry, the VI Corps numbered as many men as Early's entire army, but staying the Rebels' momentum proved to be a difficult task. General Horatio G. Wright, commander of the corps, was acting as army commander that morning in Sheridan's absence. Wright deserves far more

As the winter of 1864–65 drew to a close, Petersburg's days as the last bastion of the Confederacy were starkly numbered. Federal thrusts farther and farther west to Burgess' Mill and Hatcher's Run had stretched Lee's lines impossibly thin. A final Confederate offensive at Fort Stedman on 25 March won brief, illusory success, before ending in a costly repulse. At Five Forks on 1 April and all around Petersburg on 2 April, Northern troops broke the Confederate line and forced the abandonment of the city. A desperate stand by a handful of Southern troops in Fort Gregg bought time for Lee's army to slip away and dash westward in a vain attempt to escape from Virginia and continue the war in North Carolina.

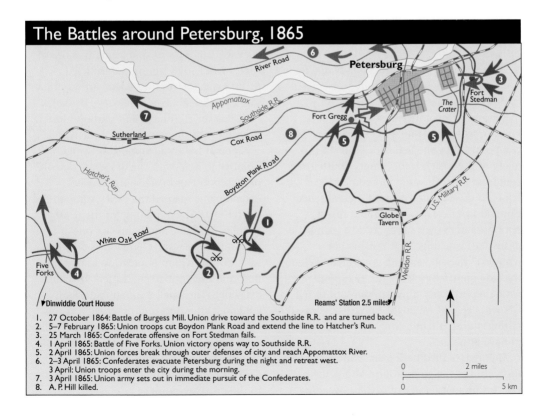

## The Battles around Petersburg, 1865

1. 27 October 1864: Battle of Burgess Mill. Union drive toward the Southside R.R. and are turned back.
2. 5–7 February 1865: Union troops cut Boydon Plank Road and extend the line to Hatcher's Run.
3. 25 March 1865: Confederate offensive on Fort Stedman fails.
4. 1 April 1865: Battle of Five Forks. Union victory opens way to Southside R.R.
5. 2 April 1865: Union forces break through outer defenses of city and reach Appomattox River.
6. 2–3 April 1865: Confederates evacuate Petersburg during the night and retreat west.
   3 April: Union troops enter the city during the morning.
7. 3 April 1865: Union army sets out in immediate pursuit of the Confederates.
8. A. P. Hill killed.

At dawn on 19 October 1864, Confederates dashed across
the Shenandoah river and surprised camps full of sleeping
Federals. For several hours they maintained their
momentum and came near to winning the Battle of Cedar
Creek despite being outnumbered more than three-to-one.
(Public domain)

credit than he has been given for his calm,
courageous stand that diluted Confederate
momentum and restored the day for
his army.

Early has received considerable blame for
not pressing Wright more firmly to keep
astride the momentum that was his only
major advantage under the circumstances.
The Confederate commander's quandary was
compounded by the behavior of his troops:
many of the weary, lean, hungry Southerners
could not resist the array of food and
booty in the captured camps. Their absence
thinned Early's ranks and limited his
options. Early's own summary to a member
of his staff is telling: 'The Yankees got
whipped,' he said, 'and we got scared.' When
the aide prepared to leave for Richmond
with a report, Early directed him 'not to tell
General Lee that we ought to have advanced'
farther during the morning, 'for ... we ought
to have done so.'

Sheridan dashed back from Winchester to
the sound of the guns around Middletown,
sent his immense force of cavalry sweeping
around the Confederate left (for the third
time in three battles), and advanced all
across the line. With the momentum of the
Southerners' surprise attack evaporated, there
could be no doubt whatsoever about the
outcome. Early's survivors fled south once
more. All the bright hopes of the morning
had vanished in the face of unchecked
disaster. The Confederates had captured
20 cannon in their triumphant attack; now
they lost all of them, and as many more of
their own. Early's troops had inflicted
5,700 casualties on the Federal army, and
lost 2,900 themselves. They also, by day's
end, had for all intents and purposes lost
the valley for the remainder of the war.

General Lee recalled most of Early's
infantry to help with the desperate defense
of Richmond and Petersburg. Cavalry
detachments roamed the valley through the
winter of 1864–65, raiding for the scant
supplies available and harassing one another
without major results. Both sides afflicted
such of the civilian population as had not
fled, and eked out a cold, bitter, costly
existence. The small remnant with Early
collapsed after only a faint struggle at the
Battle of Waynesboro, in the southern valley,
on 2 March 1865. The General himself was
among the handful who escaped. By then,
Lee's lines beyond the mountains were close
to the breaking point.

# From Richmond and Petersburg to Appomattox

Winter weather and its effect on a bad road system stymied Grant's steady probing westward toward the railroads through the war's last winter. The only major operation through that period unfolded on 5–7 February 1865 in the Battle of Hatcher's Run. Once again the Federals hoped to seize and hold the Boydton Plank Road; and once again they coveted the invaluable South Side Railroad, which ran just beyond the road. A strong Federal force moved into the area. It included II Corps, now under General Andrew A. Humphreys (long-time, much-admired corps commander Hancock had left the army), and Warren's V Corps returning to familiar ground.

On 5 February, Humphreys battered Confederates who had hurried out from Petersburg. The next day, further Southern units swarmed over Warren and inflicted serious damage, but without lasting results. On the 7th, Lee concluded that he could not evict the Federals from their new perch, so both sides once more went back to entrenching. This latest extension of the line left Lee with 35 miles (56km) to defend. About 1,500 Federals had fallen, and 1,000 Confederates.

General John B. Gordon entered service in 1861 without any military training or background whatsoever, but advanced steadily on merit until by the war's end he was among Lee's most important subordinates. Gordon designed and led the desperate attack on Fort Stedman on 25 March 1865. (Public domain)

Among the Southern casualties was General John Pegram. One contemporary remembered him fondly, if oddly as 'a delightful & artistic whistler.' The handsome young officer had been married in Richmond at St Paul's Church on 19 January to Hetty Cary, a widely admired belle – 'the most beautiful woman I ever saw in any land,' enthused a Confederate officer. Five days later John celebrated his thirty-second birthday. Two more weeks and he was back at St Paul's in a casket.

By mid-March, Lee's options had all but vanished. He accepted a desperate scheme hatched by the innovative General Gordon, back with the main army after leading the secret march at Cedar Creek in the Shenandoah valley. Gordon would marshal as many men as could be spared from the

Confederate General John Pegram married a young woman acclaimed as among the most beautiful in the South, then was killed a few days later at Hatcher's Run. (Public domain)

attenuated lines and lead them in a
late-night assault against the Federals at
Fort Stedman, not far from the Crater and
on precisely the ground where the 1st Maine
Heavy Artillery had been slaughtered the
preceding June.

Careful planning and steady bravery
brought Gordon initial success. Picked troops
silently removed the defensive obstructions
in front of the Confederate works opposite
Stedman, then crawled up a ravine toward
their enemy. Small detachments of
volunteers silenced Federal pickets and deftly
opened a corridor through the enemy
obstacles near the fort. Storming parties
followed and burst upon their surprised foe,
capturing the fort and spreading down the
line on either side. More Southern infantry
followed, Gordon in their midst, to exploit
the breakthrough.

A major Federal supply depot only a mile
(1.6km) behind Fort Stedman must have
seemed to some of the starving Confederates

Federals stand in review as their defeated foemen march
past at Appomattox, en route to surrendering their arms.
(Painting by Don Troiani, www.historicalartprints.com)

to be the quintessential prize. Daylight
brought stunning reality, however, as
Federals farther down the lines on both sides
brought artillery to bear. By 8.00 am Yankees
were swarming back toward Stedman. 'The
whole field was blue with them,' a dismayed
Southerner wrote. In the succinct summary
of a disappointed North Carolinian, the
fleeting success resembled a 'meteor's flash
that illumines for a moment and [then]
leaves the night darker than before.'

The Confederate horizon would darken
even further during the next fortnight, then
flicker out permanently. The advent of early
spring gave Grant the chance to push west
and southwest again. Lee obviously could
not hold out much longer in Petersburg and
Richmond, but the Federal commander
feared that his wily adversary might find a

way to slip away through the lines and head for North Carolina to join forces with another retreating Confederate army there.

Before Lee could attempt such a stratagem, his thinly manned lines snapped. Fighting by Union cavalry around Dinwiddie Court House on 31 March went well for Confederate General George E. Pickett, but to Lee's dismay Pickett fell back north to the invaluable Five Forks intersection on the White Oak Road. On 1 April, Pickett, ever the dilettante, played host at a fish fry. Generals Fitzhugh Lee and Tom Rosser joined him at what became infamous as 'The Shad Bake.' While the generals enjoyed the respite from winter's short rations, Warren's diligent V Corps crashed into the exposed Confederate left and completely shattered it. Instead of applauding Warren's coup, Sheridan, commanding on the field, relieved him from command and assumed the mantle of the hero of Five Forks.

With Five Forks in Unionist hands, there remained nothing to keep them from the long-sought South Side Railroad. The next morning Grant ordered attacks all along the line and ended the siege of Petersburg. Horatio Wright's VI Corps rolled through A. P. Hill's troops almost at will. In a random encounter in the woods, two Federal enlisted men met Hill, who ranked behind only Longstreet among Lee's subordinates, accompanied only by a courier. After a nervous exchange of challenges, one Yankee fired a bullet that went through Hill's thumb and into his heart.

Farther northeast, closer to Petersburg, a tiny Confederate detachment held desperately to Fort Gregg to buy time for Lee to knit together a new line, and for the Confederate government to evacuate Richmond. Fort Gregg's defenders counted only two Mississippi regiments, one section of Louisiana artillery, and a handful of artillerists pressed into service as infantry – perhaps 300 men in all. The entire fresh Federal XXIV Corps attacked across an open field against the small work. Although it seemed to one witness that the Federal flags created 'a solid line of bunting around the fort,' the

Southerners repulsed the first assault. Another fell back in confusion, leaving a bloody wake behind. Attacking Northerners wrote of 'withering fire' that 'mowed down our men most unmercifully.' Finally the defenders collapsed under an overwhelming assault from all sides. They had shot more than 700 Federals. Only a handful of unwounded Southerners survived to be captured.

The sacrificial stand in Fort Gregg bought Lee time to protect Petersburg by means of a hastily connected interior line, but that night he had to abandon the city that for so long had been a focus of military operations in Virginia. For six days, 3–8 April 1865, Lee's Army of Northern Virginia wove a weary trail westward, hoping against hope to find a means of escape. Federal detachments, both infantry and cavalry, darted in and out of the desperate Southern columns, snaring prisoners and disrupting the retreat. Lee hoped to find rations for his men near Amelia Court House and Farmville; there were none. On 6 April the last pitched battle of the war in Virginia broke out on the banks of Sayler's Creek. The fighting did not rage hot or long. Federals closing in from three sides captured about 8,000 men, including eight general officers. Lee fought off pursuit at Cumberland Church on 7 April and kept heading west.

On the night of 8 April, near Appomattox Court House, Lee found the enemy directly in his path as well as closing in from all sides. The next day he surrendered to Grant. The ceremony took place in the home of Wilmer McLean. By remarkable coincidence, four years earlier McLean had moved to Appomattox from his farm along Bull Run, to get away from the war that the Battle of Manassas had brought to his property. Not coincidentally, and entirely characteristically, Grant did not even invite Meade to the ceremony.

With four years of bloodshed at last ended in Virginia, other Confederate forces across the South faced imminent surrender. It now remained for Northerners to implement their hard-won victory, and for Southerners to find the means of sustenance in a destroyed country.

# McHenry Howard's war

In September 1814, Francis Scott Key of Maryland wrote a poem as he watched British ships bombard Fort McHenry in the harbor of Baltimore. When an actor sang Key's 'The Star-Spangled Banner' to the tune of an old drinking song, it at once became a popular patriotic air, and many years later the official national anthem of the United States.

Francis Scott Key's grandson, McHenry Howard, did not hesitate about going to war against the Star-Spangled Banner when Northern troops invaded his hometown of Baltimore in 1861. Federal authorities simply threw into jail those of Maryland's elected legislators who would not do as they were told. Howard and thousands of other young men from the state hurried southward, eager to fight for restoration of self-government. Their purpose, Howard wrote, was 'not merely to aid the cause of the Confederacy as it was constituted, but believing that they were serving their own State – in subjection – in the only way that was left to them.' Francis Scott Key had about 60 descendants living in 1860, and 'every man, woman and child was Southern,' Howard recalled, although 'I cannot recall that any owned slaves in 1861.'

When war interrupted Howard's civilian pursuits, he had been studying law after graduating from Princeton University. The 22-year-old lawyer in training belonged to a volunteer organization, the 'Maryland Guard,' that served purposes at least as much social as military. The guardsmen affected gorgeous uniforms of the 'Zouave' variety, modeled after the outfits of French colonial troops who had caught the popular fancy in North America. Howard later described his garb with amusement provided by hindsight:

*The full dress was a dark blue jacket, short and close fitting and much embroidered with yellow; a blue flannel shirt with a close row of small round gilt buttons (for ornament merely,) down the front, between yellow trimming; blue pantaloons, very baggy and gathered below the knee and falling over the tops of long drab gaiters; a small blue cap, of the kepi kind, also trimmed with yellow; and, finally, a wide red sash ... kept wide by hooks and eyes on the ends.*

Private Howard would soon discover, in the world of a real soldier in the field, that 'this gaudy dress, which made a very brilliant effect on street parade ... was totally unsuitable for any active service.'

For nearly a year Howard served (more suitably attired, of course) in the ranks as an enlisted man with the 1st Maryland Infantry, Confederate States Army, made up of 1,000 young men who had escaped across the Potomac River to join the Southern cause. In the spring of 1862 he won a commission as lieutenant and aide-de-camp to fellow Marylander General Charles S. Winder. Lieutenant Howard remained at that lowest of the commissioned ranks for the final three years of the war. In his staff role, he had an opportunity to observe much of the conflict's most dramatic events, and many of its most significant leaders. After a Federal shell killed General Winder at Cedar Mountain in August 1862, Howard did staff duty with Generals Isaac R. Trimble, George H. Steuart, and George Washington Custis Lee, son of army commander General Robert E. Lee.

When Lee's Army of Northern Virginia headed north after the Battle of Chancellorsville, Lieutenant Howard followed as a supernumerary. His chief, General Trimble, had not reported back to the army after convalescing from a bad wound. That left Howard without a role, but he could not ignore his comrades' aggressive move northward and headed across country toward the Potomac to catch up with the army. When he splashed up the left bank of the river, the exiled Marylander noted sadly that it was the first time he had been on the soil of his native state in one month more than two years.

In Greencastle, Pennsylvania, Howard and a half-dozen other stray Confederates wound up in a hot street fight against mounted Yankees. Pistol bullets shattered windowpanes on all sides, dust obscured galloping horses, and the little band of Rebels had to flee. Later Howard and his mates chased a lone horseman for miles, only to discover that he was a Confederate major and an old friend.

During the army's subsequent retreat back toward Virginia, Howard rode through a Maryland town and thought wistfully, 'Oh, that it was Baltimore!' On 14 July, as the

McHenry Howard, 1838–1923. (Public domain)

Army of Northern Virginia abandoned Maryland, Howard wrote in his diary: 'Feel very much depressed at the gloomy prospect for our State. I look around me constantly to see as much of it as I can before leaving it.' As the army crossed the Potomac into Virginia, bandsmen gladly struck up 'Sweet Home,' but that seemed 'a mockery' to the Marylanders. Howard 'could not refrain from some bitter tears as I … looked back to our beloved State.'

For 10 months after Gettysburg, the exiled lieutenant performed staff duty under General George H. Steuart, a West Point graduate with 'Old Army' ideas about organization and discipline. The summer after Gettysburg passed without a major engagement. During the lull, Howard and his mates fought against the elements and against logistical defects – just as has every army in every era. In September 1863, he wrote disgustedly in his diary: 'Raining like

pitchforks – very disagreeable ... Regular equinoctial storm – have had nothing to eat for almost twenty-four hours.' Violent downpours had drowned every fire for miles. Through one uncomfortable day, Lieutenant Howard, General Steuart, and three others huddled unhappily in a storm-shaken tent all day long, hungry and miserable.

Howard missed the campaigning around Bristoe Station in October 1863 because he had gone to the Confederate capital for

religious reasons – to be confirmed in the Episcopal faith in Richmond's elegant St Paul's Church. He had returned to duty by the time of the Battle of Mine Run, where his staff chores brought him under heavy fire: 'the bullets coming through the switchy woods sounded somewhat like the hissing of a hail or sleet storm.' He also noticed in that engagement one of the benchmarks of the war's evolution. Confederate soldiers had reached the conclusion that substantial protective fortifications made really good sense in the face of rifled musketry. They used 'their bayonets, tin cups, and their hands, to loosen and scoop up the dirt, which was thrown on and around the trunks of old field pine trees' that they cut down and stretched lengthwise.

During the winter of 1863–64, genuine hardship became a constant companion of Southern soldiers. Lieutenant Howard described his diet, at a point in the food chain well above the privates and corporals, as consisting mostly of 'corn dodgers' – corn meal cooked with water – for both breakfast and dinner. In good times, dinner also included 'a soup made of water thickened with corn meal and mashed potatoes and cooked with a small piece of meat, which ... was taken out when the soup was done and kept to be cooked over again.'

Events in the spring campaign in 1864 threw McHenry Howard into the cauldron of combat, then yanked him out of action as a prisoner of war. At the Wilderness, the night of 5 May echoed mordantly with the 'moans and cries' of wounded men from both armies who lay between the lines and beyond succor. 'In the still night air every groan could be heard,' Howard wrote, 'and the calls for water and entreaties to brothers and comrades by name to come and help them.' The next morning, fires started in the underbrush by muzzle flashes spread through the Wilderness and burned to death some of the helpless wounded.

Spotsylvania followed Wilderness immediately. On 10 May 1864, a brutal

The burning of Richmond. (Ann Ronan Picture Library)

cross-fire caught and pinned down Howard and his friends. They had no option but to hug the ground and wait for darkness. 'A more disagreeable half hour,' he wrote in retrospect, 'with a bullet striking a man lying on the ground every now and then, could not well have been spent.' Two days later a Federal assault swept over the nose of the Confederate works near the point soon to be christened 'the Bloody Angle.' Yankee bayonets surrounded Howard and he went into a captivity that would last for six months. Howard's concise sketch map of the Angle at Spotsylvania remains an important artifact for studying the battle.

As his captors herded Lieutenant Howard to the rear at Spotsylvania, he began a prison experience shared by hundreds of thousands of Civil War soldiers. Howard wound up at Fort Delaware, in the middle of the Delaware river downstream from Philadelphia. There he enjoyed reasonably civilized treatment, by the uncivilized standards of the day. The fort's commander liked Howard and others of the Confederates, but some of his subordinates took the opportunity to abuse their power, as humans are wont to do. In November 1864, Howard went back south under a program for the exchange of prisoners. Once released in Georgia, he used a flask of brandy to bribe his way into a good railroad car on a Confederate train and by the end of 1864 had reached Richmond again.

Through the war's waning weeks, young Howard assisted General G. W. C. Lee in the effort to turn an accumulation of home-front troops, raw levies, and naval ratings into a hodge-podge brigade for emergency use. The emergency arose on 2 April 1865. The lieutenant was sitting in a pew at St Paul's, where he had been confirmed a few months earlier, for the 11.00 am Sunday service, when a courier informed Jefferson Davis that the army's lines had been broken. Richmond must be

abandoned. For four days the *ersatz* brigade under G. W. C. Lee took part in the retreat west and south from Richmond. In a mix-up that especially depressed and horrified Howard, the green troops loosed a volley against friends that killed several men, victims of mistaken friendly fire just a few hours before the army surrendered.

Howard fell into enemy hands again on 6 April at Sayler's Creek. This time his prison camp was Johnson's Island in Lake Erie. There he took the oath of allegiance to the United States on 29 May and made his long way home. Awaiting him in Baltimore was a demand, dated September 1862, that he report to Yankee conscript officers to be drafted into Federal service. Men had come to his mother's house and asked the names and occupations of all the family's males. McHenry's mother responded that her husband and eldest son were being held unconstitutionally as political prisoners in northern Bastilles. Four sons were serving in the Confederate army. 'McHenry,' she told her interrogators, was 'with Stonewall Jackson and I expect he will be here soon.' The officials wrote out the conscription demand and left. McHenry kept the souvenir the rest of his life.

Lieutenant Howard enjoyed a long and fruitful career after the war. He completed his legal training and practiced law in Baltimore for decades, finding time also to write extensively about his Confederate experiences. McHenry's lively, urbane recollections appeared in periodicals both North and South. He eventually turned his story into a charming and important – and sizable, at 423 pages – book that is a classic piece of Confederate literature: *Recollections of a Maryland Confederate Soldier and Staff Officer under Johnston, Jackson and Lee* (Baltimore: Williams & Wilkins Company, 1914). Howard died in his native Maryland on 11 September 1923, two months before his eighty-fifth birthday.

# 'This horrid and senseless war…'

While soldiers carrying arms under both flags faced death or maiming at the battle front, their families at home coped with a wide variety of fundamental changes and challenges. Some home-front Americans met with fabulous economic opportunities; others with dire economic suffering. Millions of civilians struggled with numbing grief at the loss of loved ones, and millions more faced personal danger from scavengers – both 'friendly' troops and invaders.

'The world around war' chapter of Gallagher, *The American Civil War,* describes those trends on a war-wide basis, including the impact of the war on the growth of government; women's roles in society and commerce; inflation and wages; speculation; corruption in the production of war materials; taxation; refugees; slavery and freed ex-slaves; and politics. In every context, the impact of the war upon civilians became broader and deeper during 1863–65 in the Virginia Theater than it had been during the war's first half.

Since all but a few days of the armies' campaigning in the theater unfolded on Confederate terrain, the impact on Southerners was far greater. Millions of Northern firesides mourned deeply and bitterly when the casualty lists from Virginia arrived, but on the economic and social front most Northern institutions actually gained strength, while the Confederacy was in the process of utter destruction. Southerners carefully watched the news about the price of gold in New York, and relished evidence of inflation. They were deluding themselves. The North thrived, as victorious nations' war economies generally do. Only on the battlefield could Confederates hope to create circumstances in which they might generate enough war-weariness to win their independence.

Southern civilians faced war's brutality on a far more intimate level than their quondam fellow-citizens in the North. Until fairly recently it had been conventional wisdom that mid-nineteenth-century mores kept occupying soldiery in check. A recent careful survey and indexing of United States Army courts-martial during the war has banished that old-fashioned notion. More than 83,000 Union soldiers came before courts. Nearly 5,000 of them were charged with crimes against civilians, including 558 for murder and 225 for rape. The number of formal trials, of course, only begins to reflect the volume of untried crimes, especially in areas where civilians were utterly powerless to protect themselves.

For millennia, European wars have trampled the citizens of the continent, shattering property and minds and leaving millions of non-combatant dead. In the two and a quarter centuries that comprise the relatively short life span of the United States however, no large body of American civilians has ever felt war's horrors up close –except Confederates during the final stages of the Civil War. As a direct result, soldiers from desolated areas of the South came under immense pressures to go home and protect their families. A letter from home came into evidence at a desertion trial of one of Lee's men. 'I have always been proud of you,' wrote Mary to Edward, 'and since your connection with the Confederate army, I have been prouder of you than ever before … but before God, Edward, unless you come home we must die.' Edward went home. Provost guards brought him back to the army. After the trial Edward was returned to duty, perhaps on the strength of the emotions provoked by the letter. Soon thereafter he was killed in action.

Margaret Junkin Preston, whose condolence letter to a stricken friend was one of many millions written during the American Civil War. (Virginia Military Institute Museum)

The personal suffering and loss would gradually heal in many instances, but the destruction of more than 620,000 lives could not be erased. Margaret Junkin Preston, one of the leading female authors in the country, wrote a condolence letter to a friend whose brother had just fallen victim to what Preston called 'this horrid and senseless war.' Maggie's heart-felt emotions capture what so many millions of others went through.

*I cannot refrain from mingling my grief with yours ... It is dreadful to have our loved ones die ... [We are] utterly shaken by the uncontrollable outthrusting of our mere human grief at seeing the pleasant face never never more ... the tender eyes shut, not to be opened again – the sweet interchange of thought, feelings, emotions – all all over! ... The Blessed God comfort you under this sense of loss which will press upon you so agonizingly.*

A few weeks after she wrote this tender letter, Maggie faced the same ordeal when her own 17-year-old stepson fell mortally wounded in action.

# Ella Washington and the Federal Army

George Armstrong Custer became forever famous when he led more than 250 cavalrymen to annihilation on the Little Big Horn river in 1876. A dozen years earlier he had been infamous among Virginians for destruction of civilian property and executing prisoners. Before either of those notable episodes of Custer's life and death, he had been the gallant savior of a hard-beset Virginian woman who lived near Richmond.

Ella Bassett grew up on her father's sizable plantation 'Clover Lea,' a dozen miles northeast of Virginia's capital city. She had been born in September 1834 at another family estate, 'Eltham,' in New Kent County.

In May 1862, the Civil War came to Eltham, and the next month it washed up on the grounds of Clover Lea as well. Two years later the war, by then a hard-eyed, unforgiving monster, descended on Clover Lea in an episode fraught with terror for Ella. Her descriptions of the ordeal she experienced in May and June 1864 serve as an example in microcosm of the suffering of hundreds of thousands of civilians at the mercy of invading troops.

By 1864, Ella had been a married woman for 3 years. Her husband, Colonel Lewis

Ella Bassett Washington, 1834–98. (Courtesy of the Mount Vernon Ladies' Association)

Washington, was a direct descendant of the first President, George Washington (through George's wife and family; he had no natural children). So was Ella. She and Lewis each had ancestry back to the first President's family on both sides of their own parentage, and accordingly Lewis and Ella were themselves distant cousins by multiple connections. Lewis was more than two decades older than Ella and had been married before. Ella evidently had little or nothing to do with his two daughters, who lived with relatives in Maryland, but she was fond of stepson James Barroll Washington.

The war's preliminaries had fallen on Lewis Washington with alarming savagery the year before he married Ella. On an October morning in 1859, several men used a fence rail to batter down the door of Washington's home, 'Beall Air,' near Harpers Ferry, Virginia. The intruders – a detachment from the marauding party directed by John Brown – knew that Lewis owned relics of George Washington and demanded them as booty. They carried Lewis off as a hostage. He witnessed, as a prisoner, the storming by United States Marines of Brown's hideout at Harpers Ferry. Directing the storming party was Colonel Robert E. Lee, United States Army. Among the first men to the door of the stronghold was Lieutenant J. E. B. Stuart, United States Army, acting as an aide to Lee.

The year after Lewis's brief ordeal at the hands of Brown's merry band, his new bride, cousin Ella, moved into Beall Air. In late 1861, the couple moved from Beall Air to Ella's family place at Clover Lea. She attributed the need to relocate to 'the critical condition of my health.' Since Lewis's home stood in a mountainous region, and Clover Lea plantation lay in the relatively swampy ground near Richmond, contemporary notions would have suggested (not inaccurately) that health considerations would actually militate in favor of Beall Air. Perhaps Ella's concern was to be near her own family to secure their assistance. Not

long after the Washingtons relocated to Clover Lea, their baby daughter Betty died. In June 1863, Ella bore a son, William D. Washington.

The 1862 campaign around Richmond nearly resulted in the capture of the Confederate capital and an early end to the war. Fortunately for the Southern army, its timid commander fell wounded at the end of May and General R. E. Lee assumed command. In a week of fighting denominated the 'Seven Days' Campaign,' Lee slowly and at great cost drove away the besieging Northerners and bottled them up against the James river. Lee won the week's biggest battle with the largest charge he ever launched during the war, at Gaines' Mill, just five miles (8km) from Clover Lea.

In the aftermath, suffering wounded men clogged the entire countryside. A major hospital mushroomed next to the Bassett-Washington property. The Richmond *Whig*

'Clover Lea,' home of Ella Bassett Washington, photographed in the 1930s. (Author's collection)

three times published appreciative notices of the kindness bestowed on sick and wounded soldiers by women of the neighborhood, 'especially … the ladies of "Clover Lea."' A few weeks later, the same newspaper reported the death of baby Betty. It is hard to avoid the speculation (but impossible to prove) that microbes from the hundreds of sick, wounded, and infected soldiers convalescing in the vicinity might have brought on the infant's demise.

Although the Federals failed to capture Richmond during that spring of 1862, they did capture Ella's stepson, Lieutenant James Washington. The youngster, who had been serving on the staff of Confederate army commander Joseph E. Johnston, found himself in the hands of a friend from West Point days, George A. Custer. The quondam classmate treated Washington to a cigar and something to drink, and rounded up some other friends serving in the Union army.

That evening, Ella wrote later, the prisoner and his captors enjoyed 'rather a jollification in one of the headquarters tents,' reminiscing about their cadet days at the famous Benny Haven's Tavern near the military academy grounds.

When the provost guard took young Washington away to head for a prisoner-of-war camp, Custer stuffed some US currency in his friend's vest pocket to help smooth his captivity. 'You must have some money, Jim,' Custer said, 'those pictures in your pockets [Confederate currency] don't pass up there.' The cartel for exchange of prisoners had not yet broken down at that stage, so James went back to Confederate service upon exchange after a short period in captivity. Two years later, George Custer would be in a position to help James Washington's stepmother in a more substantial fashion.

War's mailed fist went rampaging northward for nearly two years after the

fighting around Richmond in May and June 1862 – but in May 1864 hostile troops swept across the grounds of Clover Lea and threatened to destroy everything that the Bassetts and Washingtons owned. On 28 May, Ella could hear rifles rattling in the near distance. It was a time 'of dreadful suspense and anxiety.' She wondered in her diary that evening whether her brothers had been in the fighting, and whether they had survived. A few Confederates galloped past, pausing only briefly. 'God bless you, boys,' Ella's father said as they hurried away. As their horses' hoofbeats faded, Ella thought they left behind 'a strange silence, brooding over nature like a pall.'

The next morning, after a terrified night and little sleep, Ella had to face the invasion of her property by swarms of uncontrolled enemy foragers. This 'most horrible set of creatures I ever saw' took everything in sight and made the women fear for their safety. Ella longed for a guillotine to 'take their heads off in just as rapid a style' as they were killing the farm animals.

In desperation, Ella Washington sent notes off to her stepson's friend, General Custer, hoping that he might come to assist her. One of the messages did reach the Federal cavalry general and on the 30th he arrived in person at Clover Lea, where he at once promised to protect the stepmother of his friend James Washington, and her property. Custer behaved gallantly with the pretty Virginian, who despite being his school chum's stepmother was not much beyond his own age. Ella wrote of the pleasure of finding someone, in the midst of 'this host of enemies, with whom we can feel some human sympathy.'

Even though they enjoyed intermittent protection afforded by the connection with Custer, Clover Lea and its civilians still suffered under the hostile occupation. Despite her gratitude for Custer's aid, Ella told her diary: 'In wickedness and impudence no nation ever equalled the Yankees.' Years later, in contrast, she still wrote warmly of the enemy general's 'generous and kindly deeds done under trying circumstances.'

Mrs Washington's experience as a helpless pawn on the chessboard of war was of a kind shared by countless thousands of other women. Her own vivid words describe some of what she saw and felt:

*the dreadful Yankees ... I feel so much fatigued I can scarcely dress ... What a day of horrors and agony, may I never spend such another ... The demon of destruction [was] at [our] very door, surrounding, swallowing [us] up in its fearful scenes of strife ... How can such an army of devils not human beings ever succeed? ... I fancied (though it seems a very ridiculous idea) that there was something almost human in [the dying farm animals'] screaming voices ... I was glad when the last had been killed ... I am feeling physically and mentally oppressed, never found my nerves so shaken, and my courage so tried.*

As General Custer took his leave of Clover Lea and went back to war, Ella described to him the frustration of being helpless to affect her own fate. 'You men don't know how much more intolerable the martyrdom of endurance is than the martyrdom of action.' 'Some of us,' he replied, 'can comprehend, and sympathize, too. War is a hard, cruel, terrible thing. Men must fight, and women weep.' Ella gave Custer as a token of her appreciation a button from George Washington's coat. The General set the button as a brooch and presented it to his wife, who eventually donated the relic to the US Military Academy. It survives today in the collection of Custer Battlefield National Monument, Montana.

Custer subsequently played a role in making war 'a hard, cruel, terrible thing' in the Shenandoah valley. In September, his troopers murdered six Confederate prisoners in a churchyard and the streets of Front Royal. One was a 17-year-old youngster whose widowed mother screamed in horror as she pleaded in vain for his life. A girl in the village wrote of how that 'dark day of 1864 ... clouded my childhood' and haunted her dreams forever. The famed Confederate partisan leader John S. Mosby ordered execution of a like number of Custer's captive men, but the Southerners blanched after carrying out half of the brutal job and let the rest go. Twelve years later, Custer himself wound up at the mercy of merciless men and died with scores of his troopers at the Battle of the Little Big Horn.

James Barroll Washington became a railroad president after the war and died in 1900. His father, Ella's husband, died in 1871, leaving the widow without many resources. Ella used her Washington connections to assist ex-Confederates in procuring Federal pardons after the war. When that lucrative but short-term business died down, she subsided into genteel poverty and died in New York in 1898.

Lieutenant James Barroll Washington and Captain George Armstrong Custer in 1862, while Washington was a prisoner of war in the keeping of his old friend from the US Military Academy. (Little Bighorn Battlefield National Monument, National Park Service)

# From Appomattox to Liverpool

Lee's surrender at Appomattox Court House on 9 April 1865 essentially ended the war in the Virginia Theater. Many thousands of men had slipped out of the weary, retreating, Confederate column as the cause became patently hopeless, thus escaping the final surrender. Some of those soldiers attempted to head south into North Carolina to join the Southern army still fighting there under General Joseph E. Johnston. That forlorn hope evaporated when Johnston surrendered to General William T. Sherman near Durham Station on 26 April, after complicated negotiations involving Washington politicians.

In the weeks that followed, Confederates who had not signed paroles at either Appomattox or Durham Station gradually made their way to occupied towns and took the oath of allegiance to the United States. Some troops from the deep South took weeks or even months to reach homes, many of them desolated, in Alabama or Louisiana or Texas. Soldiers who surrendered with Lee, or took the oath separately later, missed the ordeal suffered by their comrades who had been taken prisoner just a few hours before the Appomattox ceremony. Confederates captured during the retreat from Richmond and Petersburg, including thousands of men who surrendered at Sayler's Creek, went off to prison camps as though the war still raged on. Most did not secure their freedom until mid-June 1865.

Meanwhile, the triumphant Federal armies converged on the national capital for a mass celebration of the war's end. On 23 and 24 May, hundreds of thousands of blue-uniformed veterans marched in serried ranks. As the victorious divisions and brigades and regiments began to muster out of service, far-flung Confederate detachments continued to fight forlornly, and finally to give up the struggle. On 2 June, General E. Kirby Smith formally accepted terms at Galveston, Texas, and surrendered the Confederate forces in the Trans-Mississippi. Weeks later the Confederate cruiser CSS *Shenandoah* was still capturing whalers in the Bering Sea. Lieutenant James I. Waddell, CSN, finally surrendered the *Shenandoah* to British officials at Liverpool on 6 November 1865.

The reconstruction of the desolated Southern states remained to be done, and the healing of divisions, and the reunion of the United States in fact as well as in law. None of those tasks would be easy; nor could they be accomplished to the satisfaction of everyone.

# Recovery and reconstruction

Fighting in the American Civil War included more than 10,000 recorded battles, engagements, and skirmishes. Virginia served as the stage for more of those than any other state – some 2,200; Tennessee ranked next with about 1,500. At least 620,000 soldiers and sailors died during the war, more than 365,000 of them Federals. Microbes wreaked more havoc than bullets did, in an age of primitive notions regarding sanitation and medical science. Postwar calculations by the Federal Surgeon General, for instance, tabulated 45,000 Northern deaths from dysentery and diarrhea; 20,000 from pneumonia; and more than 9,000 by drowning or other non-battle accidents.

Political consequences of the conflict wrought fundamental changes in the nature

Defeated Confederates went home to face an ordeal of a different sort in a shattered land bereft of food and sustenance. Military 'Reconstruction' lasted more than a decade in some places in the South. (Public domain)

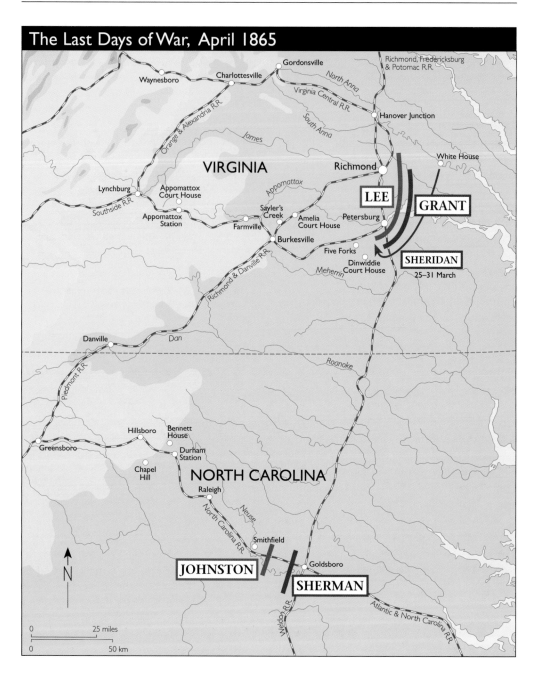

## The Last Days of War, April 1865

When Lee's attenuated lines around Petersburg finally snapped at the beginning of April, he hoped to slip west along the railroad, then turn south to join the Confederate army in North Carolina under General Joseph E. Johnston. Federal columns hounded the Southern remnants on all sides. At Appomattox Court House on 8 April, Lee found a substantial force of the enemy in front of him, eliminating his last hope of escape. He surrendered the next day. Johnston did likewise on 26 April at Durham Station, North Carolina, effectively ending the war in the Virginia Theater.

of institutions and culture in North America. The results of the war ensured prompt freedom for some 3.5 million black slaves, and also opened an entirely new chapter of restructuring American society and economy. Triumphant Northern politicians had the opportunity to remake the South in their own image, and for their own purposes, in what is usually styled the Reconstruction era.

Perhaps the most significant event in that process came just five days after Appomattox when pro-Confederate actor John Wilkes Booth assassinated President Abraham Lincoln at Ford's Theater in Washington. Lincoln's death removed his pragmatic, conciliatory influence and left control in the hands of radical politicians of vindictive temper. The President of Harvard University sounded a prevailing tone when he declared pompously, 'The task for the North is to spread knowledge and culture over the regions that sit in darkness.' On a more visceral level, anti-Confederate activists such as the Rev. James W. Hunnicutt advocated violence: 'The white men have houses and lands ... you can apply the torch to the dwellings of your enemies ... the boy of ten and the girl of twelve can apply the torch.' Considerable political and racial violence swept the desolated South.

With virtually every local citizen banned from office as a conquered rebel, Southern states fell under the control of venturesome Northerners who came south with little luggage but a carpetbag (a traveling bag made of carpeting), and who came to be known colloquially as 'carpetbaggers.' Some surely brought with them altruistic agendas; others surely came to loot from prostrate and powerless individuals and localities. General John M. Schofield, a veteran Union officer assigned to duty in postwar Virginia, called the eager immigrants 'ignorant or unprincipled' and summarized their behavior in a letter to U. S. Grant: 'They could only hope to obtain office by disqualifying everybody in the state who is capable of discharging official duties, and all else to them was of comparatively slight importance.'

The ruling political bloc in Washington welcomed the vacuum and operated gleefully within its embrace. Congressman Thaddeus Stevens of Pennsylvania summarized his goals succinctly: 'Unless the rebel States ... should be made republican in spirit, and placed under the guardianship of loyal men, all our blood and treasure will have been spent in vain.' A Federal soldier stationed in

Alabama expressed his view of the Southerners in his power: 'There is not 9 out of 10 of these so called "Whiped" traitors that I would trust until I saw the rope applied to their Necks, then I would only have Faith in the quality of the rope.' The carpetbag Governor of South Carolina (the last state returned to home rule) defended the record of his administration, insisting that he had observed 'steady progress toward good government, purity of administration, reform of abuses, and the choice of capable and honest public officers in those States in which the colored race had the most complete control.'

Southerners powerless under carpetbag government faced concerns far more basic than political institutions. A quest for food and shelter and minimal financial security ruled their lives in a barren land reduced to ashes. A 28-year-old woman living in central Virginia described her feelings in a letter to her sister written in August 1865. The entire region had been 'reduced almost to indigence ... I sometimes feel as if it could not be reality, and that I have been the victim of some hideous nightmare.' Returning survivors from the army were so 'heart broken' that it 'wrung your very soul.' She hoped that somehow the fight might be renewed. Feeling against the North was 'intense ... It will never pass away.' The distraught woman closed her letter by expressing the hope that small children would be taught to 'Fear God, love the South, and *live to avenge her*.' In 1867 a former Confederate colonel wrote with bitter nostalgia of 'that blissful time, for the return of which I most devoutly pray, when it was lawful to kill Yankees.'

Virginia completed 'Reconstruction' before most other ex-Confederate states, seating representatives in Washington in January 1870 who had been elected by broad popular vote. The North meanwhile enjoyed a fabulous explosion in wealth, fed by the war's profits and building upon industrialization generated by war contracts. As a direct consequence, hundreds of thousands of Southerners emigrated north for work or west for fresh opportunities on the frontier.

For the first time in United States history, veterans became a basic force in politics. Northern veterans touted their honorable service in what came to be known as 'waving the bloody shirt.' In Virginia, political pundits noticed that it was almost impossible to be elected governor without the stigmata of a visible war wound. Union veterans lobbied for National Cemeteries, the first in the country's history, and especially for pensions. Federals with any sort of disability drew pensions from Washington. As a byproduct, books full of memoirs of horrors suffered in Southern prisons began to appear. They soon blossomed into a virtual cottage industry. Most included significant exaggerations; some contained not even a kernel of truth.

Pensions for all veterans followed. Southern survivors, of course, had no access to benefits from the Federal government, so their states inaugurated local pension systems. Virginia pensions began under an Act dated 1888. Subsequent laws in 1900 and 1902 expanded coverage. Civil War pensions marked the first large-scale government welfare system in the country's history. By the 1920s and beyond, pensions had become so attractive during the Great Depression that fraudulent applications abounded. Recent scholarship that examined the stories of the final 10 self-announced survivors of the war (five from each side) discovered that every one of them was entirely bogus.

The war resulted in a revolution in North American medical practices.

European scientists such as Pasteur and Lister had been making strides in germ theory and antiseptic practice. Americans caring for their millions of soldiers gradually absorbed some of that important new technique. Hard experience produced other empirical changes in treatment.

Military art and science underwent an even more profound evolution. The Civil War was the first major conflict in which: most participants used rifled shoulder arms; percussion caps replaced less efficient ignition systems; railroads played a major role, both logistically and strategically, with dramatic increases in army mobility; field entrenchments became (by 1864) a routine but significant defensive mechanism; ironclad warships ruled naval affairs; general-staff functions began to receive adequate attention; telegraphy was used; standardization of production became effective (in the North); and some soldiers (almost exclusively Federals) employed repeating weapons and breech-loaders. The contending armies began the war employing techniques akin to those of the Napoleonic Wars. By 1865, combat was being waged in a manner that foreshadowed the First World War. Only the following year, Prussia was employing a skilled general staff, the telegraph, rifled arms, and a thoroughly planned railroad network, together with the other new features of warfare, to crush the Austrians. The Civil War had initiated a wide array of changes in the conduct of war that was to dominate battlefields for the next 60 years.

# Further reading

## Primary sources

Brown, Varina Davis (ed.), *A Colonel at Gettysburg and Spotsylvania*, Columbia, South Carolina, 1931.

Chesnut, Mary Boykin, *A Diary from Dixie*, New York, 1905.

Grant, Ulysses S., *Personal Memoirs of U. S. Grant*, 2 vols, New York, 1886.

Holt, David, *A Mississippi Rebel in the Army of Northern Virginia*, Baton Rouge, Louisiana, 1995.

Lee, R. E., *The Wartime Papers of R. E. Lee*, Boston, Massachusetts, 1961.

McClure, A. K. (ed.), The *Annals of the War Written by Leading Participants North and South*, Philadelphia, Pennsylvania, 1879.

Meade, George Gordon, Jr, *The Life and Letters of George Gordon Meade*, 2 vols, New York, 1913.

Wainwright, Charles S., *A Diary of Battle*, New York, 1962.

Worsham, John H., *One of Jackson's Foot Cavalry*, New York, 1912.

## Secondary sources

Catton, Bruce, *A Stillness at Appomattox*, New York, 1953.

Coddington, Edwin B., *The Gettysburg Campaign*, New York, 1968.

Davis, William C., *The Battle of New Market*, Garden City, New York, 1975.

Dowdey, Clifford, *Lee's Last Campaign*, Boston, Massachusetts, 1960.

Dyer, Frederick H., *A Compendium of the War of the Rebellion*, Des Moines, Iowa, 1908.

Freeman, Douglas S., *Lee's Lieutenants*, 3 vols, New York, 1942–44.

Furgurson, Ernest B., *Not War But Murder: Cold Harbor 1864*, New York, 2000.

Gallagher, Gary W. (ed.), *The Spotsylvania Campaign*, Chapel Hill, North Carolina, and London, 1998.

Gallagher, Gary W. (ed.), *Three Days at Gettysburg: Essays on Confederate and Union Leadership*, Kent, Ohio, and London, 1999.

Hattaway, Herman, and Archer Jones, *How the North Won: A Military History of the Civil War*, Urbana, Illinois, 1983.

Henderson, G. F. R., *The Science of War*, London, 1905.

Humphreys, Andrew A., *The Virginia Campaign of '64 and '65: The Army of the Potomac and the Army of the James*, New York, 1883.

Johnson, Ludwell H., *Division and Reunion: America, 1848–1877*, New York, 1978.

McPherson, James M., *Battle Cry of Freedom: The Civil War Era*, New York, 1988.

Marvel, William, *A Place Called Appomattox*, Chapel Hill, North Carolina, and London, 2000.

Pfanz, Harry W., *Gettysburg: The Second Day*, Chapel Hill, Northern Carolina, and London, 1987.

Pfanz, Harry W., *Gettysburg: Culp's Hill and Cemetery Hill*, Chapel Hill, North Carolina, and London, 1993.

Rhea, Gordon C., *The Battle of the Wilderness*, Baton Rouge, Louisiana, 1994.

Rogers, H. C. B., *The Confederates and Federals at War*, London, 1973.

Trudeau, Noah Andre, *The Last Citadel: Petersburg*, Boston, Massachusetts, 1991.

Warren, Robert Penn, *The Legacy of the Civil War*, New York, 1964.

Wert, Jeffry D., *From Winchester to Cedar Creek: The Shenandoah Campaign of 1864*, Carlisle, Pennsylvania, 1987.

Wiley, Bell I., *Confederate Women*, Westport, Connecticut, and London, 1975.

Wilson, Edmund, *Patriotic Gore: Studies in the Literature of the American Civil War*, New York, 1962.

# Part 2

## The war in the West

# Defining freedom

During his Gettysburg Address in November 1863, President Abraham Lincoln reminded his listeners that in 1776, people had come together to form a new nation, one 'conceived in liberty and dedicated to the proposition that all men are created equal.' Eighty-five years later, their descendants fought a great civil war to ensure 'that the nation shall, under God, have a new birth of freedom, and that government of the people, by the people, for the people, shall not perish from the earth.' The American Civil War was, in fact, a struggle over the final draft of both the Declaration of Independence and the United States Constitution, to define freedom and to settle the longstanding dispute over the compatibility of slavery and the purpose of the nation.

By the time of Lincoln's speech, the war had assumed an entirely new dimension. Initially, men on both sides had rushed to arms, fearful of missing out on the great event of their lives. In time, the savagery and the bloodshed, the hunger and the cold, the disease and the death, had altered all that. Banished were naive notions of a short war, a single, decisive battle to prove who was superior. Gone, too, were foolish assumptions about the individual's ability to transform the battlefield. The reality of 1860s warfare, with massive armies using rifled weapons and sustained by the fruits of 1860s industrialization and mechanization, had stripped away much of the glory. Only the starkness and brutality remained. Yet, somehow, those lofty goals that Lincoln had proclaimed still lived in the hearts and minds of the people. Despite hardships, suffering, and losses, soldiers and civilians clung tightly to their cause.

Although the Rebels never had someone whose words so elegantly encapsulated their cause as Lincoln's did, Southern whites also clung to their cause with deep passion. They had seceded to protect the institution of slavery, bequeathed to them by their ancestors. Secessionists may have voiced their cause in words of freedom and rights, but the rights they believed that the Lincoln administration would threaten were their right to own slaves, their right to take those slaves as property into the territories, and their right to live with those slaves in the security that fellow countrymen would not incite those slaves to insurrection. In comparing his new nation to the United States, Vice President of the Confederate States of America Alexander Stephens explained its purpose best when he declared, 'Our new government is founded upon exactly the opposite idea; its foundations are laid, its cornerstone rests, upon the great truth that the negro is not equal to the white man; that slavery … is his natural and normal condition.'

Northerners, by contrast, rallied around the flag for the lofty goal of preserving the Union. They believed that the Union was inviolate, and that the Republican candidate Abraham Lincoln had won the presidential election fairly. If they accepted the right to secession, Northerners argued, then how could any people ever preserve a democratic republic? Implicit in the Constitution, and understood by every one of the Founding Fathers, was the concept that all Americans must respect the outcome of a fair election. If a minority feared the results of the election, Northerners justified, then its supporters could rely on the system of checks and balances in the Constitution to secure and protect their rights.

Ulysses S. Grant rose from relative obscurity to be the commanding general of the Union armies and directed ultimate Federal victory. His Vicksburg campaign may have been the most brilliant of the war. This photograph, from 1864, was taken during the Overland campaign, when he served as commanding general. (Library of Congress)

By 1863, Lincoln had helped to provide something more tangible to the Union war aims than the sanctity of the Union. He signed the Emancipation Proclamation on New Year's Day, which granted freedom to all slaves in Confederate-held territory.

Back in 1858, Lincoln had proclaimed his belief that 'this government cannot endure, permanently half *slave* and half *free*.' While he did not divine civil war, he did predict:

*Either the* opponents *of slavery, will arrest the further spread of it, and place it where the public mind shall rest in the belief that it is in the course of ultimate extinction; or its* advocates *will push it forward, till it shall become alike lawful in* all *the States,* old *as well as new,* North *as well as* South.

Slavery was incompatible with Northern versions of freedom. Based on his constitutional powers as commander in chief, Lincoln decreed that if the Union won, its people could rest assured that they had sowed the seeds for slavery's destruction.

The Emancipation Proclamation also converged with a new approach to warfare that had begun to surface, particularly in the west. Two Federal generals, Ulysses S. Grant and William Tecumseh Sherman, had exchanged ideas on the problems and the conduct of the war. From these communications emerged the rudiments of a new approach to the war, a raiding strategy that would target Confederate civilians and property, in addition to their soldiers, as the enemy. Federal armies would seize slaves, confiscate food and animals, destroy railroads, factories, mills, and anything else of military value, and demonstrate to Confederate soldiers in the ranks just how vulnerable their loved ones were. 'They cannot be made to love us,' Sherman justified to Grant, 'but may be made to fear us, and dread the passage of troops through their country.'

Hardened veterans, too, had replaced raw recruits as the dominant force in these armies. Those who had survived the first two years had formed a different perspective on the war. Like Grant and Sherman, Northern veterans discarded outmoded notions about respect for private property and about treating delicately Southern civilians who supported the men in Rebel uniform. They wanted secessionists to feel the hard hand of war. Confederates, too, had toughened physically, mentally, and emotionally. Unfortunately for them, they had to exhibit that change on battlefields alone. Rarely did they have an opportunity to give Northern civilians a taste of the real war.

Representative of this new attitude was an event that occurred in the last weeks of the fighting, when a Union corps commander arrived at an assigned location a dozen hours behind schedule. Major-General Philip Sheridan promptly ordered his arrest and relieved him from command. Earlier in the war, the Union high command would have celebrated the arrival of a corps in the Eastern Army of the Potomac just 12 hours late. But Sheridan had spent his first three years out west, where a harder breed had emerged as military commanders. They tolerated errors of aggressiveness, not those of caution or tardiness. That spirit in the Federal western armies had begun to infuse soldiers in the east as well.

Part 2 of *The American Civil War 1863–1865* highlights this vital transformation. Here we explore the Western Theater, where Ulysses S. Grant rose to prominence and where Union armies developed an unstoppable momentum. The volume opens with the conclusion of the Vicksburg campaign, perhaps the most masterly of the entire war. It focuses on the burgeoning partnership between Grant and Sherman and their rise to power and influence over the Union war effort. Ultimately, the war in the west came under Sherman's direction, and he left his distinct mark on the way Federal armies would conduct their campaigns. At the same time, these soldiers from the west had their own vision of the way the Union needed to fight this war, and by their conduct they forced their views on officers and men. With the Federal stalemate in the east, this successful collaboration in the west assured Lincoln's re-election and guaranteed four more years of war, if necessary.

For the Federals, too, this section witnesses the decline of a slow yet capable commander, Major-General William Rosecrans, who committed a blunder based on faulty information, and the rise of a talented replacement, Major-General George H. Thomas, whose stellar service saved the army that day. Thomas continued to earn accolades for his generalship throughout the war, culminating in his decisive victory at Nashville.

On the Confederate side in the Western Theater, no Robert E. Lee emerged. Neither Braxton Bragg, Joseph E. Johnston, nor John Bell Hood proved themselves even pale imitations. Disastrous infighting at the highest levels of the army undermined fine Confederate soldiery, and by the end of the war, Federals had marched right through the heart of the Confederacy and accepted surrender in central North Carolina, not far from Raleigh.

While Abraham Lincoln accomplished his principal goals – the restoration of the Union and the destruction of slavery – he never fully witnessed those achievements. An assassin's bullet struck him down just days after Lee's surrender and almost two weeks before Johnston capitulated in North Carolina. Without Lincoln at the helm, his dream of a new freedom was only partially realized. The United States largely embraced the direction that Northerners had staked out, but it would be another century before African-Americans began to share fully in the rights and benefits of the Republic.

# War takes its toll

When the war broke out, the Northern states possessed a vast superiority of resources, so much so that some scholars have depicted Confederate efforts at independence as doomed from the start. That argument, however, draws on the critical knowledge that the Confederacy ultimately lost. In wartime, nations must be able to tap their resources, to convert them into military strength, and to focus and sustain that force at the enemy's critical source of power, what Prussian military theorist Carl von Clausewitz called the center of gravity. The task is easier said than done. In an industrialized world, it takes prolonged periods to mobilize manpower, to convert manufacturing to wartime purposes, and to replace valuable personnel who have rushed off to arms but who had produced on farms and in factories. Then, political and uniformed leaders must map out strategy, train and equip armies, and finally oversee the successful execution of military operations.

Certainly the advantage of resources rested with the Federals. Four of every five white persons lived in the Northern states, and the region held 90 percent of all manufacturing. The Union was home to two of every three farms, and possessed a modern and efficient transportation system.

But the Confederacy had advantages as well. The seceding states encompassed over 700,000 square miles (1.8 million km²) of territory. Since the Union sought to conquer the Rebels, its armed forces must overcome a hostile people over an enormous land mass. That huge Southern coastline – some 3,500 miles (5,600km) – no doubt could serve as an avenue of invasion. At the same time, it also offered easy access for imported goods, which could compensate for limited manufacturing capabilities. The Confederacy had a well-educated segment of the population who could design and build factories. And while the North had an overwhelming advantage in population, the Confederacy hoped to rely on three and a half million slaves. Their labors could offset the loss of productivity when white men took up arms and actually enable the Confederate states to place a higher proportion of their population in uniform.

After 27 months of fighting, Union armies had seized control of the Mississippi River, severing the Confederacy and reducing further contributions to the area west of the river to a trickle. Grant alone had captured two Rebel armies, totaling nearly 50,000. Federal forces had secured Kentucky and much of Tennessee, in addition to large portions of Missouri, Mississippi, and Louisiana. Tens of thousands of slaves had flooded Union lines. Early in the war, these laborers had produced for the Confederacy; now, they would work to defeat it. With the Emancipation Proclamation in effect, the Union armies would make a conscientious effort to strip Southerners of their slaves and to recruit them to work for or serve in the Federal armies. As Lincoln assessed pithily to Grant, 'It works doubly – weakening the enemy and strengthening us.'

By mid-1863, too, Northern might had just begun to weigh into the equation. There were twice as many Federals present for duty as Confederates, and the Union could replace its losses much more easily than the Confederacy. These Yankees, moreover, were better clothed, better fed, and better equipped than their Rebel opponents. It took a while, but the preponderance of Union resources began to take effect. Factories in the North churned out enormous quantities of military and civilian products, and imports continued to pour into New York, Boston, Philadelphia, and other port cities.

President Abraham Lincoln struggled to find someone who could exploit the Northern superiority in resources and lead the Union army to victory. Eventually he found that person in Ulysses S. Grant. (National Archives)

Relying on farm machinery to offset manpower loss, Northern farmers grew bumper crops, despite inclement weather. And after some initial struggles, Northerners had mastered the art and science of logistics – the supply and transportation of its armies – to ensure that soldiers in the field received much of that productive bounty.

The conversion of Northern industry to wartime production also advantaged the Union. After the war, Confederate Chief of Ordnance Josiah Gorgas boasted that the Confederacy never lost a battle because its armies lacked ammunition. Yet Northern factories churned out vastly more ammunition and weapons, and the quality was superior. The Northern states forged as many field and coastal artillery guns in a single year as did the combined productivity of the entire Confederacy for the war. Yankee munitions makers manufactured 50 percent more small-arms cartridges in one year than the Confederacy made for the entire war. Had Confederate ports been open, the Rebels could have offset the imbalance through imports, but Northern shipbuilders crafted ironclads and wooden vessels in such prodigious numbers that the once porous blockade had begun to tighten significantly.

While momentum had shifted to the Federals, two critical questions remained. Would the Union place individuals in high command who would direct the armies and resources skillfully against the Confederate center of gravity – its people's willingness to resist Union authority in order to create an independent nation? Second, would the Northern public and the armies in the field continue to support the cause in the face of huge losses, sacrifices, and hardships?

From the Confederate standpoint, despite losses in manpower and territory in the first 27 months of fighting, most Southern whites retained a powerful commitment to the war. Morale had rolled up and down, based largely on battlefield successes and failures. Still, Confederates realized that the Union had to conquer them to win, and in mid-1863, the secessionists were a long way from being defeated. Most Confederate land remained in Rebel control. No massive slave rebellions had taken place, and although large numbers had fled to the enemy, millions remained behind and produced for the Rebel cause. The primary armies stood intact, and the one in Virginia appeared unbeatable on home soil. No doubt, soldiers and civilians suffered shortages, but Southern farms and factories produced enough to sustain both sectors. If the Confederacy could resist stoutly for another 16 months, till the Northern presidential election, perhaps its people could force a political decision by swaying Northerners into voting a peace party into power.

# Overview and final stages

On 1 April 1863, a pleasant yet unimpressive-looking man – medium height, medium build with brown hair and trimmed whiskers – cast his eyes across the Yazoo River in Mississippi at the high ground called Haines' Bluff. It would not work, he concluded sadly.

For six months, Major-General Ulysses Simpson Grant had attempted to seize the Confederate bastion of Vicksburg, located high up on the bluffs overlooking the Mississippi River. He had tried scheme after scheme to get at the Confederate forces there, and each one failed. From this observation point 11 miles (18km) from Vicksburg, Grant realized that an attack here would result in 'immense sacrifice of life, if not defeat.' He had exhausted all options. 'This, then, closes out the last hope of turning the enemy by the right,' he admitted the next day to Admiral David Dixon Porter, Commander of the Mississippi Squadron. He must concentrate on turning the enemy left.

Since Lieutenant-General Winfield Scott, the Union Commanding General early in the war, had prepared his concept for Federal victory – derisively called the 'Anaconda Plan' by the media – control of the Mississippi River had been a top priority. If the Union held the river, it would slice off part of the Confederacy, thereby severing the Eastern Confederacy from the bountiful supply of cattle and horses that Texas possessed and virtually isolating Rebel troops there. Federal forces could move up and down the Mississippi with impunity, launching raids that could penetrate deeply into rebellious states. Once more, too, Midwestern farmers could ship their produce downriver to New Orleans and on to ocean-going vessels for distant markets, providing a cheaper transportation alternative to expensive railroads.

Despite Grant's frustration over Vicksburg, the Union war effort in the west had achieved significant results after two years of fighting. And at the heart of those successes had been that fellow Grant.

After Confederate gunners had fired on Fort Sumter, Federal President Abraham Lincoln called out the militia to put down the rebellion. Virginia, North Carolina, Tennessee, and Arkansas used that as their cue to secede from the Union and join fellow slaveholding states of South Carolina, Florida, Georgia, Alabama, Mississippi, Louisiana, and Texas in the Confederate States of America. They would resist by force of arms any attempt by the old Union to enforce its laws or maintain control of its property.

Four other slaveholding states did not officially join the Confederacy. Delaware, with a tiny slave population, remained solidly pro-Union. The other three, however, were more problematic. Lincoln employed legal and illegal means to keep Maryland from seceding. Missouri erupted in a nasty civil war of its own, and even though the Federals gained dominance there, guerrilla fighting plagued its population for years. The last one, Kentucky, was the worst combination of the other two. The situation in Kentucky was as complicated as Missouri, and its handling required even more delicacy than Maryland.

Early on, Kentucky declared its neutrality. While a majority of the people in that commonwealth probably preferred to remain in the Union, Kentuckians feared that their homes would become the battleground if they declared themselves for either side. Lincoln, who was born in Kentucky, knew just how valuable it was to the Union. He reportedly told someone that, while he hoped to have God on his side, he must have Kentucky. With its large number of livestock, its agriculture, its manufacturing and mining, and its almost 500 miles (800km) of banks along the Ohio River, the Union could not afford a hostile Kentucky. Lincoln raised substantial forces and positioned them to strike into the commonwealth, but only if the Confederacy violated its neutrality first.

Fortunately for Lincoln, he did not have to wait long. In one of the great blunders of the war, Major-General Leonidas Polk, a former West Point classmate of Confederate President Jefferson Davis, who had gone on to become an Episcopal bishop, violated Kentucky neutrality. Fearful that Federals might seize Columbus, Kentucky, Polk ordered its occupation in September 1861. Union Brigadier-General U. S. Grant responded by sending troops to Paducah and Smithland, where the Tennessee and Cumberland Rivers meet the Ohio. The Union-leaning legislature of Kentucky condemned Polk's act and proclaimed that the Confederate invaders must be expelled. By acting with restraint, Lincoln kept Kentucky in Union hands. And it paid great dividends. While some 35,000 Kentuckians served in the Confederate army, 50,000 fought for the Federals.

Leonidas Polk, a West Point graduate and bishop of the Louisiana. Polk violated Kentucky's neutrality in one of the great blunders of the war. As a corps commander, he promoted unrest with Bragg. Polk was killed during the Atlanta campaign. (Library of Congress)

Grant, a West Point graduate with considerable combat experience in the war with Mexico, had grasped the value of aggressiveness in warfare. Two months after his move into Kentucky, he gained his first Civil War combat experience at Belmont, Missouri. Grant's forces surprised a Confederate command there and drove them out of camp. Then, the lack of discipline among Grant's inexperienced troops wreaked havoc. They broke ranks and began plundering, setting themselves up for a Confederate counterattack that drove them back. At Belmont, Grant exhibited dash and recorded an important lesson about the nature of his volunteers.

Grant's first major campaign brought him back to the Tennessee and Cumberland Rivers. The Tennessee River dipped down through Kentucky and Tennessee and into northern Alabama. The Cumberland extended not quite as far south, but it did course through the Tennessee state capital of Nashville. Union control of these rivers would offer excellent naval support for invading armies.

The Confederates, who recognized the value of these waterways, erected forts along both rivers to block Federal movements, but with a huge area stretching from the Appalachian Mountains to southwest Missouri to protect, they lacked the troop strength to repel a large and effectively managed attack – exactly what Grant delivered.

In February 1862, Grant had obtained permission from his superior officer, Major-General Henry Wager Halleck, to transport his command of 15,000, accompanied by naval gunboats, down the Tennessee River and to secure Fort Henry, which blocked waterway traffic and military penetration into central Tennessee. By the time he arrived there, winter rains and ensuing floods had swamped Fort Henry, making it indefensible. Instead, Confederate forces concentrated on firmer ground at Fort Donelson, a dozen miles (19km) east on the banks of the Cumberland River, leaving behind only a paltry garrison of artillerists.

Those remnants at Fort Henry quickly succumbed to US navy shelling.

The new Confederate commander of the Western Department, General Albert Sidney Johnston, had no delusions about the overextended nature of the Confederate defenses. Located at Bowling Green, Kentucky, with about 25,000 troops, Johnston worried that the Federals would pierce his weak cordon and then outflank or trap a large portion of his manpower among Grant's command, a smaller one to the east under Brigadier-General Don Carlos Buell, and the Union river gunboats. After meeting with senior officers, Johnston decided to fall back to a Memphis–Nashville line, but also sent reinforcements to Fort Donelson to delay Grant's advance. Even worse, the two ranking commanders at Donelson were military incompetents yet well-connected politicians, John B. Floyd and Gideon Pillow.

Grant, meanwhile, immediately shifted his focus to the Confederates at Fort Donelson. Unlike so many Union officers, Grant grasped the value of initiative in warfare. He directed two divisions to slog their way through mud to the outskirts of the Confederate positions. The succeeding day, a third division arrived by transport along the Cumberland River, and with the aid of Federal gunboats, Grant invested the Rebel forces.

At Fort Donelson, the Confederates suffered from dreadful leadership. They launched a surprise attack that pried open an escape route, but Pillow grew squeamish over the losses and convinced Floyd to cancel the breakout. Seizing the opportunity, the aggressive Grant launched a counterattack of his own which not only sealed the breakthrough but occupied some vital positions in the old Confederate line as well. Unable to withstand another Federal assault, the Confederate commanders realized that their situation had become hopeless. Floyd fled, followed by Pillow. Also refusing to surrender was a disgusted colonel named Nathan Bedford Forrest, who would prove to be a Union scourge for the next three years. Forrest took 700 horsemen with him.

That left Brigadier-General Simon Bolivar Buckner, an old friend of Grant's, to request terms for capitulation. Grant's terse reply, wholly in character with his approach to warfare, captured the imagination of the Northern public: 'No terms except an unconditional and immediate surrender can be accepted. I propose to move upon your works immediately.' Buckner angrily relented, and Grant had gained the first important Union victory of the war, taking nearly 13,000 Rebels prisoner.

With the fall of Forts Henry and Donelson, the door opened for a rapid advance on Nashville. Grant and Buell both made haste, and by late February the city had fallen into Union hands. Grant's columns then pushed on to the Tennessee River, where they awaited reinforcements for a large-scale advance on Corinth, Mississippi, the site of a major rail intersection.

After abandoning Nashville, Johnston fell back to Corinth. There, he gathered some 40,000 Rebel troops and hatched a scheme to crush Grant's command before it united with Buell. Grant's soldiers, positioned largely on the south side of the Tennessee River, had failed to fortify. An effective Confederate attack might be able to pin the Yankees against the riverbank and crush them. With his army prepared to assail the Union lines the next day, Johnston vowed they would water their horses in the Tennessee River tomorrow.

In the early morning of 6 April, Johnston's troops struck Brigadier-General William Tecumseh Sherman's division, catching them largely without fortifications. Sherman and most of the Federals fought valiantly that day, but the Rebel onslaught was too much. Even though thousands of Federals cowered under the riverbank, Union troops had resisted enough for the Yankees to regroup and prepare a defensive position, aided by ample artillery. There, they received help from portions of Buell's army, which began arriving in the late afternoon. Among the staggering number of casualties, close to 20,000 that April day, was Albert Sidney Johnston, who bled to death from an untreated leg wound.

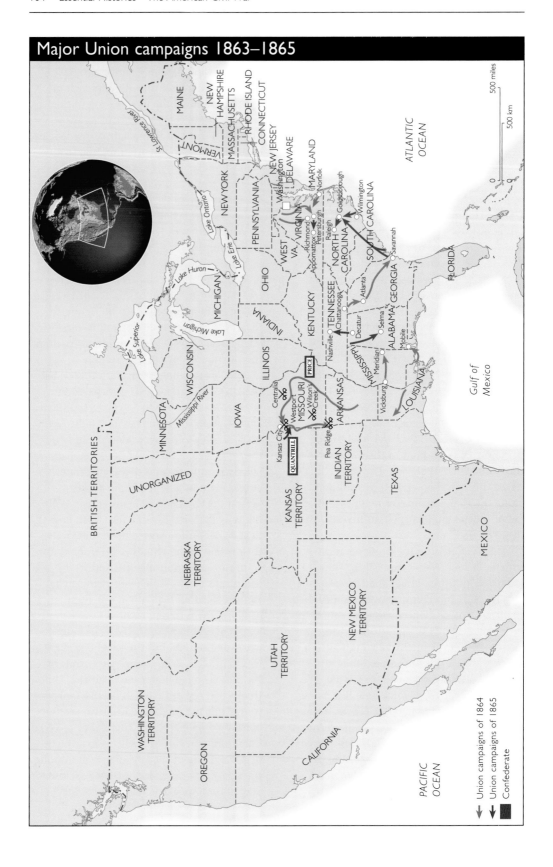

# Major Union campaigns 1863–1865

Union campaigns of 1864
Union campaigns of 1865
Confederate

With reinforcements from Buell's command, Grant seized the initiative early the next morning, attacking and eventually sweeping the field by afternoon. Sherman then attempted to organize an effective pursuit, but it was too late. The Federals were as confused in victory as the Rebels were in defeat.

What Grant won on the battlefield at Shiloh, however, he lost in the eyes of the Northern public. The unprepared state of the army, and the massive casualties at Shiloh, over 13,000 on the Union side and 10,600 Confederates in two days, appalled Northerners, and cries for Grant's removal radiated from all around the country. Halleck stepped in, stilling the public clamor against Grant but also displacing him. While Grant stewed in his nominal post of second-in-command, Halleck cautiously maneuvered his ponderous army of over 100,000 and eventually occupied Corinth.

By mid-June 1862, the Union had achieved extraordinary success in the West. Kentucky and central and western Tennessee had fallen into Union hands, as had a part of northern Mississippi. Brigadier-General John Pope had crushed Rebel defenses at New Madrid, Missouri, and Island No. 10, removing obstacles to Mississippi River passage all the way down to northern Mississippi. Naval forces advancing downriver blasted past Fort Pillow, and by early June they had shelled Memphis into submission. Farther to the south, a Union fleet led by David Farragut had pounded its way upriver and compelled the Confederacy's largest city, New Orleans, to surrender. Occupation troops followed.

When Lincoln called Halleck to Washington as commanding general the following month, it looked on the surface as if the Confederacy in the west was in dire straits. But before Halleck left, he slowed the advance and began to consolidate Federal gains, dispersing his massive army for some occupation duty and an advance under Buell on Chattanooga, Tennessee. It did not take long for the initiative to shift to the Confederacy.

Admiral David Farragut became the first great naval hero for the United States in the war. A bold commander, Farragut forced his fleet up the Mississippi River and compelled New Orleans to surrender in 1862. Later, he forced his way into Mobile Bay and closed a valuable Confederate port. (Library of Congress)

After Johnston's death, his second-in-command, General P. G. T. Beauregard, took over. Beauregard successfully evacuated Corinth, but then took an unauthorized leave when he fell ill. Confederate President Davis, already irritated with Beauregard for his unprofessional conduct in Virginia, used this as the basis for Beauregard's replacement. Davis chose General Braxton Bragg, a Mexican War hero with a reputation for quarrelsomeness, as the new commander.

Confederate cavalrymen in the area taught Bragg a valuable lesson. While Buell's army crept east toward Chattanooga, Forrest's cavalry struck his railroad supply line, and later another mounted raid under Kentuckian John Hunt Morgan did so as well. Both Rebel horsemen made Buell's life extremely difficult. Bragg realized that a larger, coordinated movement in the Federal rear might wreak havoc on Federal troops in

Mississippi and Tennessee, and force them to yield the territory they had taken since February. Once Confederate troops trod on Kentucky soil, Bragg was sure thousands would flock to his army and take up arms against the Union.

By rail, Bragg shifted 30,000 men to Chattanooga, where they began an advance. From Knoxville, Tennessee, Edmund Kirby Smith with 21,000 men, including a division of Bragg's, left in mid-August, passing through the Cumberland Gap and driving deep into Kentucky. Yet the march into the Bluegrass State was not much cause for local celebration. Few volunteers rushed to the Rebel banner.

Prodded by military and political officials, Buell finally undertook pursuit in early October. After much maneuvering on both sides, portions of the two armies collided in

The despised commander of the Army of the Tennesssee, Braxton Bragg had been a hero in the Mexican War, where he made a favorable impression on Jefferson Davis. His failure to follow up at Chickamauga may have been one of the greatest mistakes of the war. He resigned command of the army after the débâcle at Missionary Ridge. (Library of Congress)

some hilly terrain around Perryville, Kentucky. Because of an acoustic shadow, neither Bragg nor Buell heard any shots and they did not know the battle was taking place. As a result, soldiers who were literally a few miles from the battlefield did not participate. Despite 7,500 casualties, neither side gained an advantage, and Bragg withdrew his forces back to Tennessee.

The raid into Kentucky exposed serious flaws in both the Confederate and the Union commanders. Grumbling over Bragg filtered back to Richmond, and Confederate President Davis, himself a man of considerable military experience and accomplishment, proposed an interesting solution. General Joseph E. Johnston, who had suffered a serious wound at the Battle of Seven Pines several months earlier, had recovered enough to return to active duty. He could not get his old command back; General Robert E. Lee had been so effective with it that the soldiers and the public viewed the army as his. But Johnston possessed leadership skills and experience that the Confederacy needed. Rather than replace Bragg or the new commander around Vicksburg, Northern-born Lieutenant-General John C. Pemberton, Davis superseded them.

All along, Davis hoped his commanders could assume the offensive, but when the Federals advanced, the Confederate President wanted army commanders to concentrate manpower and other resources by tapping neighboring departments. Johnston's new assignment was to oversee military forces from the Appalachian Mountains to the Mississippi River. Davis expected him to coordinate their military activities, help them formulate plans, inspect, critique, and advise. Of course, when he was present, Johnston should command, but Davis wanted him to focus on the strategic and operational, not the tactical, levels. Johnston never grasped the concept.

Similarly, on the Union side, Lincoln had soured on Buell. Cautious to a fault, Buell followed Bragg hesitantly as the Rebel army escaped from Kentucky. By late October, an exasperated Lincoln had had enough. When Buell announced that he preferred to restore his supply base in Nashville instead of chasing Rebels, the President replaced him with Major-General William Rosecrans.

Lincoln wanted generals who would seize the initiative and, for a while, it appeared as if he had chosen the wrong man. Rosecrans planned painstakingly, and when Lincoln urged him to advance on the enemy, he refused to budge until everything was in order. Finally, Rosecrans moved out of Nashville with 42,000 men the day after Christmas. Despite skillful harassment by Rebel cavalry, Rosecrans pressed on toward Chattanooga and Bragg's army. On 30 December 1862, the armies confronted each other around Stones River, just north of Murfreesboro.

Strangely enough, Rosecrans and Bragg formed the same plan: to turn their opponents' right flank and get in their rear. Bragg got a jump on the Federals the next day, attacking first. His people roared down on the Yankee flank and pushed it back, but the Confederates could not get around Rosecrans's rear. On New Year's Day, the two sides skirmished. On the following day, though, Bragg attacked on the other side of the field. Although his men gained some high ground, they suffered heavy losses from Yankee artillery. As Union reinforcements arrived the next day, Bragg knew he must fall back.

At the Battle of Stones River, Rosecrans suffered 31 percent casualties, while Bragg lost a third of his men. Together, these were the highest proportionate losses in a single, major battle throughout the war. In victory, it took months for Rosecrans's Army of the Cumberland to recover. In defeat, dissension over Bragg worsened, but Johnston refused to take over, fearing the perception of him replacing Bragg with himself.

Farther to the west, Grant's reputation plummeted after the débâcle at Shiloh. When Halleck stepped in to oversee the Corinth campaign, Grant had nothing to do. After pondering for some time, he decided to ask Halleck to relieve him. Fortunately, Sherman talked Grant out of leaving, and six weeks later, authorities ordered Halleck to

Henry W. Halleck, who was Grant's commander during the Forts Henry and Donelson campaign, supplanted him after Shiloh. A critic of Grant, his appointment as commanding general restored Grant to command. He later served under Grant as chief of staff. (Library of Congress)

Washington and appointed him general-in-chief. Grant resumed charge of his old army. Patience had won Grant an opportunity to restore his name.

Back east, too, Grant won a reprieve. Halleck's ascension to the office of general-in-chief in the summer of 1862 improved his standing with the authorities in Washington. The new commanding general arrived in the nation's capital as a moderately strong Grant proponent. Halleck publicly exonerated him for his actions at Shiloh. After his own experiences in command at Corinth, Halleck had softened his initial criticism of Grant. Although he 'is careless of his command,' Halleck commented to Secretary of the Treasury Salmon P. Chase, he evaluated Grant 'as a good general and brave in battle.'

## The Vicksburg campaign

For several months afterward, Grant did little but combat raiding parties and guerrilla bands. After Halleck had scattered his mammoth army, Grant lacked sufficient force to launch another offensive. Runaway slaves, cotton trading, guerrillas, Confederate raids, and offended civilians absorbed his time and energy. Campaigning, it seemed, had taken a back seat to occupying secessionist territory.

But by late October 1862, pressure for a campaign against Vicksburg had begun to build. Nestled on a 200ft (61m) bluff overlooking the Mississippi River, Vicksburg dominated passage along the waterway. In Confederate hands, some cleverly positioned cannon could block Union transit. For the Federals, Vicksburg and Port Hudson, Louisiana, represented the last two Rebel strongholds along the Mississippi River. Once Vicksburg fell to Union forces, Port Hudson would become untenable. Then the Federals would control the entire length of the river and would slice off and isolate the Trans-Mississippi Confederacy.

A politician turned general, John A. McClernand, had received authority from Lincoln to raise a command to capture Vicksburg. Grant, who knew McClernand well, had serious doubts about McClernand's ability and temperament to lead such an expedition, judging him 'unmanageable and incompetent,' and at the urging of Halleck he decided to preempt McClernand's Vicksburg campaign by attempting it himself.

Grant's plan called for two separate forces to advance simultaneously and without communication, a risky proposition at best. While Grant personally led an army south along the Mississippi Central Railroad toward Jackson, hoping to draw Confederate forces out for a fight, Sherman would slip down the Mississippi River on transports and land near Chickasaw Bluffs, just north of Vicksburg. Sherman's troops then would brush aside the light Confederate opposition and seize the city. But the scheme quickly fell awry.

Two Rebel cavalry raids severed Grant's supply line, and he fell back under the misapprehension that his feint had succeeded and Sherman had captured Vicksburg. The Confederates at Vicksburg, however, did not budge from their works, and when Sherman tried to storm the bluffs in late December, Confederate shells and balls cut bluecoats down by the hundreds.

The new year brought a blend of headaches and hope for Grant and Sherman. On 2 January 1863, McClernand arrived by transport north of Vicksburg with his newly created army. Commissioned a major-general of volunteers that ranked him above Sherman, McClernand took command of all forces there. They had no prospects of capturing Vicksburg from below Chickasaw Bluffs. Sherman, therefore, proposed a joint army–navy operation against Fort Hindman, often called Arkansas Post, on the Arkansas River, from which Confederates had launched raids against Federal transit along the Mississippi River. McClernand endorsed the concept so warmly that he eventually claimed the idea as his, while Admiral David Dixon Porter needed coaxing from Sherman. Porter had all the confidence in the world in Sherman and none in McClernand, and as a result he extracted a promise from McClernand that Sherman would run the operation. On 9 January, the Federal expedition reached the vicinity of Arkansas Post, and within two days, Porter's bombardment had compelled the defenders to raise up the white flag. Nearly 5,000 prisoners fell into Union hands.

Grant, meanwhile, had resolved some important questions in his own mind about the upcoming Vicksburg campaign. Since McClernand lacked the fitness to command, he would direct operations personally. McClernand, Sherman, and a Grant protégé named James B. McPherson, a personable engineer officer who graduated first in the West Point class of 1853, would command corps.

The overland advance along the Mississippi Central Railroad had failed, so Grant explored a variety of options to get at Vicksburg. He

John A. McClernand, a politician from Illinois before the war, commanded a division at Forts Henry and Donelson and again at Shiloh. He raised troops that helped him capture Arkansas Post. McClernand commanded a corps in the Vicksburg campaign, fighting at Raymond, Champion Hill, and the assaults on Vicksburg. Quick to claim glory, he failed to gain the trust of Grant or Sherman and was removed. Later, he led a corps under Banks in the disastrous Red River campaign. (Library of Congress)

tried bypassing it, and seeking waterways that could position his army on the bluffs to the northeast of the city. 'Heretofore I have had nothing to do but fight the enemy,' a dejected Grant commented to his wife. 'This time I have to overcome obstICES to reach him.' When the last effort to turn Vicksburg on the right failed, Grant, Sherman, and Porter reconnoitered to select the best places to land troops.

But on that April Fool's Day, as he gazed across the Yazoo at the opposite slopes, he realized just how costly an attack here would be, and with no assurance of success. Lately, he had contemplated an unconventional movement that would take his army around to the enemy left flank. It was a risky proposition, but in a very different way from the frontal attack against Confederates occupying high ground. As he stood there, mulling it over in his mind, Grant determined that it was worth a try.

Grant began the campaign by asking the ever game Porter to run gunboats and barges past the Vicksburg batteries. For deception, Grant sent a cavalryman named Colonel Benjamin Grierson to launch a raid through the interior of Mississippi and come out at the Union army around Port Hudson, and he called on Sherman to feign an attack at Haines' Bluff. Meanwhile, the other two corps would march along the western side of the Mississippi River and Porter's people would shuttle them across the river to Bruinsburg, below Vicksburg. Eventually, Sherman's men would follow.

Once on the eastern side, Grant launched one of the most brilliant campaigns in American military history. By rapid marches, he continually confused his enemy. His army pounded the Confederate forces protecting Vicksburg, and then moved quickly to the northeast, where they hammered a Rebel command accumulating near the capital city of Jackson under General Joseph E. Johnston. Grant then turned back on Vicksburg, and had McClernand not attacked prematurely, he might have interposed Sherman's corps between Vicksburg and its defending columns. All told, the Union army fought five battles, and even though there were more Confederates in the campaign than Federals, Grant placed superior numbers on each battlefield and won every one of them. By mid-May, he was laying siege against Vicksburg.

The Confederate commander at Vicksburg, Pemberton, had a chance to escape. Johnston urged him to do so, but Pemberton had also received explicit instructions from President Davis to hold the city at all costs. After a council of war, Pemberton chose to hunker down and await succor from Johnston. It would never arrive.

Shortly after he besieged Vicksburg, Grant attempted to storm the Rebel works twice and was repulsed on both occasions. He also removed McClernand from command for violating a War Department directive and for general incompetence. Otherwise, he supervised a traditional siege that slowly strangled Pemberton's army. By early July, it became apparent to the Confederate general that his cause was lost. On 4 July, Pemberton

David Dixon Porter, whose father also raised David Farragut, proved to be a wonderful naval commander. Intolerant of red tape, Porter's aggressiveness and spirit of cooperation with the army won him lifetime friendship with Grant and Sherman. Porter was invaluable in the Vicksburg campaign and the fall of Fort Fisher. (Library of Congress)

surrendered almost 30,000 Rebels and 172 artillery pieces. For the second time, Grant had captured a Confederate army.

The fall of Vicksburg left one last Confederate toehold on the Mississippi River – Port Hudson, Louisiana. Located some 25 miles (40km) north of Baton Rouge, Port Hudson consisted of extensive man-made works and natural obstructions, especially swamps. Like Vicksburg, its commander, Major-General Franklin Gardner, hailed from the North. Gardner, who had fought at Shiloh and in Bragg's Kentucky campaign, had a mere 7,000 troops to hold the position.

Against Gardner and his defenders, the Union sent Major-General Nathanial P. Banks and 20,000 troops, accompanied by Farragut's warships. From 8 to 10 May, Union gunboats shelled and ultimately silenced the batteries. Banks maneuvered his troops around the Confederate defenses,

taking a horseshoe-shaped position, with the ends stretching to the riverbank. On 27 May, Banks launched an uncoordinated assault. Among the participants were two black regiments, the 1st and 3rd Louisiana Native Guards. Charging well-defended fortifications, and part of the way through floodwater, the black infantrymen exhibited courage, even in the face of severe losses. The Union attack was repulsed everywhere. Again on 11 June and then 14 June, the Union columns attacked and failed. Banks resigned himself to siege, hoping to starve out the defenders. One Confederate recorded in his diary that he and his comrades ate 'all the beef – all the mules – all the Dogs – and all the Rats' they could find.

Once word of the fall of Vicksburg reached the Port Hudson defenders, Gardner knew his cause was hopeless. He surrendered on 9 July. Banks suffered 3,000 casualties in the campaign, while the Confederates lost 7,200, of whom 5,500 were taken prisoner. Lincoln could now announce proudly, 'The Father of Waters again goes unvexed to the sea.'

## Crisis in Missouri

The conflict in Missouri stretched back long before the firing on Fort Sumter in April 1861. Violence first erupted in 1854 when Congress passed the Kansas–Nebraska Act, creating those territories, repealing the Missouri Compromise, which stated that all territories north of 36° 30' latitude would be free soil, and substituting popular sovereignty – a vote of the people there – to determine whether slavery could exist or not. As settlers poured into the Kansas Territory, a Northern, antislavery flavor was discernible. To tilt the balance toward slaveholders, Missourians crossed the border and cast ballots illegally and intimidated antislavery voters. Antislavery Kansans responded to violence with more violence, and soon Kansas was aflame in brutality. Border Ruffians from Missouri launched raids that resulted in rapes, murders, pillaging, and home burning. Among those who retaliated, John Brown of Osawatomie, Kansas, led a band that savagely murdered five pro-slavery neighbors.

Strangely enough, the secession crisis of 1860–61 brought matters to a lull, as both sides struggled to size up the situation. Missouri Governor Claiborne Jackson advocated secession and called for the state to join the Confederacy. Pro-Union opposition, centered around the German-American community in St Louis and led by Francis P. Blair, a member of one of the most prominent families in Missouri, resisted. When the governor mobilized pro-secession militia and positioned them to seize the US arsenal in St Louis, Blair acted. He encouraged a fiery red-headed US army officer named Nathaniel Lyon to surround and disarm the militia, which Lyon accomplished. But as he marched his

prisoners back, a crowd of civilians gathered and harassed and abused Lyon's militiamen. Finally, someone shot and killed one of Lyon's officers, and his troops retaliated by blasting into the crowd. When the smoke cleared, 28 people lay dead.

From this moment on, the violence took on a life of its own. Union troops and opponents of slavery in Kansas and Missouri began sacking towns and seizing slaves and other property from Missourians. These acts inflamed old passions and drove many neutrals or pro-Union advocates, among them a Mexican War veteran named Sterling

John S. Pemberton (right), a Northerner by birth, commanded Confederate forces at Vicksburg. Caught between orders from President Davis and General Johnston, Pemberton could not decide whether to try to save Vicksburg or his army. He lost both. (Ann Ronan Picture Library)

Price, into the secessionist camp. After an attempt to broker a peace failed, Lyon assumed the offensive and began driving Price and pro-Confederate forces from the state. In his wake, Lyon stirred up all sorts of guerrilla bands. William Quantrill and 'Bloody Bill' Anderson led the Rebel bushwhackers. Among their followers were acclaimed robbers Frank and Jesse James and Cole and Jim Younger. From Kansas, pro-Union guerrillas included the diminutive 'Big Jim' Lane and Charles Jennison.

By August 1861, Price had accumulated 8,000 Missourians, augmented by some 5,000 Confederate soldiers under Ben McCulloch. Before he could attack, though, Lyon struck first. Unwilling to retreat and yield all the territory he had secured, Lyon elected to surprise the enemy at a place called Wilson's Creek. Initially, his attack on both flanks made headway, but a Confederate counterassault drove both back. The Rebels then focused on the Union center, where Lyon directed the fight. Although the Union commander was killed, his line repelled Price's attacks. When the smoke cleared, the Confederates had called off the fight, but the Union forces had lost 20 percent of their men and had been so badly damaged that they retreated. Price, whose command suffered slightly fewer casualties, slowly marched northward, collecting recruits and pressing all the way to Lexington, between St Louis and Kansas City.

In St Louis, the recently appointed commander of the Western Department, Major-General John C. Fremont, overreacted. The Republican Party candidate for president in 1856, Fremont declared martial law, proclaimed the death penalty for all

guerrillas, and freed all slaves of Confederate supporters. Although the emancipation directive caused outrage in the North, Lincoln privately asked Fremont to modify his order, to save the General from embarrassment. With unparalleled temerity, Fremont refused, and Lincoln had to order it.

Having irritated his commander-in-chief and many others, Fremont needed a victory to restore his reputation. He accumulated a large force, some 38,000, and began a pursuit of Price. The militia commander fell back, a good portion of his army melting back into the countryside to complete the fall harvest. An order relieving Fremont reached him before he caught up with Price.

Price's retreat into Arkansas did not quash Confederate designs on Missouri. In March 1862, Major-General Earl Van Dorn gathered 16,000 men, including some Indian troops, with Price and McCulloch as division commanders. His plan was to brush aside Union opposition and capture St Louis, a prize that would earn him accolades throughout the Confederacy. Union commander Brigadier-General Samuel Curtis, a tough old West Pointer, had other ideas. Van Dorn attempted to swing around Curtis's rear, but Yankee scouts including 'Wild' Bill Hickok spotted the movement. When the Rebels attacked at Pea Ridge, Arkansas, they made little headway. The next

Sterling Price, a Mexican War veteran and an original opponent of secession in Missouri, soured on the Union after Frank Blair and others took aggressive action to block the governor's pro-Confederate policies. He commanded Missouri's secessionist militia in 1861, led a Confederate division as a major-general at Pea Ridge in 1862, and directed the last raid into Missouri in 1864. After suffering a defeat at Westport near Kansas City, he began his retreat, enduring Union harassment along a roundabout route back to Arkansas.

day, Union artillery silenced Confederate guns, and a Federal assault swept the field.

Had the Union authorities only confronted organized armies in Missouri, they would probably have eliminated the threat in 1863. But longstanding tensions, ideological differences over slavery, and the conduct of Union troops stirred up a hornets' nest of trouble from guerrilla bands. Although many Rebel guerrillas there had strong ties to slavery, quite a few others exhibited a passion for violence and destruction that may have been pathological. Helping to ignite this tinderbox were Kansans who combined fervent abolitionism with a passion for plundering.

During the Missouri campaign of 1861, there were pockets of fighting in which neither side gave quarter. Yet raids from Kansas fueled the violence when they extended from confiscation of slaves and livestock to arson, robbery, and murder. These Kansans insisted they were merely retaliating for the slaughter of seven of their people by guerrillas a few days earlier, but acts of savagery begat more acts of savagery, and soon the entire region was ablaze in deeds of violence or brutal reprisals.

In an effort to check the acts of partisans, Union occupation troops under Major-General David Hunter and John Schofield nearly ruined their careers with repeated failures. They tried building forts in guerrilla-infested areas, but local partisans blended into the community and struck when they discovered soldiers at a disadvantage. Next, they experimented with population removal. Because guerrillas drew from friends and families for support, Brigadier-General Thomas Ewing had arrested the wives and family members of notorious guerrillas as leverage against them. Not long afterward, in August 1863, Ewing announced he would transport those under arrest as well as the families and other supporters of the Confederacy to Arkansas. Before he could do that, though, the rickety building where he housed some of the women collapsed, killing five and crippling another. Two victims were sisters of William

A West Point graduate and a former Republican congressman from Iowa, Samuel R. Curtis led a successful operation into southwest Missouri and northern Arkansas, and defeated Confederates at Pea Ridge. After heading the Departments of Missouri and Kansas, Curtis led Union forces that helped to defeat Price's Missouri Raid in 1864. (Library of Congress)

Anderson, already known for his violence. He now vowed to kill every Yankee he could find, and it was not long before he earned the nickname 'Bloody Bill.'

In retaliation, Quantrill led his party of 450 on a raid against Lawrence, Kansas, a hotbed of abolitionism. En route, they forced Kansas farmers to act as guides and then executed them. On 21 August, they slipped into town and disposed of the small number of soldiers there. The town soon surrendered, but those words meant nothing to Quantrill and his followers. All told, they murdered 150 males, wounded 30 more, and torched 185 buildings.

Federals responded to the raid by ordering all western Missourians who did not live in certain cities to migrate. Those who pledged loyalty to the Union could settle around forts, and all others would have to abandon the area. Union authorities hoped to deprive guerrillas of local support and establish free-fire zones in the area, thereby eliminating much of the worry of distinguishing friend from foe. The policy had little if any effect on the bushwhackers.

What ultimately led to the demise of guerrilla activities actually stemmed from their own success. Various partisan activities had impressed Price, particularly the work of Quantrill, and when they insisted that Missourians would rise up in support of the Confederacy if he raided into the state, Price jumped at the opportunity. With 12,000 cavalry, half of whom lacked arms, Price crossed into Missouri in mid-September 1864.

In support of the movement, various pro-Rebel bushwhackers had attacked isolated posts, towns, and pockets of soldiers, massacring troops and civilians, armed and disarmed alike. Simmering divisions began to bubble to the surface among guerrilla leaders. Anderson wanted to attack the fortified garrison at Fayette; Quantrill opposed it as too dangerous. When Anderson and his men suffered a repulse and the loss of 13 men, it only infuriated them more. A few days later, they entered Centralia in search of plunder and news of Price's whereabouts. There they pulled 25 unarmed Union soldiers off the train and executed them. When some Missouri militiamen stumbled on the guerrillas, they attacked and suffered a horrible defeat. Out of an original 147 militiamen, 129 were cut down. The guerrillas then committed a host of atrocities, including cutting off the genitals of a living soldier and placing them in his mouth.

Price, meanwhile, had advanced well into Missouri. The same day as the Centralia Massacre, his command attacked Federals under Ewing at Pilot Knob, suffering heavy losses in the repulse. As Union reinforcements arrived in Missouri, Price pressed westward along the south bank of the Missouri River. Anderson and his people met up with them, and Price sent them on a destructive spree north of the river. Before October ended, Anderson fell to two militiamen's balls. They placed his body on display, then severed his head, and eventually buried him in an unmarked grave.

As Price's columns pressed toward Kansas City, Union forces closed in on them. With Curtis to his front and Major-General Alfred Pleasanton closing from his rear, Price attempted to beat them in detail. He attacked Curtis first, and pushed the Union command back initially, but the Federals stiffened and launched their own counterattack. To the rear, Pleasonton drove back the Rebel cavalry, and Price began his retreat. Federals continued to press him, capturing 1,000 men in Kansas. Eventually, his command limped into Arkansas with only half of his original 12,000.

Price's raid was the last major Confederate undertaking west of the Mississippi River. Guerrilla fighting continued in Missouri, however, and extended well after the war, as unreconstructed bands like the Jameses and Youngers continued to rob and plunder. Quantrill, having suffered the humiliation of a rebellion in his ranks, elected to shift his base of operations to Kentucky. In May, he was shot in the back and paralyzed by Union troops. He died almost a month later.

## The Tullahoma campaign

During the Vicksburg campaign, Halleck and even Grant pleaded with Rosecrans to advance. Since early in the war, the idea of liberating Unionists in East Tennessee had intrigued Lincoln. Once Grant had crossed the Mississippi River and engaged Pemberton's forces, the administration had even more reason to demand that Rosecrans attack: Union leaders feared that Bragg's army would rush reinforcements west to defeat Grant. If 'Old Rosy,' as his men called him, would advance on the Confederate Army of the Tennessee, Bragg would be compelled to hold on to all he had. In fact, Johnston did draw troops from Bragg, as well as units from the Atlantic coastal defense. Yet Rosecrans would not be rushed. Finally, after word that Union troops under Major-General Ambrose P. Burnside would push toward East Tennessee, the Union Army of the Cumberland moved out, 169 days after the Battle of Stones River.

Rosecrans may have been slow, but he was not without skills. He used a portion of his army to swing around and threaten the Confederate rear. In an effort to protect the Confederate base at Tullahoma, Bragg pulled his forces back, thereby uncovering valuable gaps in the Cumberland Plateau. With powerful Union columns pressing through them and then in on his flanks, and a raid that threatened his rear, Bragg decided to abandon Tullahoma and fall back to Chattanooga.

At comparatively little cost, Rosecrans had driven his enemy back 80 miles (129km). But he deemed further pursuit impossible. Heavy rains had impaired movements on both sides, converting roads into muck. 'Tulla,' so noted one Confederate officer, was Greek for 'mud,' and 'homa' meant 'more mud.' The halt, however, did not sit well with authorities in Washington. They could neither see rainfall nor experience the mud; all they could envision was a delay that would allow Bragg to fortify. And when Old Rosy took time to repair the railroad from Nashville, they interpreted it as his usual temporizing behavior and balked. Finally, under threat of removal, Rosecrans's army rumbled forward again in mid-August 1863, in conjunction with Burnside's advance on Knoxville.

Bragg, meanwhile, had lost the faith of his army and had begun to lose confidence in himself. His corps commanders, Polk and Lieutenant-General William J. Hardee, had voiced displeasure over his leadership. For the most part, Bragg's soldiers despised him for his strict discipline and lack of battlefield success. Under stress, especially during campaigns, he himself grew ever more despondent. Rather than view the mountains

around Chattanooga as a defensive advantage, Bragg transformed them in his own mind into a Federal asset.

Because those mountains and the Tennessee River provided strong protection for Chattanooga and its defenders, Rosecrans executed a march of deception, as he had done in the Tullahoma campaign. He sent a portion of his army north of the city, to convey the impression that he was uniting with Burnside. The bulk of his army, though, crossed the Tennessee River to the southwest. By the time Bragg realized what had happened, Union forces were barreling down on his rear. On 8 September, he abandoned Chattanooga to the Federals.

To this point, in spite of delays, Rosecrans had conducted a skillful campaign. But then he got sloppy. He assumed the Rebels would fall back once again, and he divided his army for another maneuver campaign, spreading it out far too wide for the hilly terrain. Fortunately for Old Rosy, Bragg could not exploit the opportunity. Twice the Rebel commander tried to pounce on portions of Rosecrans's isolated forces, and in both instances subordinates failed to execute. In

After fighting at Iuka and Corinth, Rosecrans assumed command of the Army of the Cumberland. He led the army at the bloody engagement at Stones River. He directed the army skillfully in the Tullahoma campaign, but suffered a disaster at Chickamauga when he pulled troops from his line based on an erroneous report. Rebels attacked through the opening and routed his army. Grant replaced him with Thomas. Rosecrans finished out the war as head of the Department of Missouri. (Library of Congress)

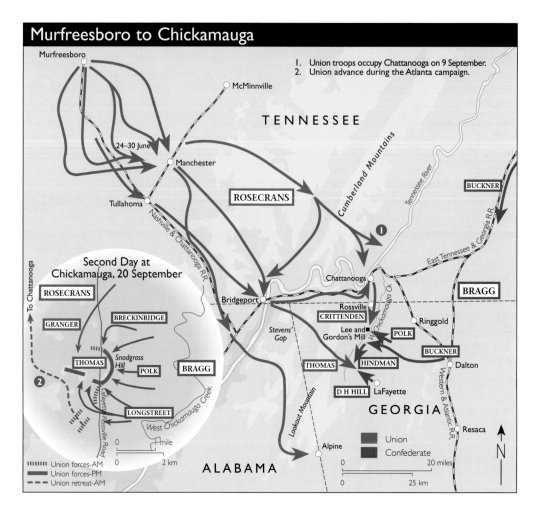

## Murfreesboro to Chickamauga

1. Union troops occupy Chattanooga on 9 September.
2. Union advance during the Atlanta campaign.

Union forces-AM
Union forces-PM
Union retreat-AM

Union
Confederate

haste, Rosecrans consolidated his command near a stream known as Chickamauga.

Since the spring, Confederate officials had debated the possibility of reinforcing Bragg or Pemberton from Lee's army. At the time, Lee had his own plans, a raid into Pennsylvania, and he demurred. With Bragg in need that fall, and the Union Army of the Potomac exhibiting little initiative, President Davis sent west two divisions from Lee's Army of Northern Virginia, under the command of Lee's 'Old War Horse,' Lieutenant-General James Longstreet. Traveling in a roundabout way, it took them nine days to reach Bragg's army. Major-General John Bell Hood's division arrived the day before the fight, giving Bragg numerical superiority. The next evening, Major-General Lafayette McLaws's division reached the battlefield.

On 19 September, Union and Confederate troops began to skirmish over control of a clearing. Reinforcements joined the fray piecemeal. Each time that one side extended beyond the enemy flank, a fresh batch of troops stretched beyond them. Neither Bragg nor Rosecrans could coordinate anything effective, in part because of the heavy timber around the battlefield. All they had to show for the day of fighting were lengthy casualty lists.

That night, Longstreet arrived with McLaws's division. A frustrated Bragg gave him command of the Rebel left wing and directed Polk to initiate the fight on the right the next morning. As usual, Polk made little progress, due partly to his tardiness and partly to the stout resistance of Major-General George H. Thomas's corps. In exasperation, Bragg called on Longstreet to launch an assault.

Never before on a battlefield had Longstreet fallen into such good fortune. Rosecrans had begun to pull units over to his beleaguered left, as additional support for Thomas. When a Union staff officer mistakenly reported a gap in the line on the right – the troops were actually well concealed in some woods – Old Rosy shifted some units over, this time creating a gap. Into this breach Longstreet's men fortuitously charged. Two Union divisions collapsed, racing back to Chattanooga. In their flight, they took the Union army commander with them. Once the Rebels penetrated the line, Longstreet ordered them to wheel right, to envelop the bulk of Rosecrans's command. Union units melted away, until the old stalwart, Thomas, held firm. With some timely reinforcements, the native Virginian Thomas refused to budge from Snodgrass Hill, and repeated Rebel attacks could not drive him off. At dark, he withdrew his men, earning the sobriquet 'Rock of Chickamauga' for his efforts.

In triumph, Bragg emerged in lower standing than before the battle. No one was impressed with his leadership during the course of the fight, and the bloodbath – over 18,000 casualties on the Rebels' side and more than 16,000 for the Yankees – seemed to have paralyzed him. He contributed nothing after the breakthrough, and despite pleas by Forrest and others to follow up the victory, he stalled. The Federal troops made good their escape and fortified. Eventually, Bragg took up positions to lay siege, attempting to cut off all supplies, but he lacked the resources to do so completely.

After Bragg wasted a splendid opportunity to crush the bulk of the Army of the Cumberland, old and new wounds began to fester among the Confederate high command. Bragg suspended Polk and two others for refusing to obey orders. Several generals petitioned Davis to remove Bragg, and Longstreet penned the Secretary of War, pleading with him to send Lee. Forrest rejected such niceties. He threatened Bragg to

George H. Thomas, a Virginian by birth, served as corps commander under Rosecrans. His defense at Chickamauga saved the Army of the Cumberland and earned him the nickname of the 'Rock of Chickamauga.' Appointed its commander before the Chattanooga battles, he served in the Atlanta campaign. Late in 1864, Thomas routed Hood's army at Nashville. (Library of Congress)

his face. 'I have stood your meanness as long as I intend to,' thundered the brilliant cavalryman. 'You have played the part of a damned scoundrel, and are a coward, and if you were any part of a man I would slap your jaws and force you to resent it.' Forrest then made clear that if Bragg ever interfered or crossed paths with him, 'it will be at the peril of your life.' Bragg, as well as everyone else in the army, knew Forrest would do it, too.

Finally, Davis traveled out to Chattanooga to resolve matters himself. The Rebel President relieved D. H. Hill, a good yet cantankerous officer, and transferred Polk to Mississippi. With Davis's assent, Longstreet took 15,000 men to recapture Knoxville. Yet the President failed to address the major problem, Bragg.

On the other side, Rosecrans's days were numbered. Officials in Washington tolerated his seemingly interminable delays as long as

The best cavalry commander in the Western Theater and probably on either side in the war, Nathan Bedford Forrest was a scourge to Union soldiers. Forrest's disgust for Bragg was so great after Chickamauga that he threatened to kill him. Forrest also gained notoriety when his cavalrymen slaughtered black soldiers at Fort Pillow. (Library of Congress)

he won, but after the Chickamauga débâcle they lost all faith in him. Lincoln thought Rosecrans acted 'confused and stunned like a duck hit on the head.' The Assistant Secretary of War, Charles A. Dana, visited Chattanooga and reported that the army lacked confidence in him. What the

administration needed was someone to take charge. That man was Grant.

## Battles around Chattanooga

Secretary of War Edwin M. Stanton caught a speedy train westward to rendezvous with Grant in Louisville. Instead, he caught up to him at Indianapolis, and the two rode together that last leg. The administration had decided to create the Military Division of the Mississippi from the Appalachians to the river, and it assigned Grant as the commander. Stanton then gave Grant a choice: he could keep Rosecrans as commander of the Army of the Cumberland, or replace him with Thomas. Grant chose Thomas.

Before Grant arrived at Chattanooga, the administration had already taken steps to improve the situation there. It had transferred the XI and XII Corps under Major-General Joseph Hooker from the idle Army of the Potomac by rail, and Sherman, with another 17,000, had been on the march from Mississippi. Rosecrans and his staff had prepared plans for opening supply lines. Grant's presence instilled confidence, and he soon had the 'cracker line' open.

With reinforcements under Sherman and Hooker there, Grant implemented his plan. Additional manpower had doubled Union

This is the crest of Missionary Ridge, where Thomas's men charged without orders. The steepness of the hill, and the Confederates in flight, provided protection for the attackers, who dislodged and routed Bragg's army. (Library of Congress)

strength, while Bragg depleted the size of his command by detaching Longstreet and 15,000 men. Grant could use this considerable numerical superiority to his advantage. He ordered Hooker to attack up Lookout Mountain on the Rebel left, while Sherman's forces would roll up the right. Thomas's army, which, Grant assumed, suffered from a lack of confidence after Chickamauga, would play a less active role. It would threaten the enemy center, a long, steep hill called Missionary Ridge.

The battle opened up well for the Federals. On 23 November 1863, Thomas's people attacked and secured Orchard Knob, from which they threatened an assault on Missionary Ridge. The next day, Hooker assailed a lightly defended portion of

LEFT The Union plan did not call for Federal forces to break through the Confederate line in the center, but men from the Army of the Cumberland did just that. In the excitement of battle and their desire to restore their reputation after the disaster at Chickamauga, these Federals exploited the steep incline along Missionary Ridge, pursuing the defenders so closely that Rebels near the top could not fire for fear of hitting their own men. In a massive rush, depicted here in the sketch, Yankees carried the heights in one of the greatest assaults of the entire war. (Library of Congress)

Lookout Mountain with almost three divisions. The successful operation amid pockets of fog created quite a spectacle and gained the nickname 'The Battle Above the Clouds.' Sherman, meanwhile, had crossed the Tennessee River and planned to roll up the Rebel right at Missionary Ridge, while Hooker rushed down on the left.

Yet two factors operated against Sherman. The narrow ground and rough terrain limited his options and restricted the amount of troops he could deploy for battle. The second factor was a superb Confederate division commander named Patrick Cleburne. An Irishman by birth, Cleburne had run afoul of officials in Richmond by proposing the use of blacks as soldiers. Although he was the best division commander in the army, authorities somehow managed to overlook him for advancement, no doubt as a result of his controversial suggestion. As usual, Cleburne's

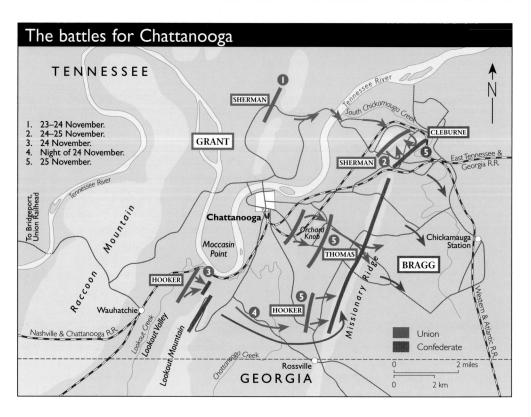

## The battles for Chattanooga

TENNESSEE

1.  23–24 November.
2.  24–25 November.
3.  24 November.
4.  Night of 24 November.
5.  25 November.

SHERMAN

GRANT

SHERMAN

CLEBURNE

East Tennessee & Georgia R.R.

Tennessee River

To Bridgeport, Union Railhead

Chattanooga

Moccasin Point

Orchard Knob

Chickamauga Station

THOMAS

BRAGG

HOOKER

Wauhatchie

HOOKER

Raccoon Mountain

Nashville & Chattanooga R.R.

Lookout Creek

Lookout Valley

Lookout Mountain

Chattanooga Creek

Rossville

GEORGIA

Missionary Ridge

Western & Atlantic R.R.

Union
Confederate

0        2 miles
0      2 km

men fought like tigers, and Sherman could make little headway against such a determined and well-led foe.

With Union plans stymied, Grant directed Thomas to order his men forward. The Union commander hoped that if men from the Army of the Cumberland seized the first row of rifle pits, it would draw Confederate reinforcements from the flanks and assist Sherman and Hooker. To the shock of both Grant and Thomas, who were standing together, soldiers in the Army of the Cumberland not only crashed through the first line of defense, they kept on going. An annoyed Grant asked who gave that order, saying there would be 'hell to pay.' Thomas admitted knowing nothing. As the defenders fell back, the Yankee troops pursued so closely that Rebels higher up the slope could not fire for fear of shooting their own men. Confederates, moreover, had chosen their primary line on the actual, not the military, crest, which created dead spaces where gunfire could not touch anyone. Federals discovered that as they clambered up the

incline, they gained these pockets of protection from enemy fire, and Rebels could not depress their artillery guns enough to hit them. On 25 November, the Army of the Cumberland exacted revenge for the Chickamauga disaster. They utterly shattered the center of Bragg's line.

Cleburne's division acted as rear guard and blocked Union pursuit. Still, Bragg had to fall back 30 miles (48km) to Dalton, Georgia, to regroup. The men in the Army of the Tennessee had no confidence in Bragg's leadership; the turmoil of high command and the detachment of Longstreet's men had caused severe damage to the morale of the men. A week after the débâcle at Chattanooga, Bragg resigned as army commander.

Nor did Longstreet's Knoxville expedition reap benefits to the Confederate cause. He advanced on Burnside, delayed, and when he did finally attack, it failed. After the rout of Bragg's army, Grant rushed Sherman with two corps to help relieve Burnside. As the Federals approached, Longstreet slipped away.

## Shake-up in the high commands

Now that Chattanooga was firmly in Union hands, Grant hoped to revive plans for a major campaign against Mobile, a valuable port still under Rebel control. Instead, the administration offered a litany of missions, none of which would significantly advance the Union toward its ultimate goal of defeating the Rebels. What Grant wanted to do was launch a campaign from New Orleans to Mobile, and from there press northeast toward Atlanta, while Thomas moved from Chattanooga to Atlanta. The administration countered with a proposal that he strike into Texas.

Before they worked out their differences, though, Lincoln and Congress had concluded that the nation's most successful combat commander should direct the war effort. Congress passed legislation to create the rank of lieutenant-general, and Lincoln signed it into law. There was no disagreement over who should receive the promotion. They established the law with Grant in mind.

Major-General Joseph Hooker and his troops drove the Rebels from Lookout Mountain. Grant's plan called for Hooker to pinch the Confederates from the west, while Sherman pressured them from the east, and Thomas threatened their center. As it turned out, Hooker carried Lookout Mountain, Sherman bogged down in narrow and well-defended terrain, and Thomas's men stormed the heights of Missionary Ridge, gaining a resounding victory for the Federals. (Library of Congress)

In early March, Grant traveled to Washington to receive the promotion in person. Originally, he had intended to stay in the nation's capital briefly, just long enough to draft plans for the spring campaigns and resolve some command issues. Before he went, Sherman had advised him to return west. The politics in Washington were poison; all Grant had to do was look at Halleck to see how the pressures had affected him.

Once there, Grant soon realized that he must establish his headquarters in the east. Everyone from the politicians to the press to the public at large expected him to oversee the campaign against Lee. In their eyes, Lee's

A hero in the Mexican War, Confederate President Jefferson Davis designed a sensible strategy for the Confederacy. Unfortunately, he never found a commander in the Western Theater to match Robert E. Lee in the east. (Ann Ronan Picture Library)

Halleck would be Grant's connection to various field commanders, summarizing their messages and relaying them to Grant for decisions and instructions. Occasionally, Halleck would issue orders or advise field commanders on his own. In the shake-up, Sherman replaced Grant as head of the Military Division of the Mississippi. Trusted subordinate McPherson took charge of the Army of the Tennessee, Sherman's old command.

The Confederates, too, underwent a command change. With Bragg's resignation, Jefferson Davis needed a new army commander, someone in whom the soldiers had faith. Hardee agreed to act as commander until the President secured someone, but he would not do it permanently. Hardee proposed Joe Johnston. Davis's old friend, Polk, also suggested Johnston, as did Robert E. Lee. Although Davis still harbored resentments for Johnston's failure in Mississippi, he had little choice. It was either him or Beauregard, and Davis opted for the lesser evil, Johnston.

## Banks's Red River operation

Because of French presence in Mexico, a desire to seize valuable cotton, and a distant hope to secure complete control of Louisiana and to begin the reconstruction process, in spring 1864, Lincoln called for an expedition under Banks up the Red River. Banks would march overland to Alexandria, Louisiana, where he would link with 10,000 veterans from the Army of the Tennessee under Major-General A. J. Smith, whom McPherson would loan temporarily. Their goal was Shreveport. Admiral Porter with an assortment of ironclads and gunboats accompanied Smith. In addition, Major-General Frederick Steele would march from Little Rock, Arkansas, with another 15,000. To oppose this force, the Confederates had some 15,000 men under Major-General Richard Taylor, Davis's former brother-in-law and one of Stonewall Jackson's old brigade commanders.

army had come to symbolize the viability of the rebellion, and until Grant vanquished the Army of Northern Virginia, the revolt would continue. At the same time, Grant knew that he could not endure the endless distractions of life in the nation's capital.

As his solution, Grant formulated a novel command structure. To avoid the continual barrage of visitors and to oversee the operations of the Union forces against Lee's troops, he elected to travel alongside the Army of the Potomac. There, he could observe and, if necessary, supervise the army and its generals directly, while leaving Major-General George G. Meade in command. At the same time, he could remain relatively close to the political epicenter, Washington, DC. To handle everyday military affairs, Grant would retain former commanding general Halleck under a new title, chief of staff. A superb staff officer,

After a disastrous campaign in the Shenandoah valley, in which he earned the nickname of Stonewall Jackson's quartermaster, the ante bellum politician Nathaniel P. Banks took over command of the Department of the Gulf. He oversaw the fall of Port Hudson, but then led the Federal forces in the disastrous Red River campaign. Banks's late start also deprived the Army of the Tennessee of 10,000 of its men for the Atlanta campaign. He was succeeded by E. R. S. Canby. (Library of Congress)

Even though Sherman instructed Banks that he must conduct the campaign promptly and return McPherson's troops for the spring offensive, Banks began late and arrived at Alexandria eight days after Smith's men had taken the town. Taylor's Confederates fell back beyond Natchitoches and halted around Mansfield, forming their defense at Sabine Crossroads. On 8 April, Federals stumbled into an unanticipated fight and suffered a rout, losing 2,500 as prisoners. Yankees fled pell mell to Pleasant Hill, where Banks prepared a defense built around Smith's corps.

The next day, Taylor attacked, and although Federals blocked the advance, Banks withdrew the next day. The Rebels pursued, harassing Banks's command and Porter's fleet at every opportunity. By the time the Yankees had reached Alexandria, low water trapped the vessels. An ingenious

engineer, Major Joseph Bailey from Wisconsin, erected a dam to build up the water level. When they broke the dam, the rushing water carried Porter's fleet to safety. Still, Confederates continued to strike at retreating Union columns until 18 May. Not only had Banks suffered a severe repulse, and nearly lost Porter's expeditionary force, but delays deprived McPherson of critical manpower in the early days of the great spring campaign. Banks's retreat allowed the Confederates to concentrate on Steele's command and defeat it as well.

Poor leadership was only part of the Federal problem, though. The Red River campaign was the product of misdirected strategy on the part of Lincoln and Halleck. They ordered the expedition over the objections of Grant and Sherman, and even Banks preferred an advance on Mobile. The administration committed (and risked) valuable resources to an enterprise that, in the final analysis, would not have brought the rebellion appreciably closer to its conclusion, even if it had been extremely successful.

The son of Zachary Taylor and Jefferson Davis's former brother-in-law, Richard Taylor led a brigade under Stonewall Jackson and was one of the few who earned his admiration. He returned west, where he served out the war. As lieutenant-general, he skillfully opposed Banks's Red River campaign and whipped the larger Union force. Taylor surrendered his command to E. R. S. Canby in May 1865. (Library of Congress)

## The Red River campaign

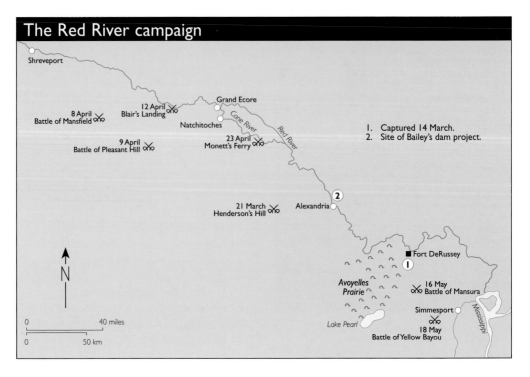

Shreveport

Grand Ecore

12 April
8 April    Blair's Landing
Battle of Mansfield

Natchitoches    Cane River

9 April    23 April
Battle of Pleasant Hill    Monett's Ferry    Red River

1. Captured 14 March.
2. Site of Bailey's dam project.

21 March    Alexandria
Henderson's Hill

2

N

Fort DeRussey
1

Avoyelles    16 May
Prairie    Battle of Mansura

Simmesport    Mississippi

0    40 miles    Lake Pearl    18 May
0    50 km    Battle of Yellow Bayou

## Plans for the spring campaign

The appointment of Joe Johnston sent a
bolt of electricity through the Army of
Tennessee. After a year and a half of the
obstreperous and unsuccessful Bragg, the
men felt as if they had finally secured a real
leader. Johnston possessed an extraordinary
charisma that drew soldiers to him. Troops
felt as if he cared about them, and at least
initially, the men in the Army of Tennessee
rejoiced over his appointment. Unlike the
Commander-in-Chief, the soldiers did not
blame him for the loss of Vicksburg, and he
had the great fortune of having been
removed well before the Bragg fiasco of mid
to late 1863.

Johnston's mere presence revived the
Confederates' sinking morale, but despite
his prewar experience as the Quartermaster-
General of the US army, he could not
conjure supplies from nothing. He
addressed basic necessities like food and
clothing as well as he could, but the army
suffered from serious shortages of mules,
horses, and wagons, none of which he
could overcome.

Johnston took on the job of
commanding general with a legacy of
mistrust between him and Davis that
virtually doomed the assignment from the
start. He believed that Davis installed him
in positions that would inevitably fail,
thereby ruining the General's reputation.
Davis thought Johnston did not live up to
his potential as a military man. He was too
immersed in petty command prerogatives,
and he dabbled far too heavily in the
opposition to Jefferson Davis.

The Confederate President instructed
Johnston to communicate freely and call on
him for advice. He wanted Johnston to
produce a campaign plan, particularly one
with an offensive punch to it. Davis had
read and digested only the misleading,
positive reports of the army and convinced
himself that it should assume the offensive
that spring. Johnston kept his own counsel
and refused to provide the kind of
information his Commander-in-Chief
expected. The Army of Tennessee, moreover,
did lack the essential resources to undertake
major offensives. The best it could hope for,
Johnston believed, was to fight on the

defense, repulse a major attack by Sherman, and then counterattack.

Johnston determined to fight on the defensive around Dalton, seeking an error by the enemy to exploit. Yet in the event he had to fall back to Dalton, he failed to prepare alternate defensive positions to his rear and to design traps for Sherman's army. Throughout the campaign, when his army retreated, he and his staff had to scramble to find new defensive locations. Inevitably, he yielded the initiative and sacrificed the operational level of war for strictly tactical defensive positions.

On the Union side, upon Grant's return from Washington, he summoned Sherman from Memphis to discuss plans for the campaign season. Sherman would succeed him out west. To save time, they took the train to Cincinnati together, plotting strategy and discussing personnel changes. Two weeks later, Grant issued his plan in writing. He intended to assume the initiative on as many fronts as possible, 'to work all parts of the army together, somewhat toward a common center,' something the Union had attempted yet failed to accomplish for two years. 'You I propose to move against Johnston's army, to break it up, and to get into the interior of the enemy's country as far as you can, inflicting all the damage you can against their war resources.' Grant refused to dictate the specifics of the campaign plan; he merely requested that Sherman submit a general plan of his operations.

Rather than a single army, Sherman commanded what modern soldiers would call an army group. At his disposal for the campaign against Johnston, he had Thomas's Army of the Cumberland, McPherson's Army of the Tennessee minus A. J. Smith's people, and a small corps under Major-General John M. Schofield, head of the Department and the Army of the Ohio. Hooker remained with Sherman's forces, commanding the XI and

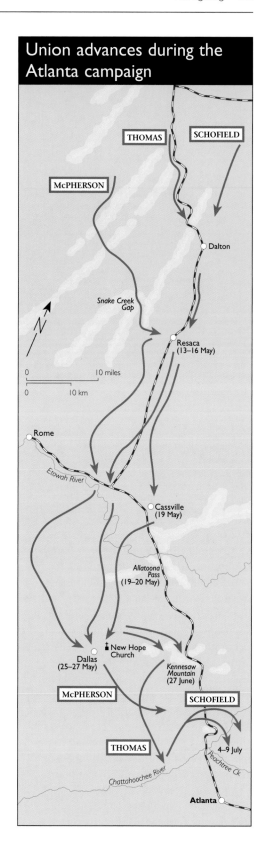

**Union advances during the Atlanta campaign**

THOMAS
SCHOFIELD
McPHERSON
Dalton
Snake Creek Gap
Resaca (13–16 May)
0   10 miles
0   10 km
Rome
Etowah River
Cassville (19 May)
Allatoona Pass (19–20 May)
New Hope Church
Dallas (25–27 May)
Kennesaw Mountain (27 June)
McPHERSON
SCHOFIELD
THOMAS
4–9 July
Peachtree Ck
Chattahoochee River
Atlanta

This map shows the movements of the combined armies of Major General William T. Sherman during the Atlanta campaign, from early May through mid-July 1864.

Joseph E. Johnston was one of the great enigmas of the Civil War. The Confederacy expected great things from Johnston, but he never seemed to rise to meet those expectations. He fell afoul of President Jefferson Davis, who blamed Johnston for the loss of his beloved Vicksburg. Johnston returned as commander of the Army of Tennessee, only to be removed at Atlanta. (Library of Congress)

the climactic battle, especially against a competent opposing commander like Johnston, was a bootless one. Large armies, sustained by industrialization, advanced agriculture, and more modern supply methods, could withstand great losses, as the Rebel Army of Tennessee and the Yankee Army of the Potomac had, and still be effective forces. Where Sherman could damage the Rebel war effort was by taking Atlanta. A manufacturing city second only to Richmond, it was also a critical rail nexus.

Originally, Sherman had planned for Thomas and Schofield to hold Johnston in place while McPherson's Army of the Tennessee sliced down from northern Alabama to seize Rome, Georgia. The move might compel Johnston to fall all the way back to the Atlanta defenses. When it became clear that Banks could neither return A. J. Smith's men to McPherson nor undertake a strike on

XII Corps, which he merged to form the XX Corps. Sherman's total force, infantry, cavalry, and artillery, totaled around 100,000.

Extremely sensitive to logistical issues, Sherman worried about Confederate cavalry raids striking his lengthy supply line on the campaign. He gathered large numbers of locomotives and rail cars to service his army. During the months before the campaign began, Sherman accumulated supplies and stockpiled all sorts of other necessities, such as rails, ties, and material for bridging. He directed the construction of blockhouses to protect vital positions along the rail route, and he devoted considerable numbers of troops to protecting that line of support.

After three years of active service, and years of army experience and contemplation, Sherman had concluded that the search for

A Grant and Sherman protégé in the war, James B. McPherson graduated first in his class at West Point. He began the war as an engineer and rose to command the Army of Tennessee. He was killed in the Battle of Atlanta. (Library of Congress)

Mobile, which would help protect the Army of the Tennessee in its isolated march, and that two more of McPherson's divisions were delayed up north, Sherman had to revamp everything. Thomas, who had honed intelligence gathering to a fine art, ascertained that gaps in the mountainous country to the south and west of Johnston's army were lightly defended. Sherman determined that a bold flanking movement might be able to push into Johnston's rear, sever his rail link to Atlanta, and then strike the Rebel flank as the army retreated.

In early May, in conjunction with Grant's campaign against Lee, Sherman opened the offensive. Thomas held Johnston in place with an excellent feint, while McPherson slipped around the Rebel left flank. On 8 May, Union troops advanced into Snake Creek Gap, not far from Resaca and the railroad. But the next day, Federal troops discovered a body of Confederates in a fortified position. Uneasy over his isolated situation, McPherson decided that he lacked the strength to assail the enemy. He withdrew to the gap, but this alone forced Johnston to retreat. Had McPherson's army possessed its full complement of troops, or had Sherman accepted Thomas's offer of lending some of his army, the campaign might have proved disastrous for Johnston. As it was, the flanking movement dislodged the Rebels from a great defensive position.

As Johnston's command retreated, it picked up some valuable reinforcements. Polk brought what amounted to another corps, to join with those under Hardee and Lieutenant-General John Bell Hood, who had earned a great reputation in Lee's army as a brigade and division commander and had possessed the great fortune of spearheading the drive through Rosecrans's gap at Chickamauga.

Johnston took a defensive position around Resaca and then to the southwest along the northern bank of the Oostanaula River. After some fighting, especially on the Confederate right, Sherman's men forced a crossing over the Oostanaula, and by 15 May, Johnston had to fall back again.

The pattern of Sherman fixing and turning his enemy continued. When Johnston planned a counterstroke, as he did at Cassville, Hood hesitated. The corps commander accepted a report that Union troops were approaching his rear and canceled the attack. Johnston then fell back to the Etowah River and a formidable defensive position at Allatoona. But he could not lure Sherman into an assault. The Union command slipped again to the west, and the Rebels retreated to the area around Dallas and New Hope Church, tossing up strong field works for protection. The Federals followed suit. The two sides then skirmished with each other, but neither launched a major attack.

By shifting to the west, Sherman had drawn Johnston away from the Western & Atlantic Railroad, the Confederate supply line to Atlanta. The Union commander tried to swing his army around the Rebel right flank, gain control of the railroad, and compel the Confederates to attack him. Instead, Johnston beat him there and occupied some high ground near Marietta. In mid-June, Sherman's command butted up against the Rebels, probing for any weaknesses or opportunities. Finally, on 27 June, Sherman committed the kind of blunder that Johnston had sought weeks earlier. Believing that the Confederates had extended their line so far that it was weak in the center, Sherman hurled men up slopes in two locations. Troops in both Thomas's and McPherson's army were repulsed. At these encounters, collectively called the Battle of Kennesaw Mountain, the Union suffered 3,000 casualties, while inflicting only 600.

With Johnston and much of the Confederate army distracted by the attack around Kennesaw Mountain, Schofield's troops slid past the Rebels on the Union right and, again, Johnston had to fall back toward Atlanta, occupying a prepared line. By 5 July, McPherson had bypassed that position, and the Union flanks touched the Chattahoochee River. To get his army over the river, Sherman feigned a crossing on his right, had Thomas fix Johnston's army, and directed Schofield to cross the river

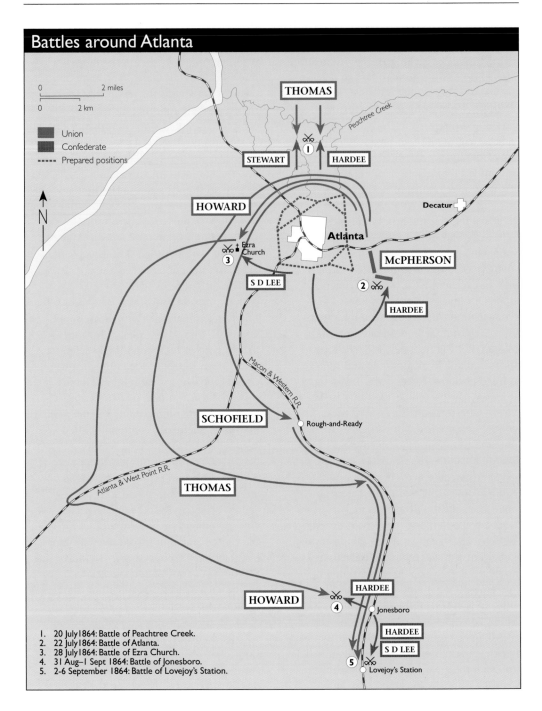

## Battles around Atlanta

0 _____ 2 miles
0 _____ 2 km

■ Union
■ Confederate
----- Prepared positions

N

THOMAS
Peachtree Creek
STEWART
HARDEE
1

HOWARD

Decatur

Ezra Church
3

Atlanta

S D LEE

McPHERSON
2
HARDEE

Macon & Western R.R.

SCHOFIELD
Rough-and-Ready

Atlanta & West Point R.R.

THOMAS

HARDEE
4
HOWARD
Jonesboro

HARDEE
S D LEE
5
Lovejoy's Station

1.  20 July 1864: Battle of Peachtree Creek.
2.  22 July 1864: Battle of Atlanta.
3.  28 July 1864: Battle of Ezra Church.
4.  31 Aug–1 Sept 1864: Battle of Jonesboro.
5.  2–6 September 1864: Battle of Lovejoy's Station.

upstream. As Federals worked their way over the river, Johnston had to abandon yet another powerful defensive position. He retreated to the south side of Peachtree Creek, only 3 miles (5km) from the heart of Atlanta.

As Johnston fell back closer to Atlanta, people began to lose faith in their highly touted commander. Soldiers grumbled; some cast aside their weapons and went home; still others turned themselves in to the Yankees. How far Johnston would retreat, no one knew, but soldiers and civilians alike grew more and more concerned.

LEFT

20 July, Hood executed Johnston's plan by trying to strike Thomas's army as it crossed over Peachtree Creek, using men from Stewart's and Hardee's corps. Thomas repulsed the attack.

22 July, Hood pulled Hardee's corps out of the trenches around Atlanta and sent it on a wide march around the Union flank. Scouts saw the movement, but Hardee's late arrival convinced the Federals that the movement had been canceled. McPherson's army fought off the attack. McPherson was killed in the battle.

28 July, Sherman sent Howard around to the west, to sever the railroad connections to Macon and the west. Stephen D. Lee's corps attacked him and was repulsed. When cavalry raids failed to destroy the railroads effectively, Sherman secured his hold on his supply line,

the Western & Atlantic Railroad, and shifted the bulk of his army to the south. Schofield struck the Macon & Western Railroad near Rough and Ready. Part of Thomas's army advanced about halfway between Rough and Ready and Jonesboro, and Howard's army moved on Jonesboro. On 31 August, Hardee's and Lee's corps attacked Howard and were repulsed. Lee had to withdraw, and Sherman tried to destroy Hardee's corps. He called down Thomas and part of Schofield's commands. Although the Union attacks were successful, Hardee withdrew south with most of his corps. On 2 September, men from Thomas's and Schofield's commands attacked Hardee at Lovejoy's Station. Later that day, the remainder of Hood's army arrived, and the forces skirmished for a few days before Sherman withdrew his troops to Atlanta.

ABOVE

The Western & Atlantic Railroad, which ran from Chattanooga to Atlanta, became part of Sherman's and Johnston's lifeline during the Atlanta campaign. From a military standpoint, Allatoona Pass proved extremely important. The photograph, looking northward, demonstrates the narrowness of the area and indicates how important control of it was for both sides.

Back in Richmond, Davis worried about the loss of Atlanta. He had received reports, including private messages from Hood, complaining that Johnston refused to fight. From the army commander himself, Davis learned little. Johnston grumbled that he lacked the manpower to assume the offensive, or that he needed additional cavalry to strike Sherman's supply line, the Western & Atlantic Railroad. In fact, the disparity between the two armies was not that severe. During Johnston's retreat, he shortened his supply line to Atlanta and

picked up some additional defenders. Sherman, meanwhile, had to peel off almost 20,000 soldiers to guard his supply line.

To get at the real situation, and to explain the issues from Richmond's perspective, Davis sent his military advisor, Bragg, to Atlanta to meet with Johnston. After speaking to subordinate commanders and Johnston over a few days, Bragg reported to the President, 'I cannot learn that he has any more plan for the future than he has had in the past.' Bragg did suspect, though, that Johnston 'is now more inclined to fight.'

enable me to anticipate events.' In reply, Johnston insisted, 'As the enemy has double our number, we must be on the defensive. My plan of operations must, therefore, depend on that of the enemy. It is mainly to watch for an opportunity to fight to advantage.' He then expressed a hope to employ the Georgia militia in the Atlanta defenses, to free up his army for movements.

That was the last straw. Davis needed to hear that he would defend the city and that he had a plan of action. Johnston offered neither. The next evening, 17 July, Davis removed Johnston and placed Hood in command.

By all accounts, Hood was an aggressive fighter. Personally courageous, he fought in the front and suffered the consequences. A ball had shattered his arm at Gettysburg, and he suffered the amputation of his leg from a wound at Chickamauga, which impaired his ability to move about and afflicted him with

The Confederacy could not afford to lose Atlanta, and Davis had to act. He needed assurance from Johnston that he would hold the city. 'I wish to hear from you as to present situation,' telegraphed Davis, 'and your plans of operation so specifically as will

John Bell Hood gained early acclaim as commander of Hood's Texas Brigade and for his breakthrough at Chickamauga. He commanded a corps throughout the Atlanta campaign, and he replaced Joe Johnston outside Atlanta. Davis assigned him to command because he would fight, and Hood did just that, but he still lost Atlanta. He was also defeated at Franklin and Nashville. (George S. Cook)

With the help of slave labor, the Confederates erected some stiff defensive works around Atlanta. The photograph, taken from the viewpoint of the Rebel cannoneers by George Barnard in 1864, shows the protection afforded them, the open terrain for effective firing, and some obstructions to impede attackers. (Library of Congress)

chronic and severe pain. He also lacked experience at high command. Yet despite his disabilities, there was no denying his aggressive spirit.

With Johnston's plan, Hood attacked Thomas's army on 20 July, as it tried to cross Peachtree Creek. Veterans in the Army of the Cumberland beat them back. He then attempted to send Hardee's corps on a lengthy march around Sherman's left to roll up the flank. Even though Federals had seen them on the march, Hardee's late attack caught them off guard. In the battle, the Yankees lost McPherson, who accidentally

John A. Logan, a former Democratic congressman from Illinois, proved to be one of the truly exceptional politician-generals of the Civil War. An excellent brigade and division commander, Logan earned the trust and respect of Grant and Sherman. The XV Corps commander, he filled in as army commander in the Battle of Atlanta when McPherson was killed. Logan commanded the XV Corps for the remainder of the war. (Library of Congress)

rode into advancing Confederates and was shot and killed. Major-General John A. Logan, probably the best of the political generals on the Union side, replaced the fallen leader and repulsed the assault. When Sherman then swung to the southeast, stretching for the Macon & Western Railroad, Hood struck once more at Ezra Church. The new commander of the Army of the Tennessee, a pious, one-armed West Pointer named Oliver Otis Howard, repelled the attack. In three battles over six days, Hood had done what Davis had asked him to do: fight. But in the process, he had suffered two and a half times as many casualties as Sherman's army, and he was in a worse position to hold on to Atlanta.

At the Battle of Atlanta, Hood attempted to roll up the Union flank. Federals observed the wide flanking movement, but Rebel delays misled Federal troops into believing that no attack would occur. Hardee's men drove the Union forces back, but Federals eventually counterattacked and held the line. Major-General James McPherson was killed while riding to the sound of gunfire, and Major-General John A. Logan oversaw the victory. (Ann Ronan Picture Library)

Sherman knew that if he could just cut the Western & Macon Railroad, Hood would be compelled to abandon the city. His cavalry failed to do the job, and he planned to pull back part of his army for defense, freeing up others for offensive operations to the southwest. Slowly, he wheeled his forces toward the railroad. In order to protect that last, vital line, Hardee launched a vicious attack against Howard's men at Jonesboro, but he could not dislodge them. With Thomas's and Schofield's columns gaining parts of the line, too, Hood had no choice but to abandon Atlanta. He exploded rail cars loaded with ammunition and evacuated his armed forces from the city. On 2 September 1864, a gleeful Sherman wired, 'Atlanta is ours, and fairly won.'

RIGHT William Tecumseh Sherman rebounded from a nervous breakdown to become Grant's most trusted subordinate. His victory in this Atlanta campaign assured Lincoln's re-election, and his revolutionary March to the Sea and through the Carolinas helped bring the war to a speedy conclusion. (Ann Ronan Picture Library)

BELOW Before Hood's army abandoned Atlanta, it destroyed an ordnance train. The explosion and fire caused massive destruction. (Library of Congress)

## The presidential election of 1864

No doubt, Sherman knew just how important the fall of Atlanta was to the cause of reunion. More than a precious industrial and transportation center, Atlanta signaled the success of the commanding general, Grant, and the Commander-in-Chief, Lincoln. It could not have come at a more vital time.

Both the Union and the Confederacy understood the consequence of battlefield decisions that year. The year 1864 would see a presidential election, and by choosing Grant as his commanding general, Lincoln had linked his political future to Grant's military success. The Rebels, too, recognized its significance. If they hoped to win independence, they must extract a political decision from antiwar forces in the North at the polls. And the key to that would be military success in 1864.

The year opened with Banks's Red River fiasco, followed by stalemates in the two major campaigns. Grant incurred staggering losses in his campaigns in the east – some 60,000 casualties in seven weeks – and eventually locked into a siege with Lee around Petersburg. Sherman's columns did not suffer the same number of losses as Federals back east did, but to observers it appeared as if the Rebels under Johnston were holding their own for quite a few weeks.

More than just the antiwar supporters, more than just the loyalists of the Democratic Party, Lincoln had generated a fair amount of opposition within his own party. Conservative Republicans saw him as caving in to the Radicals, while the Radicals believed that Lincoln catered too much to the opponents of abolitionism and to those who interpreted the Constitution narrowly. Secretary of the Treasury Salmon P. Chase tested the political waters with certain elements of the Republican Party, and Major-General John C. Fremont, the party's nominee for president in 1856, openly courted support to replace Lincoln on the ticket. Both insurgencies failed, but they represented uneasiness with Lincoln's candidacy.

During the summer months, the situation grew tense for Lincoln. After the President withheld his signature and prevented the Wade–Davis Bill, a congressional plan for reconstruction, from becoming law, Wade and Davis drafted a critical manifesto that stoked the fires of opposition against Lincoln. In July, Jubal Early's raid northward nearly seized Washington. The value of Union currency plummeted. And for a while, a sullen Lincoln believed his defeat at the polls was a real possibility. He drafted a letter which he required every cabinet member to sign unseen, declaring,

*This morning, as for some days past, it seems exceedingly probable that this Administration will not be re-elected. Then it will be my duty to so co-operate with the President elect, as to save the Union between the election and the inauguration; as he will have secured his election on such ground that he can not possibly save it afterwards.*

But just as quickly, the tide shifted. The Wade–Davis manifesto went too far, and it pulled Republicans together, at least for the election. The Democratic Party endorsed a peace platform, and then nominated Major-General George B. McClellan, who promptly announced his continued support for the war. The fall of Atlanta sent assurances to the Northern public that the Union was going to win the war, and that Lincoln was the nation's proper steward. Then, three weeks later, a large Federal force under Major-General Philip Sheridan delivered a powerful blow against Early's raiders and followed it up with yet another.

Lincoln won re-election with overwhelming support from the army. Although not all soldiers were old enough to vote, and some states prohibited their troops in the field from participating, they rallied behind their commander-in-chief and aided his election cause any way they could. Of those who could vote, close to 80 percent cast their ballot for Lincoln, compared to 53 percent of the civilian population. In Sherman's army, about 90 percent cast their ballots for Old Abe. And whether they could vote or not, they clearly expressed their preferences to the folks at home. A Wisconsin man explained to his brother that every man who voted against Lincoln was 'a soldier's enemy.' An Illinois fellow coached his dad to 'Shun all disloyal company and do not vote the copperhead [Democratic] ticket, no matter who might say it is right.' But the bluntest talk came from an Ohioan, who instructed his sister, 'Tell Ben if he votes for Mc[Clellan] I will never speak to him again.'

Bursting with confidence after their victory at Atlanta, soldiers were assured that they would win by Lincoln's victory at the polls. 'We go with our Hartes contented,' an infantryman explained to a friend, 'nowing that we have a President that will not declare peace on no other tirmes then an Uncondishnell Surrender.'

## Planning for the great march

After the fall of Atlanta, Sherman decided not to pursue Hood's army. The two forces had been in continuous contact for over 100 days, and Sherman believed his men needed a rest. He doubted that the Rebel Army of Tennessee possessed enough strength to be much of a threat to the Union cause, and he much preferred to recuperate, refit, and then undertake a very a different type of campaign from the grind toward Atlanta.

Hood's army, badly worn down but not whipped, eventually limped to Palmetto, about 25 miles (40km) from Atlanta. Morale declined over the loss of the campaign, but some rest, hot food, and time for reflection away from the boom of guns helped to restore their attitude, as did a religious revival that roared through camp. With a rejuvenated spirit, members of the Army of Tennessee began to look at the past campaign in a different light. The fall of Atlanta, concluded most of the troops, was merely a setback. Through a vast numerical superiority, the Federals had forced them out of the city, but had by no means crushed the Army of Tennessee.

During this hiatus, the Confederate President decided to pay the army a visit. Jefferson Davis had heard reports of dissatisfaction with Hood's performance throughout the Army of Tennessee and had also sensed a dramatic decline in public morale throughout the region. He hoped that a personal inspection of the army and a few public speeches on the way back to Richmond were just the solution. Upon his arrival, Davis immediately began to speak with Hood and several of his key subordinates, and it soon became clear that a major shake-up was in order. Davis promptly transferred corps commander Lieutenant-General William J. Hardee, at his own request, to the Department of South Carolina, Georgia, and Florida. Hood, however, stayed. Davis had always been fond of Hood's aggressive style, and he strongly approved Hood's new plan to strike at Sherman's long supply line and retake Atlanta. To silence critics Davis placed a more experienced officer, General P. G. T. Beauregard, in a supervisory position over Hood. Hood would still command the Army of Tennessee; Beauregard's job was merely to give Hood advice.

In addition to sorting out the command problems, Davis also hoped to give the members of the Army of Tennessee a lift. He spoke to them of the upcoming campaign and announced that they would soon advance into Tennessee and Kentucky. The President insisted that Atlanta, like Moscow for Napoleon, would be Sherman's downfall. For the most part, the Confederate troops responded favorably to Davis's predictions, yet a few of the more superstitious men feared that 'his coming is an omen of ill luck.' The last time Davis had spoken to the Army of the Tennessee was just before the catastrophe at Chattanooga.

While Major-General Joseph Wheeler and his cavalry looked after the Federals in Atlanta, Hood embarked upon a series of rapid marches along Sherman's supply line, the railroad from Atlanta to Chattanooga, destroying track and bridges and gobbling up garrisons en route. At first, Sherman jumped at the bait. He left one corps to occupy Atlanta and pursued the Confederates vigorously with the rest of his command, and on a few occasions they nearly cornered Hood's elusive army. Yet by the time the Rebels reached eastern Alabama, the Federal commander had decided to call off the hunt. It was useless for the Federals to surrender the initiative, particularly when they could not move as rapidly as the Confederates.

Since late 1862, when Grant and Sherman wrestled with guerrillas and civilian problems in Tennessee and Mississippi, they had thrashed out a strategy of raiding. Rebel cavalry had been effective against the Union army and its supply lines. Think how much disruption a Federal army could cause, the two generals speculated, if it could destroy the Confederate infrastructure, seize their slaves, damage or consume their property, and disrupt lives. The Union could demonstrate unequivocally to the Southern people just how futile continued resistance would be. In January 1864, Sherman had tested the concept in a march on Meridian, Mississippi, living off the land and wrecking anything of military value. The best thing to do, Sherman concluded, was to launch an even grander campaign. He proposed that he send a portion of his army back to Tennessee under Thomas, in case Hood pushed farther north, while he struck west for Savannah with 65,000 men.

Neither Lincoln nor Halleck liked the plan, and Grant was at best lukewarm. The commanding general much preferred that Sherman eliminate Hood's army first. But Sherman kept tossing out more and more reasons why he should go and, ultimately, he struck a responsive chord. 'Instead of being on the defensive, I would be on the offensive,' he reminded his friend, 'instead of guessing at what he means to do, he would have to guess at my plans. The difference in war is full 25 per cent.' From that moment, Grant blocked any challenges to Sherman's raid, even though he raised questions himself. Grant believed in Sherman.

For his campaign, Sherman retained four corps – the XV and XVII from the Army of Tennessee and the XIV and XX from the Army of the Cumberland – totaling about 60,000 infantry and artillery, along with a cavalry division of 5,000. These he grouped into two armies, the Army of the Tennessee under Howard and the Army of Georgia under Major-General Henry W. Slocum. To Chattanooga or Nashville under Thomas, Sherman sent back two corps, the IV and the X, plus some cavalry. Schofield elected to go with Thomas.

Even though Confederate scouts detected the passage of troops and supplies back and forth, Hood decided not to try to block Sherman's advance deeper into Georgia. The Confederate commander had come to the conclusion that he could inflict more damage on the Federal war effort by invading Tennessee and possibly Kentucky without Sherman's army hounding his rear than by chancing a battle with the larger Federal force. Although Hood still had doubts about his army defeating superior numbers in a pitched battle, he was fully confident in its ability to conduct an effective raid against the smaller Federal numbers to the north. Thus, in an anomaly of warfare, both the Federals and the Confederates terminated the campaign intentionally by marching in opposite directions from one another without having given battle.

## The March to the Sea

On 12 November 1864, in preparation for the campaign, Sherman's troops began to destroy anything of military value 60 miles (96km) back from Atlanta. Some private homes along the railroad were also torched. In Atlanta, Sherman's soldiers overstepped their bounds, lighting fires throughout the town and damaging an estimated 4,000–5,000 structures. Fortunately, the population in Atlanta was light. After seizing the city, Sherman had shipped out some of the inhabitants. He saw no need to strain his food supplies for Rebel supporters.

Sherman took about 1.2 million rations with his army and a couple of weeks' worth of fodder for his animals. He had studied census records before the campaign and determined that he could supply his army from the people of Georgia, as long as his army kept moving. The key to the campaign was his reliance on the experienced nature of his soldiers. Eighty percent of his enlisted men had joined the army in 1861 or 1862. Nearly 50 percent qualified as veteran volunteers, having re-enlisted for a second term of service. They knew how to handle themselves on the march, on the battlefield, and in camp. To feed his army, Sherman would have to disperse foragers into the countryside, often with loose supervision, and here that experience proved critical.

Against his army of 65,000, for much of the campaign the Confederates could only muster Major-General Joseph Wheeler and his 3,500 cavalrymen and some militia. On the march, Sherman intended to interpose his army between two valuable military targets. The Confederates could either protect one or divide their forces, weakening resistance more. Thus, Sherman positioned his army between Macon and Augusta, two valuable industrial sites. Sherman realized

Before Sherman's army abandoned Atlanta, it destroyed the railroads. Groups of soldiers picked up rails and dislodged the ties. They then started large fires with the ties and laid the rails over them. Once the rails got red hot, men twisted the rails. Since the Confederacy had no other foundries outside Richmond that could produce rails, Sherman's men did not have to undertake the backbreaking work of filling in the rail gradings. They employed this technique through the Savannah and Carolinas campaigns, destroying 443 miles (713km) of railroad. (Library of Congress)

that he did not have to capture those cities, which could prove costly and tie down his army. All he had to do was destroy Confederate facilities for moving their products, specifically the railroads, to accomplish his goal.

Sherman's army swung down as if to threaten Macon, home of an arsenal, armory, and laboratory, and then shifted up toward Augusta, which housed the great Arsenal and Gunpowder Works and the Naval Ordnance Works. Meanwhile, his army ripped up railroad track, burning ties and twisting rails. They did not have to waste time filling in the rail grade, because if his men did their work properly and twisted the rails (sometimes, they only bent them), the Confederacy had no facilities outside Richmond to melt down and roll rails. As Sherman advanced toward Augusta, he again maneuvered his army between Augusta and Savannah, confusing the Confederates as to his real destination and enabling his men to do their work. On the Savannah campaign, Sherman's troops destroyed over 300 miles (480km) of rail.

The campaign caused quite a sensation among people North and South. Few knew Sherman's true destination, Savannah, and the way he cut a swath right through the state of Georgia fascinated Northerners and terrified Southerners. By marching through the countryside, Sherman's soldiers frightened the people of Georgia. Hordes of bluecoats poured over farms, plantations, and towns, stripping the area of foodstuffs, livestock, and able-bodied male slaves, and destroying any items of military value they could not carry. Confederate soldiers in distant armies grew extremely uneasy over the welfare of loved ones and their life's work. Just as Sherman made Confederate commanders in Georgia choose between Macon and Augusta, so he forced Georgia soldiers to decide whether their ultimate responsibility lay with their beleaguered families or with the army. Before the campaign, he had vowed, 'I can make the march, and make Georgia howl.' And he did.

By the second week of December, Sherman's columns were approaching the area around Savannah. Grant had notified the Union navy of Sherman's intention, but no one knew for sure when he would surface. To open communications, Sherman's troops stormed Fort McAllister south of the city, and then stretched out to trap the garrison in Savannah. Some 13,000 Confederates under Hardee defended the city and were able to keep open one route of escape. On the night of 21 December, Hardee withdrew before Sherman could complete plans to box the Rebels inside the city. The next day, Sherman announced to the President, 'I beg to present you, as a Christmas gift, the City of Savannah.' In reply, Lincoln admitted his uneasiness over the operation and acquiesced only because 'you were the better judge' and 'nothing risked, nothing gained.' The President then insisted, 'the honor is all yours.'

## Hood's Tennessee campaign

Although Hood had lost Atlanta, Confederate President Davis retained his faith in him. Davis had appointed Hood because he was a fighter, and that was exactly what Hood did. Yet the Rebel President detected a lack of seasoning in high command, and to assist Hood, Davis assigned Beauregard as commander of the Military Division of the West. Beauregard had restored his reputation somewhat with Davis by performing well as commander of the Department of South Carolina, Georgia, and Florida, and then around Petersburg. Davis did not intend for Beauregard to supersede Hood. Rather, he wanted Hood in command, but felt that Beauregard could help shape Hood's plans and provide the kind of advice that the young, aggressive warrior needed.

Hood convinced himself that he had achieved a great success by striking Sherman's supply line, and now he planned to invade Tennessee and perhaps Kentucky. If Sherman pursued, he could give battle on his own terms. If Sherman refused to follow his army, then Middle Tennessee and perhaps more would be easy pickings. Beauregard weighed in by sending Forrest's cavalry to cooperate with Hood's army and by shifting the Rebel supply base to Tuscumbia, Alabama, on the Memphis & Charleston Railroad. Beauregard then offered some advice on how to conduct the campaign: to succeed, Hood must move rapidly.

Instead, Hood dawdled. He wasted time trying to capture a Federal garrison at Decatur, Alabama, and struggled to find an acceptable crossing at the Tennessee River. Finally, he marched to Tuscumbia and waited for fresh supplies before entering Tennessee. This indecisiveness, so uncharacteristic of the impulsive Hood, may have been purposeful. Had the Rebel army advanced into Middle Tennessee along the railroad to Nashville, Sherman might have pursued, blocking Hood's escape route southward. By shifting his army to north central Alabama, Hood discouraged Sherman from chasing him.

On the Union side, Hood's movements may have baffled Sherman temporarily, but Grant assessed the Confederate commander's intentions exactly. Once the Army of

Tennessee marched to Tuscumbia, Grant realized that any pursuit by Sherman made no sense. His trusted lieutenant must strike out for the coast with the bulk of his army, yet return enough men to Nashville for Thomas to defend Middle Tennessee.

A large part of Thomas's command came from Sherman's army during the Atlanta campaign. Major-General James Harrison Wilson took back 12,000 unmounted cavalrymen, armed with seven-shot Spencer repeating carbines, and began combing the region for fresh horses and equipment. Schofield's X Corps and the IV Corps under Major-General David Stanley gathered around Pulaski, Tennessee, to check a northward advance. Grant directed A. J. Smith's two divisions of 10,000 veterans, fresh from the defeat of Price, to move by rail from Missouri to Nashville, and

Major-General James B. Steedman brought back 5,200 men from occupation duty along Sherman's old railroad supply line. In Nashville itself, Thomas had some post guards, quartermaster troops, and 14 artillery batteries to supplement the command.

Finally, on 19 November 1864, Forrest's cavalry led Hood's advance, followed by the three corps. Scouts estimated Schofield's forces at around 15,000. With about 30,000 infantry and artillery and 5,500 horsemen, Hood hoped to push north rapidly, slip around the Federal force, and seize Columbia, compelling Schofield to fight his way to Nashville. Despite nasty weather and deep mud, the Confederates made good progress. After some initial hesitation, Schofield detected Hood's plan and narrowly beat Forrest's cavalrymen back to Columbia. The Yankees occupied some

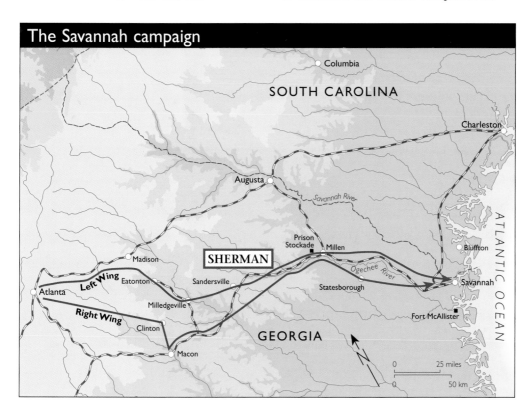

## The Savannah campaign

ABOVE Sherman's Left Wing advanced up toward Madison and swung down through Eatonton and into Milledgeville. From there, they pushed on through Sandersonville, Millen, and into Savannah. Sherman's Extreme Right Wing dipped down via

McDonough and through Jackson and Clinton to just north of Macon. They then struck out for Savannah by way of Millen and Statesborough. Once William Hazen's Division stormed Fort McAllister on 13 December, Sherman had a secure communication line to the US Navy.

The sketch is by Theodore R. Davis, an eyewitness of Brigadier-General William B. Hazen's division of the XV Corps storming Fort McAllister, near Savannah, Georgia. Sherman needed Hazen to seize Fort McAllister in order to open supply lines with the Union navy. Hazen used sharpshooters to pin down the defenders, and he assembled his men in a relatively thin line to reduce casualties. In 13 minutes, Hazen's troops captured the fort, with a loss of 24 killed and 110 wounded, mostly from land mines. His men inflicted 250 casualties. The sketch appeared in *Harper's Weekly*, 14 January 1865.

prepared trenches on the south side of Duck River. Several days later, as the great Rebel horseman began to force river crossings, Schofield fell back once again.

Schofield did not believe that Hood could move his army along a roundabout and difficult course and still beat him to Spring Hill. He was wrong. Confederate cavalry and then some infantry arrived before many of Schofield's troops, yet they could not check the Union retreat. Stanley had rushed a division back in the afternoon and a second one around sunset. With the aid of some artillery, these Yankee troops repelled piecemeal Rebel attacks. That night, miscommunication among the Rebel high command and a string of unfortunate decisions enabled Schofield to march

The author of an infantry tactics manual and a corps commander in the Army of Tennessee, William J. Hardee turned down command of the army after Missionary Ridge. He served under Johnston and Hood in the Atlanta campaign, and was transferred at his own request to the coastal defense, where he opposed Sherman's army at Savannah. Hardee also fought at Averasborough and Bentonville. (Library of Congress)

unhindered right past the Confederate forces and through Spring Hill. By morning, weary Federals had stumbled into Franklin, on the south side of the Harpeth River, 18 miles (29km) from Nashville. Immediately, officers put them to work fortifying some old, overgrown trenches, while engineers built two pontoon bridges across the river.

When Hood realized that the Yankees had escaped, he seethed with anger. Everyone was to blame except, of course, himself. Hood had long believed that entrenchments stripped soldiers of their aggressiveness, and he determined to teach the officers and men of the Army of Tennessee a lesson. The Rebels pursued rapidly, and when they came upon Schofield's troops at Franklin in the mid-afternoon, Hood ordered them to storm the works.

The relatively open, gently inclined terrain offered the Yankees an excellent line of fire. Still, Hood's men struck, and did so with fury. In the center of the Federal fortifications, where the Union maintained an advanced post, Rebels penetrated by following on the heels of those in flight. A vicious counterattack restored the line. Elsewhere, despite extraordinary bravery on the part of thousands of Confederates, Schofield's men repulsed the assaults.

On the last day of November, in less than three hours, Hood's army suffered almost 5,500 casualties. It was not a matter of courage; these Rebels exhibited plenty of that. The fact was that, in most instances, attackers were no match for veteran defenders fighting from behind breastworks, well armed with rifled muskets and supported by artillery. When the Union retreated to Nashville that evening, they took with them 702 prisoners, most of them captured as Federal troops sealed the penetration. The Yankees suffered 2,326 casualties.

At Franklin, Confederate commanders fought from the front and suffered staggering losses as a result. Twelve generals went down, six of them killed, and 54 regimental commanders fell in the fighting that day. Among those who lost their lives was Patrick Cleburne, the great Confederate division commander.

The next morning, Hood's soldiers marched past the grisly sight of the previous day's débâcle, crossed over the Harpeth, and began a slow advance up near the Union defenses of Nashville. At the time, Hood assumed that Thomas had not received substantial reinforcements, but he also believed that the Battle of Franklin had cut any offensive inclinations out of his army. Lacking the strength to lay siege to the city, he stretched his army out to cover the major roads heading southward and hoped that his presence might induce Thomas to attack him. A few days later, Hood detached some infantry and cavalry under Forrest to harass a Union garrison at Murfreesboro. It was Hood's hope that fear of losing those troops might induce Thomas to abandon his works and attack the Rebels.

Back in Nashville, Thomas had worried that he might not have enough soldiers to cope with Hood's army. But on 1 December, as Schofield's columns entered the city, A. J. Smith's and Steedman's troops arrived as well. Now all Thomas needed was enough good mounts and saddles so that Wilson's cavalry could compete with Forrest's vaunted horsemen and some good fighting weather. Yet just before Wilson accumulated enough horses and equipment, snow and sleet descended on Middle Tennessee, and for five days it scarcely let up. A thick sheet of ice blanketed the ground, making it nearly impossible for land movement by man or beast.

Meanwhile, Grant and officials in Washington had become increasingly uneasy over Thomas's delay. By the Union commanding general's calculation, Hood possessed fewer than 30,000 infantry and artillery, and while he thought it was possible that Forrest had more cavalry, Wilson's men carried repeating carbines which gave them an incredible firepower advantage. At one point, Grant nearly removed Thomas. He feared Hood would swing around Nashville and raid northward, wreaking havoc wherever he went. Only when Halleck balked did Grant yield. After Grant implored him to attack, Thomas declined. The ice storm prevented

# The battle of Franklin

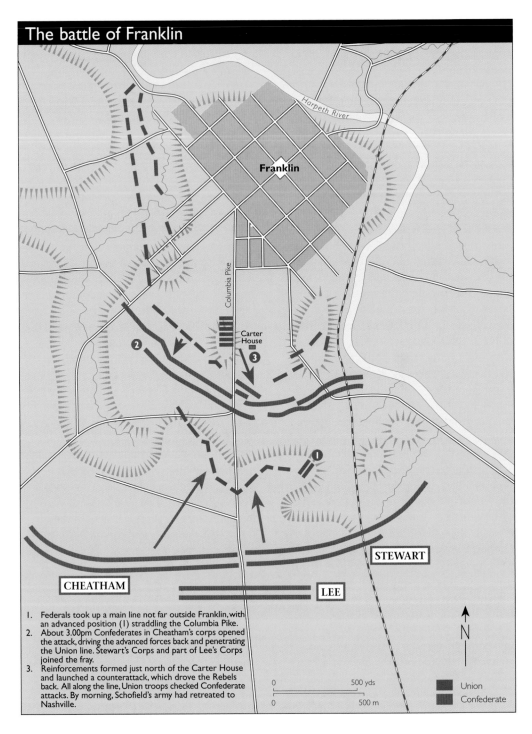

1. Federals took up a main line not far outside Franklin, with an advanced position (1) straddling the Columbia Pike.
2. About 3.00pm Confederates in Cheatham's corps opened the attack, driving the advanced forces back and penetrating the Union line. Stewart's Corps and part of Lee's Corps joined the fray.
3. Reinforcements formed just north of the Carter House and launched a counterattack, which drove the Rebels back. All along the line, Union troops checked Confederate attacks. By morning, Schofield's army had retreated to Nashville.

movement. Once it melted, Old Pap vowed to attack immediately.

For a few days, Grant accepted the explanation, but impatience got the best of him. He ordered Major-General

John A. Logan to travel to Nashville and take over from Thomas, and after some consideration, Grant decided to go himself. As Grant waited to board a train in Washington, word arrived that Thomas

## The battle of Nashville

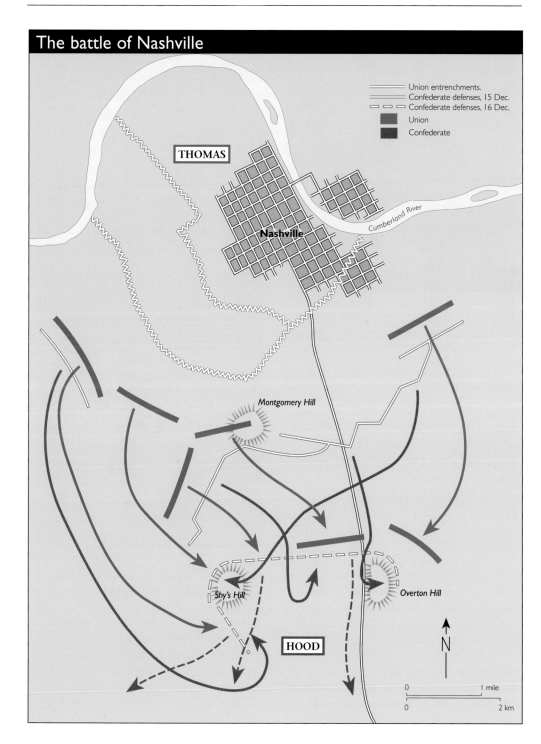

Union entrenchments.
Confederate defenses, 15 Dec.
Confederate defenses, 16 Dec.
Union
Confederate

THOMAS

Cumberland River

Nashville

Montgomery Hill

Shy's Hill

Overton Hill

HOOD

N

0        1 mile
0        2 km

had attacked and won. Grant traveled no farther.

On 15 December, Thomas launched a massive and extremely successful attack. His plan called for the Union to feint on the Rebel right and overwhelm their left. Under a cloud of fog, Steedmen's black soldiers delivered a powerful blow on the Confederate right that distracted them. On the opposite flank, A. J. Smith's troops and

ABOVE After some difficult service in Missouri, John M. Schofield served as head of the Department of the Ohio. He commanded the X Corps in Sherman's army in the Atlanta campaign. At Franklin, he repulsed a vicious Confederate assault, and his men proved critical in the flank attack at Nashville on the first day. Late in the war, Schofield commanded the expedition that seized Wilmington, and at Goldsboro his command of 40,000 united with Sherman for the final push against Johnston. (Library of Congress)

RIGHT This is a sketch by artist William Ward, who accompanied Sherman's army, of part of Logan's XV Corps as it waded across the Little Salkahatchie River in South Carolina in February 1865. Sherman's soldiers endured considerable hardships, like wading a swamp and a river in wintertime, during the Carolinas campaign. The sketch was published in *Harper's Weekly*, 8 April 1865. (Author's collection)

Wilson's cavalry crushed or completely bypassed the Rebel left. Then, late in the afternoon, Thomas hurled Schofield's men into the fight, and a massive Union assault compelled Hood's army to abandon the field.

The Rebels fell back to a new, more defensible position, but when Thomas attacked the next afternoon, the results proved even more disastrous for Hood. Once again, Thomas struck the Rebel right first, and with Rebel attention riveted there, Union infantry and cavalry swamped the left. As Federal infantry and dismounted horsemen penetrated into Hood's rear, the Rebel line crumbled, and the rout was on. Thousands of Johnny Rebs surrendered. One Confederate described the

flight as a 'stampede' and 'a sad, shocking sight to behold.' Unlike the last Confederate disaster, Wilson ordered his men back to get their mounts, and the Yankees, both cavalry and infantry, pursued with vigor.

During the two-day battle, Thomas's men took nearly 4,500 prisoners, including four generals. Wilson's pursuit snared another 3,200, of whom nearly 2,000 were wounded men at Franklin. Through Christmas Day 1864, Federal cavalry pressed the retreating Confederates. Not until Rebels crossed the Tennessee River, and Forrest assumed command of the rear guard, did Wilson ease up. Union infantry kept pace for a while, but by 22 December, Thomas had directed them

to proceed at a more leisurely speed and root out Rebel stragglers. For the campaign, Thomas's army took 8,635 prisoners and 320 Confederate deserters. As the attacking force, the Federals lost 3,061 and killed or wounded about 1,800 Rebels.

Thomas's campaign broke the back of the Army of Tennessee. While some of its members would fight again, and fight well, it no longer existed as an army in the true sense. The resounding Union victories at Franklin and Nashville, moreover, added great luster to Sherman's March to the Sea. Only such a resounding triumph would vindicate Sherman's decision to send back two corps and cavalrymen

and head to the coast on his raiding strategy.

## Campaign through the Carolinas

When Sherman arrived safely in Savannah, in December 1864, Grant had great plans to transport his army by water to the Petersburg area. With the addition of 65,000 veterans, the Federals could easily stretch around Lee's flanks and bring an end to the war in the east. But Sherman had other ideas. He hated the prospect of shipping his troops by water. Would it not be better, he proposed, to march his army through the Carolinas to Virginia, destroying railroads and anything of military value en route, as he had done in Georgia? Once Grant learned that it would take weeks and weeks to assemble enough transport ships, he authorized the Carolinas campaign.

Like their commander, Sherman's soldiers much preferred to march to Virginia by way of South Carolina. They viewed that state as the hotbed of the secession movement and blamed its people for all the lives lost, bodies maimed, and hardships endured. They were almost giddy at the prospect of exacting vengeance for instigating the war.

By comparison with the advance on Savannah, the Carolinas campaign was far more difficult. Federal troops had to march through swampy country in wintertime, often amid heavy rains. Because of the terrain, South Carolina lacked the bountiful food harvests of central Georgia. And as the Federals entered North Carolina, the Confederacy had assembled a sizable force to contest the advance, which in the previous campaign occurred only as Sherman's troops approached Savannah.

Once again, Sherman used two prized targets to confuse Rebel resistance about his initial destination. Two corps appeared as if they were marching on Charleston, while the other two threatened Augusta. Instead, Sherman employed the XV and XVII Corps to uncover the route for the XIV and XX more inland. Then, his army, often taking separate roads, advanced toward Columbia. As they destroyed railroads along the way, they isolated Charleston and compelled its abandonment.

These Yankee veterans were intent on punishing South Carolina. When a soldier in the XIV Corps crossed over the bridge into the state, he yelled back, 'Boys, this is old South Carolina, let's give her hell,' at which his comrades cheered. Without authorization, they burned parts or most of 18 towns and plundered or wrecked all sorts of private property. Sherman's troops would have their revenge.

After some skirmishing, the army entered Columbia, where the troops discovered that Confederates and civilians had begun looting shops and had left stacked bales of cotton on fire. That night, the wind kicked up and revived the flames, floating these burning projectiles to nearby buildings. In their revelry, Sherman's soldiers actively spread the fires. By morning, after the winds had died down, military officials had restored some order. One-third of the city lay in ashes. Yet Sherman's troops had not had their fill. They torched parts of five more towns in South Carolina.

Once the army crossed over into North Carolina, officers issued orders to remind the soldiers that North Carolina had been the last state to secede and had a strong Unionist minority. They urged troops to distinguish between the people of the Tarheel State and South Carolina. The army destroyed the arsenal in Fayetteville, and some firebugs burned several blocks. Generally, though, Sherman's men behaved themselves much better in North Carolina. In an army of 65,000, men plundered, especially soldiers who acted as foragers, but most soldiers eased up on their destructiveness.

By the time Sherman's troops reached North Carolina, the Confederates had begun to accumulate some forces to resist the advance. South Carolinian Lieutenant-General Wade Hampton brought cavalry from Lee's army and superseded Wheeler. Remnants of Hood's Army of Tennessee augmented Hardee's command that escaped from Savannah, and as the army fell back, they collected various coastal garrisons. On the advice of Lee, Davis restored Joe Johnston to command them all.

Despite Johnston's weakness in manpower, he had to try to block Sherman's movements. Implementing a plan devised by

RIGHT Sherman sent the XVII and most of the XV Corps by water through Beaufort. As they advanced inland, they uncovered the route for the other troops. The Right Wing (XV and XVII Corps) traveled through Orangeburg, Columbia, Cheraw, and then on to Fayetteville, North Carolina. The Left Wing passed west of Columbia through Winnesboro and then on to Fayetteville. From there, they moved on to Goldsboro, fighting at Averasborough and Bentonville. At Goldsboro, they rendezvoused with Schofield and 40,000 men from Wilmington. Joseph E. Johnston surrendered his forces near Durham.

# The Carolinas campaign

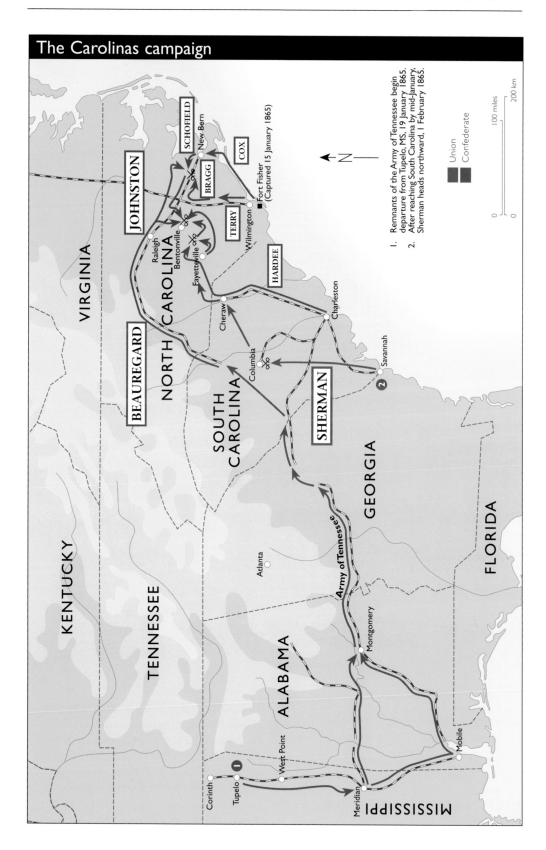

SCHOFIELD

JOHNSTON

COX

BRAGG

TERRY

HARDEE

BEAUREGARD

SHERMAN

New Bern

Raleigh

Bentonville

Fayetteville

Wilmington

Fort Fisher
(Captured 15 January 1865)

Cheraw

Charleston

Columbia

Savannah

Atlanta

Montgomery

Mobile

West Point

Meridian

Corinth

Tupelo

Army of Tennessee

VIRGINIA

NORTH CAROLINA

SOUTH CAROLINA

TENNESSEE

KENTUCKY

ALABAMA

GEORGIA

FLORIDA

MISSISSIPPI

N

1. Remnants of the Army of Tennessee begin
   departure from Tupelo, MS, 19 January 1865.
2. After reaching South Carolina by mid-January,
   Sherman heads northward, 1 February 1865.

Union

Confederate

0    100 miles

0    200 km

This sketch, prepared by an eyewitness and published in *Harper's Weekly*, I April 1865, shows men in the XIV Corps crossing the Catawba River at Rock Hill, South Carolina, on a pontoon bridge in the rain. That February it rained heavily in South Carolina, increasing water levels in rivers and making river crossings much more dangerous. Sherman's engineers and pontooneers were experts at laying bridges. (Author's collection)

Hampton, he directed Hardee to delay the advance by fighting at Averasborough, which he did successfully on 16 March 1865, at a loss of 800 men. This bought more time to accumulate additional troops and set the trap. Hampton devised a fishhook-shaped position, and some Federals walked right into it. On the morning of 19 March, when

Rebels and threatened their rear, until Sherman recalled the troops. Sherman was convinced that the end was near, and he loathed the idea of spilling any more blood. The Battle of Bentonville ended, with Johnston losing 2,606 men in the attack and Sherman suffering 1,527 casualties.

Three days later, Sherman marched into Goldsboro, North Carolina, where his troops closed the campaign. His army had marched 470 miles (756km), destroyed hundreds of miles of rail, wrecked an arsenal, burnt towns, and terrified civilians along the route. Yet like the Savannah Campaign, impact of the march through the Carolinas extended far beyond those who experienced it. Even Southerners who avoided the destruction suddenly confronted the reality that the Confederacy could no longer protect its citizenry. In effect, Southerners were at the mercy of Yankee hordes. By destroying railroads, Sherman's army impaired the ability of Robert E. Lee to draw supplies to Richmond, inflicting greater hardship on those beleaguered Confederates. The disruption of communication caused widespread anxiety about loved ones in those regions. And perhaps most importantly, Sherman's march encouraged massive desertion from Confederate armies by forcing Rebel soldiers to choose their ultimate responsibility, between their country and their family. When Confederate troops learned how their loved ones were suffering, many veterans deserted the ranks to care for them, and quite a number of their officers could not blame them. The problem reached such epidemic proportions in the Rebel army of Northern Virginia that Lee himself wrote the governor of North Carolina, alerting him that letters from home were promoting desertion and imploring him to rally the people of the Tarheel State to support the Rebel cause. In the end, neither the governor nor Lee could stem the tide of desertion. More than a campaign against an army, Sherman targeted a hostile people. Through his destructive marches, he shattered Confederate resolve to continue the rebellion.

some bluecoats reported resistance, Sherman brushed it aside as nothing more than cavalry in their front. Suddenly, Confederates sprung the trap and rocked back the advancing Federals, but as additional Union units rushed to the sound of gunfire, the Yankees stiffened. Two days later, a Union counterattack cut through the

## The Battle of Fort Fisher and the arrival of Schofield's command

En route through South Carolina, Sherman's army sought revenge against the hotbed of secession, the state that, in their opinion, initiated this unnecessary war. Here, sketch artist William Waud, an eyewitness, depicted the burning of McPhersonville, South Carolina. Sherman's troops burned part of 18 different towns in South Carolina. (Author's collection)

Although the Union blockade had reduced much of the traffic flow on the high seas, the Confederacy continued to bring in goods and military supplies through Wilmington, North Carolina. A massive Rebel bastion called Fort Fisher protected the mouth of the Cape Fear River, with Wilmington just 20 miles (32km) upriver. After the débâcle on the Red River, Admiral Porter, the new commander of a flying squadron on the Atlantic, suggested to his old friend Grant a joint expedition to knock Fort Fisher and Wilmington out of the war. Grant assigned Major-General Godfrey Weitzel, a clever engineer, to work with Porter, but Fort Fisher was part of Major-General Benjamin Butler's department, and Butler took over direction of the project. Butler proposed a scheme to explode a ship loaded with gunpowder under the fort, which he thought would demolish it. When the ship explosion failed to damage the fort, Butler sent only 2,500 men ashore and then canceled the attack.

As Porter fumed, Grant dispatched a more capable officer, Major-General Alfred Terry, and an additional brigade. Porter and Terry cooperated brilliantly. After heavy naval gunfire softened the defenses, Terry's troops and 1,000 sailors and marines landed on the beach. The next day, 14 January 1865, again under cover from naval gunfire, Terry's men stormed the timber and sand bastion. By nightfall, Fort Fisher had fallen into Union hands.

To assist Sherman and secure the fall of Wilmington, Grant pulled Schofield and his XXIII Corps from Thomas's army and injected them into North Carolina with Terry's men. The combined force captured Wilmington, and in late March, Schofield rendezvoused with Sherman's army at Goldsboro, North Carolina, bringing 40,000 troops and ready access to some much-needed supplies.

# Black soldiers and POWs

'For a man to enjoy the service, he must not be averse to much strong drink, must not be encumbered with morals & must possess an insatiable appetite for confusion,' quipped a Minnesotan. The soldier was one among some three million who responded to the call of their governments. Almost all of them volunteers, they entered military service wide-eyed, anticipating glory and rapid success. Instead, they experienced a world of hardship, heartache, and frustration.

Like the America from which they came, most Civil War soldiers were from farming or rural backgrounds. These men were an industrious, self-reliant lot, an unusual blend of idealism, individualism, and practicality. They depended on their own labor and judgment for survival, which fostered confidence in their decision-making ability. Accustomed to forming their own opinion about matters, and resistant to regimentation from the outside, their sense of independence proved both the boon and bane of their military existence.

While all sorts of pressures – family, friends, community, perceptions of manhood, quests for glory – worked on them, in the end it was that ability to decide for themselves that led most to enlist. Southerners entered military service to protect hearth and home and to defend their 'rights' – to own slaves, to take those slaves wherever they saw fit, and to live without fear of others encouraging servile insurrection. Since the US government seemed opposed to protecting those rights, they seceded and formed a new government, one that would protect them. Yankees, by contrast, believed in the permanence of the Union. Barely 80 years old, the United States was the great experiment in a democratic republic. 'It was,' so argued an Indiana sergeant, 'the beacon of light of liberty & freedom to the human race.' Secession trampled on an inherent principle of any democratic government that all would abide by the outcome of a fair election. They went off to war to sustain that government and the underlying concept because, one Yankee reasoned, 'constitutional liberty cannot survive the loss of unity in the government.' Only a minority early in the war fought for abolitionism. Although many Northerners disliked slavery, most also believed that African-Americans were inferior beings.

In 1861, soldiers rushed off to war amid celebrations and cheers. Believing the war would be short, most had the misplaced fear that the fighting would end before they saw any action. Few of them anticipated just how difficult prolonged military service would be, and how demanding life in uniform could be. Most soldiers did not know how to cook or care for themselves in camp and on the march. They loaded themselves down with excess baggage, never realizing how burdensome it was on a 15 or 20 mile (24–32km) hike. Then, when winter rolled around, they shivered through cold days and nights, cursing that Indian summer day when they had discarded their overcoats. Rather than enemy bullets, they succumbed to diseases in staggering numbers. Childhood illnesses had seldom afflicted people in rural communities, but once they gathered in large armies, these pathogens spread throughout camps, and farm boys had no resistance to them. Failure to enforce proper sanitary practices took unanticipated tolls, as camps bred pestilence and promoted the transmission of diseases at epidemic rates. As one Iowan wryly concluded, 'There is more reality than poetry in a life on the Tented field.'

Nor did they correctly anticipate the scale and scope of combat. Entering battle with severe misperceptions, the killing, the maiming, and the destruction caught men on both sides unprepared. Many had visions of personal and group glory, which realities abruptly banished from their minds. 'I can inform you that I have Seen the Monkey Show at last,' a Confederate penned home after Stones River, 'and I dont Waunt to see it no more.' He went on to describe, 'Som had there hedes shot of[f] and som ther armes and legs Won was Shot in too in the midel.' He then concluded with exasperation, 'I can tell you that I am tirde of Ware.'

They were nothing more than livestock in a butcher's pen, herded forward for the slaughter by what seemed like uncaring and incompetent generals. Men in the prime of their lives were cut down indiscriminately. Friends and comrades fell on their left and right, leaving those who survived to puzzle over the question: why them? And while they may have won the battle, rarely did they advance the cause dramatically. There seemed to be no end in sight.

Eventually, that experience in camp, on the march, and in battle hardened men on both sides. They learned how to conduct themselves better on the battlefield and in camp, to husband valuable resources and to discipline themselves on important matters. Soldiers accrued some emotional immunity to the randomness of the killing and the brutality of warfare, realizing that fear and intensive examination would produce no results. They resigned themselves to the idea that it was either God's will or their time.

The men of 1861 and 1862 had become veterans, with a vast warehouse of military knowledge based on personal experience or observation. 'The experience of twenty years peaceful life,' noted a veteran on the anniversary of his first battle, 'has been crowded into three years.' After just a few years, so stated another enlisted man, he and his comrades 'had learned nearly all that was worth knowing, at least far more than [our] generals knew three years before.'

Since early childhood, family and society had taught them to make decisions for themselves, to act as they saw best. Veterans did not hesitate to put those hard-earned military lessons to good use, even without supervision of their officers. They mastered the art of selecting excellent tactical positions and throwing up breastworks to shield their bodies from the accurate fire of rifled muskets. Engineers marveled at the positions and fortifications that enlisted men built quickly and on their own initiative. While killing was an inextricable component of warfare, soldiers learned how to take steps to reduce risks, to preserve themselves and their comrades for another day. Early in the war, they advanced elbow to elbow, as the tactics manual had instructed them. As veterans, they realized that the purpose was to concentrate firepower and strength, but they could accomplish that by dispersing themselves a little more and exploiting terrain features and cover. Yet they retained the important objective: to focus their fire on specific targets and areas. In camp and on the march, they knew 'just what to do and what not to do.' They practiced good hygiene, and supplemented their diet from the countryside. As one sergeant in Sherman's army commented, 'I believe if we were as green as we were when we first came out – (as the 'Vets' say) we would starve to death.' Almost as important, veterans could teach these lessons to new troops. While they liked to play pranks and mislead newcomers, the hardened soldiers also understood that their own lives depended to some degree on how well the green soldiers performed, and they would not neglect the instruction of any who would listen.

Along with changes in behavior, veterans embraced new attitudes about the war. They began to see both soldiers and civilians as the enemy, and they recognized the destruction of property as a powerful tool in fighting the war. Rebel cavalry commander Nathan Bedford Forrest proved himself master of the destructive cavalry raid, wreaking such havoc on garrisons, railroads, and supply depots that Sherman called him 'that devil Forrest.' Confederates, too, paid less credence to notions of 'civilized warfare,' especially when it came to black soldiers. Both they and the black troops fought under the black flag, signaling their opponent that they would give no quarter, nor expect any. All too often, they executed those they captured.

While Confederates in the Western Theater exhibited that change in attitude about the war, they did not have nearly as many opportunities as the Federals to implement it. Union soldiers campaigned throughout the South and, eventually, they came to the conclusion that by making Southern whites suffer, they could contribute mightily to the war effort. In part, Northerners felt a sense of hostility over secessionists' efforts to destroy a wonderful union, but as veterans they also came around to see the linkage between the home front and the men in the field. Confederates certainly exhibited tremendous loyalty to their cause, fighting for years under adverse conditions on meager rations and in skimpy clothing. Yet the Yankees realized that many Rebel opponents had a greater loyalty than that cause – the one to their families. If Federal troops could make life miserable for loved ones at home, they would force Confederate soldiers to choose between their responsibility to their families and their obligations to their government. As Union armies penetrated deeper into the Confederacy, consuming food, confiscating slaves and other property, and terrifying the

Southern people, more and more Rebels left the ranks to care for their loved ones.

By the last year and a half of the war, these Union and Confederate troops had mastered the art and science of soldiering. Those who remained in ranks had toughened their bodies by fighting off diseases. They had learned to deal with harsh elements, to march great distances and to live amid plenty or on little subsistence. In short, these citizens had learned to think, to act, to feel, and to fight like veteran soldiers.

## Black soldiers

Early in the war, abolitionists and African-Americans urged the Lincoln administration to accept blacks for uniformed service. The President declined. He had more white volunteers than he was authorized by Congress to accept, and the Union was walking a tightrope with the Border States. Black enlistment might have driven them to the Confederacy.

Blacks, however, began to take matters into their own hands. By the end of April 1861, several slaves whom Rebels had employed in constructing defense works slipped away and sought sanctuary at Fort Monroe, Virginia. When a Confederate officer came to retrieve the runaways, Brigadier-General Benjamin Butler, a prewar lawyer and politician, refused. Federal law did not apply to Rebels, Butler explained. Furthermore, slaves had aided the Confederate army and were subject to confiscation as contraband of war. Butler then employed the runaways to build a bakery for Federal troops. In one decisive moment, Butler had freed slaves and hired them to work for the Union army. Four

The overwhelming majority of black soldiers, perhaps 150,000 of the nearly 180,000, came from slavery. Often they fled from the fields as Union armies passed nearby, or they undertook a risky trek to locate Federal lines. Here two photographs expose the uplifting nature of military service. In one, we see a boy in his slave clothes; in the other, he has transformed into a drummer boy for the US army. (Left, Library of Congress; Right, US Army)

months later, Congress endorsed Butler's policy in the First Confiscation Act.

As the Union forces penetrated into the Confederacy, more and more slaves entered their camps. Many Federal officers objected to the idea of returning slaves, especially to owners in seceded states, and the practice distracted military personnel from their primary duty of suppressing the rebellion. In early 1862, the War Department prohibited the use of soldiers in retrieving slaves. The institution of slavery broke down a bit more.

After the failure of McClellan's campaign against Richmond in mid-1862, Lincoln re-evaluated his approach to the war. Recruiting had slowed to a trickle, and the largest untapped resource, African-Americans, was not being exploited. Slavery, moreover, had been the basis of secession, and the enemy had used slaves to help their cause. If the Union planned to prosecute the war fully, it must take slaves away from the Rebels and employ them for the Federal Government, both in and out of uniform. And if Northerners hoped eventually to bring the seceded states back into the Union, they must put that one unsolvable problem, slavery, on the road to extinction. Lincoln determined to issue an Emancipation Proclamation and to recruit blacks as soldiers.

For these controversial decisions, the President had tacit support from Congress.

Aware that Federal forces were their ticket to freedom, slaves began fleeing to Union troops whenever they approached nearby. Often they grabbed whatever they could carry, but in this case the refugees were able to use a wagon and horses to convey them to freedom. (Library of Congress)

On 17 July 1862, Congress passed the Second Confiscation Act, which authorized the President to confiscate all slaves of Rebels. That same day, Congress adopted the Militia Act, which permitted Lincoln to employ blacks for any military duties that he believed they were competent to perform. Lincoln also justified emancipation by his powers as commander in chief. Slaves aided the Rebel war effort. Surely he could deprive them of their use. As it turned out, Lincoln decided to await the next major Union victory, which did not occur until September 1862 at Antietam, before issuing the proclamation. But that summer, he began bringing African-Americans into uniform.

The first black soldiers came from a New Orleans militia unit, the 1st Louisiana Native Guards. The Native Guards had black company-grade officers and even a black major. Several months later, the Union recruited the first black regiment from scratch, the 1st South Carolina (Colored) Infantry, later called the 33rd US Colored Infantry, with all white officers.

The idea of putting blacks in uniform was extremely controversial. To increase the policy's acceptability, the administration sought competent whites to command these soldiers. By the end of the war, well over 7,000 whites had received commissions in the United States Colored Troops, while only 125 or so blacks were made officers.

Although black abolitionist Frederick Douglass and others promised that blacks would make excellent soldiers, it was essential for these first regiments to fight well. And they did. At Port Hudson, the 1st and 3rd Louisiana Native Guards charged Confederate works valiantly, and suffered heavy losses. After a New York Times newspaperman witnessed the attack, the paper declared, 'It is no longer possible to doubt the bravery and steadiness of the colored race, when rightly led.'

Several weeks later, black soldiers participated in a brutal fight at Milliken's Bend, Louisiana. The black regiments had only a few days of training and many had never fired their rifles. In a vicious assault by

368                    FRANK LESLIE'S ILLUSTRATED NEWSPAPER.                    [Oct. 26, 1861.

The issue of whether to employ blacks as soldiers was hotly contested. Despite the assertion of Frederick Douglass and other African-Americans that they would make efficient troops, the Northern white public was skeptical. Here, a powerfully racist cartoon in a popular magazine expresses the belief that blacks could contribute little to the army. (*Frank Leslie's Illustrated Newspaper*)

overwhelming Confederate numbers, the white soldiers fled but the black troops stood fast. Even though they could not reload and fire effectively, they fought hand to hand and ultimately repulsed the Rebels. One black regiment suffered the highest percentage of men killed in a single battle for the entire war. 'I never more wish to hear the expression, "The niggers wont fight,"' proclaimed a white officer in the fight.

The final event that secured a place for black soldiers was the intrepid assault by the 54th Massachusetts (Colored) Infantry on Fort Wagner, South Carolina. The 54th was the brainchild of the governor of Massachusetts, and it was raised in the North with tremendous publicity. Abolitionists or their sons served as officers. Among the enlisted ranks were two of Douglass's sons.

Its colonel, Robert Gould Shaw, volunteered the regiment to spearhead the attack on the fort that helped to guard Charleston harbor. Against a withering fire, the 54th carried up to and into the fort, yet, ultimately, the defenders repulsed them. Among the 40 percent casualties that the 54th suffered was its commander, Shaw, whom Rebels gleefully announced was 'buried with his niggers.' For the second time, newspapermen witnessed the attack, and the battle received extensive coverage in the North.

Having proved their worth on the battlefield, black soldiers began to convert detractors in and out of the army into supporters. By the end of the war, almost 179,000 blacks had served in the Union army and another 20,000 had enlisted in the navy. Military service was a thrilling event in their lives, especially for former slaves. 'I felt like a man,' recalled one black soldier, 'with a uniform on and a gun in my hand.' It gave blacks, free and slave, a sense of belonging to the United States.

Black soldiers and sailors fought to destroy slavery and restore the Union, and they hoped that a grateful nation would

reward them for their devotion by giving them full and equal rights in the postwar world. Their sense of commitment sustained them through extensive discrimination by the Union army and acts of brutality, such as the Fort Pillow massacre in Tennessee, by Confederates.

At peak, one in every eight Union soldiers was black; the percentage of black sailors was even higher. Black troops fought on 41 major battlefields and in 449 minor engagements. Sixteen soldiers and seven sailors received Medals of Honor for valor. Some 37,000 blacks in an army uniform gave their lives, and untold sailors did, too. Lincoln paid them high compliments when he declared that black soldiers fought as well as whites, and that their service was indispensable to victory.

Eventually black soldiers received an opportunity to prove themselves in combat. It was only on the field of battle that they could demonstrate their manhood and earn the postwar rights that they coveted. (Library of Congress)

'Keep it and you can save the Union,' he wrote. 'Throw it away, and the Union goes with it.'

Perhaps the greatest tribute to black soldiers, though, was paid by their opponents. Desperate for manpower, the Confederacy narrowly elected to enlist its own black soldiers in the waning months of the war. Critical in the adoption of the policy was a statement from General Robert E. Lee, in which he argued that the Union had employed black troops with success and he believed they would make 'efficient soldiers.'

## Prisoners of war

In a strange way, both Grant's Vicksburg campaign and the recruitment of black soldiers negatively influenced conditions in Civil War prison camps. Neither the Union nor the Confederacy had prepared well for the massive influx of prisoners that occurred in the last two years of the war. In the first year, only a small number of soldiers were captured. Numbers escalated in the second year of fighting, and both governments threw up prison camps until they could exchange them. In 1863, however, this exchange broke down. Confederates refused to treat black soldiers and their white officers as prisoners of war, insisting that former slaves return into bondage and their officers be prosecuted for inciting servile insurrection. The unwillingness of Confederates to include black troops in any exchange program dissolved the cartel. Confederates, moreover, declared the paroles issued by Grant to Rebel soldiers at Vicksburg invalid and placed quite a number of these parolees back in the ranks without

exchanging them properly. In protest, the Federal Government refused to swap prisoners, and for much of the next two years, the number of prisoners on both sides mounted.

Since no one anticipated the breakdown of the cartel, the huge influx of captives from the 1863 and 1864 campaigns caught them unprepared. The Confederates, for example, erected Andersonville because they feared the Union army might overrun the camp on the James River in Virginia. They chose the Andersonville location for its isolation. Originally laid out on 16 acres (6.5ha) for 10,000 prisoners, they eventually expanded it to 26 acres (10.5ha). Ultimately, Andersonville served as the home for 45,000 Union soldiers, with a peak number at

As Sherman's troops passed through Millen, Georgia, the soldiers discovered an abandoned prisoner-of-war camp called Camp Lawton. Prisoners had to burrow into the ground for shelter, and they had to remain inside a 'dead line,' which was still visible. If prisoners crossed over the line, they were shot. The sight outraged Sherman's army, which also discovered a similar prison camp outside Columbia, South Carolina. (Author's collection)

The most notorious of the Civil War prison camps was the stockade at Andersonville, Georgia. Originally planned for 10,000, it was home to more than three times that number, resulting in severe overcrowding, sanitary problems, and disease. (Collection of the New York Historical Society)

33,000. Amid the filth, congestion, lack of shelter, and poor water supply, some 13,000 died there.

Large Federal prison camps existed at Point Lookout, Maryland; Elmira, New York; Camp Chase, Ohio; and Johnson's Island, Illinois. Although Elmira earned the worst reputation among Confederate prisoners, the conditions there were better than at Andersonville. Elmira housed less than one-third the number of inmates on over 60 percent more acreage. The Union also erected barracks to shelter the inmates from the brutal cold of a Central New York winter. Still, Elmira had a staggering

24 percent death rate for Rebel soldiers incarcerated there.

No doubt, more intelligent planning and effort on both sides would have alleviated much of the misery in these camps. Of the 195,000 Union prisoners of war, more than 30,000 died. Federals held 215,000 Confederates, 26,000 of whom perished. Nor did these figures include all those who endured severe or chronic ailments from prolonged hardships and exposure. Yet despite postwar accusations, neither the Union nor the Confederacy deliberately intended to inflict horrible suffering on their captives. Rebel prison camps tended to be worse than Federal pens, but Confederate soldiers fared worse than Yankees. If the Confederacy struggled to feed and clothe its own fighting men, it should have surprised no one that its prisoners would fare poorly.

# William Wilbur Edgerton

'What storyes I shall have to tell when I get home,' announced Private William Wilbur Edgerton to his mother. Born and reared in Central New York, the third of four children to Dorothy Doud and John Leffingwell Edgerton, Wilbur had enlisted in the 107th New York Volunteer Infantry illegally in July 1862, just one month shy of his seventeenth birthday.

From a tender young age, Wilbur had been on his own. His father was a ne'er do well who wandered about, searching for success and happiness, never to find it. Wilbur's two older sisters married, and his mother, financially abandoned, took the youngest boy to Sparta, Wisconsin, where she had friends. Wilbur bonded well with his mother, recalling, 'When I was a little boy, I tought nothing was so nice as to sit on mothers lap and I have not exatly [gotten] over that.'

The best thing that ever happened to him, he believed, was being thrown out to his own devices at such an early age. Wilbur started kicking around at various jobs at twelve – fiddle playing, a cooper, a farm hand, a factory worker, and then a blacksmith. Neither fiddling nor work as a cooper paid much, so he took on employment with a farmer. When the man ripped him off of nearly half his pay, he stormed off and entered factory labor. Wilbur left that to apprentice with a blacksmith, which at the time offered a much better career track. 'Blacksmithing is black work,' he conveyed to his mother in racially charged language common in that day, 'but it brings white money so I dont care.' Unfortunately, the blacksmith's explosive temper and vulgar ways convinced him to quit. He then linked up with another blacksmith; this time a good, decent man.

Edgerton enlisted for the simple reason that everyone kept asking him why he did not soldier. He was a young man, without family, in good health, and because he had been on his own so long, everyone assumed he was older than he really was. 'I made up my mind that it was my duty to fight for my country and I did so,' Edgerton justified.

Just two and a half months after the regiment was formed, the 107th New York 'saw the elephant' in the single bloodiest day of the war, at Antietam in Maryland. Lee had raided into Maryland, but his plans fell into Federal hands. When Union forces moved more aggressively against him than he anticipated, Lee retreated to the north bank of the Potomac River, near a town called Sharpsburg and a creek named Antietam. On the morning of 17 September 1862, the 107th advanced through the North Woods and into the timber, where they came under fire for the first time. As they rushed into the East Woods, a Rebel volley struck down men on either side of Edgerton. You 'have no idea what it is to be a souldier off in a strang country whare your comrades are a dieing off fast and no noing how soon before your time will come,' he explained to his younger brother. In the course of passing through the woods, 'I run over a good maney ded and wounded *Rebels*.'

A couple of hours later, the 107th advanced to protect an artillery battery. 'The balls flew around my head like hail stones and sounded like a swarm of bees,' he described to his brother. 'O Johney I tell you that you can have no conception of the thouths [thoughts] that run through a mans head about thouse times it made a man think of the good and the bad things that he ever did in his life. I know my head was full of thoughts.' People who had been in combat had tried to prepare him for it, but the experience was nothing like anything he had ever witnessed. 'I have heard it said that after the first volley that you forged [forget] all the dainger,' he elaborated. 'Unless a man is scart out of his rite sences he knowes what is going on as well as he did at first.' Still, combat affected him. 'I know that my flesh tickeld and flinched all the time expecting to feel a ball pierce it.'

Two days later, his regiment had to cross over the hotly contested battlefield in pursuit of the Rebels. 'Sutch a odor (politely speaking) I never heard tell of *nor ever do I want smell it again*,' he confessed. 'The dead layed in heaps well it made me so sick that I had to fall out and laydown beside the road.' Despite this vivid depiction, the young private felt he had failed to convey a true sense of the experience. 'It is no usee,' he insisted, 'woords have not enuf meening.'

In mid-1863, the 107th New York fought in two of the greatest battles of the war, Chancellorsville and Gettysburg, and Edgerton was right in the thick of them. At Chancellorsville, Confederate General Stonewall Jackson launched a brilliant flank attack that rolled up the Union XI Corps and threatened the rear of the XII, to which the 107th was assigned. In the course of the fighting, Edgerton had his percussion cap box shot off, and a Rebel ball passed through his cap. 'I wouldent sware that I kiled aney body,' he admitted to his father, 'but I am prety shore that a good maney were hit buy me fore the most of the time they were not more than 10 or 15 rods [55–82.5yds; 50–75m] off and I know that I can hit a hat 20 rods off every time for I have tride it so you can judg for your self.'

At Gettysburg two months later, the battle 'was as hard if not harder than aney other that I have been in.' At one point, a shell fragment knocked his rifle right out of his hand. Having fought in several major battles, Edgerton had begun to develop some seasoning in combat. 'I mad[e] up my mind that if *they* wanted me to stop fighting *hit me* fir they couldent *scare* me aney,' he told his mother after Gettysburg.

Just before Antietam, his best friend, John Wiggins, deserted, only to return under Lincoln's amnesty the next April. Edgerton

helped his friend, who had a family at home, by lending him money, but he would never have entertained that kind of conduct himself. 'I dont care about fighting,' he confessed after Chancellorsville. 'I would willingly give all I am *worth* and a *good deal more if I had it to be out of this scrape*, but never the less I am no *coward* and I *never* will *disgrace* the *name* of *Edgerton* by *desertion* or *Sneeking* out of *danger* like some have.'

That fall of 1863, after the Union disaster at Chickamauga, the War Department transferred the XI and XII Corps under Major-General Joseph Hooker to Chattanooga. It was an extraordinary logistical achievement; Edgerton and his comrades endured the 'rufiest rideing' and a derailment, but they made it in time to witness the rout of Bragg's army. For a change, the 107th saw little action, but the regiment's arrival marked a dramatic change for its men. Not until the war's end would they return to Virginia. They soon became part of the Western Army, with the XI and XII merged to form the XX Corps under Hooker.

Because of his service in both theaters, Edgerton offered some valuable insights into the way that the enemy fought. Federal commanders, he noticed, preserved the lives of their men better by placing greater emphasis on artillery fire. The Rebels, with inferior artillery, compensated with aggressive infantry. 'There is one thing that our goverment does that suits me to a dot,' he instructed his mother, 'that is we fight mostly with Artillery, The Rebls fight mostly with Infantry. They fight as though a mans life was not worth one sent or in other words with desperration.' He also believed that the western Rebels did not fight as well as Lee's troops. Around Chattanooga, he knew that the Federals confronted what he described as two-fifths of Lee's army, including two of Longstreet's divisions, *'the best fighting men the World ever saw.'* Weeks after the Union crushed Bragg's army without Longstreet's troops present, Edgerton measured the performance of Confederate eastern and western troops and concluded, 'The rebels in this country are not such fighting men as they are in Va. [Virginia].'

The hardships of campaigning and general military service wore him out, yet he refused to let them drag his morale down too far. 'Oh if I ever do get home I know I will enjoy myself,' he vowed to his mother. 'You will never hear me grumble.' Food was always substandard. He estimated to his sister that rain-soaked clothes, blankets, and knapsacks weighed about 100lb (45kg), and that a soldier on the march hauled a woolen blanket, a rubber blanket, a change of underclothes, a tent, a knapsack, three days' rations, a belt, and a rifle. In addition to combat, everyday duty exacted quite a toll from the men. As Edgerton walked guard duty in rain, high winds, and hail, 'I would satisfy my self buy saing, that it was all for the *union*.'

As he traveled more and more throughout the South, the New Yorker gained greater exposure to the institution of slavery. 'It looks horrible,' he wrote his mother. He detested the idea of people held in bondage, some of whom were as white as he was. Slavery, he felt, made Southern whites somewhat lazy. 'I am and always was an Abolitionist,' he claimed, 'and I guess I am on the right side.'

That spring, 1864, the Union army under the overall leadership of Grant determined to press the Confederates on every front, with the two major operations targeting Richmond and Atlanta. As campaign season approached, Edgerton did not want to go forward, but duty compelled him to do so. 'Of course we dont like to fight but then, if nesesary, why, there is no body knows how aney better than we do,' he elaborated to his mother. 'I shant expose myself unnesisaryly, neither shall I shirk from doing my duty as a soldier.' Just before the campaign opened, he and Wiggins had their photograph taken together. 'I dont feel very patriotic this morning for we have got to march to morrow to the frunt & I dont want to go,' he admitted to his brother. But go he did.

Sherman had to maintain continual contact with the Rebel army under Johnston, to prevent wide flank attacks or the movement of reinforcements elsewhere,

while at the same time enabling the Federals to turn the Confederates from their defensive positions. As a result, Edgerton and his comrades remained under fire nearly the entire campaign, occupying positions anywhere from 200 to 500yds (180–450m) away. In the fight at Dallas on 28 May 1864, Edgerton declared it 'the hottest plase I was ever in' – strong words from someone who had fought in the thick of battle at Antietam, Chancellorsville, and Gettysburg. His regiment lost 168 men that day. Throughout June, he reported numerous close calls. 'I have again been preserved from the leden missles of death, while so maney of my comrades have fallen,' he alerted his mother in late June. After assessing the hardships of the campaign, he announced, 'It is a wounder [wonder] to me that I am alive.'

On 14 June, a cocky Wilbur Edgerton notified his mother, 'The rebls here dont know how to fight & they never will.' Less than two months later, a Confederate sharpshooter drilled him in the right shoulder with a minie ball outside Atlanta. Edgerton went to the field hospital, where he recovered in short order and returned to his command, just in time to participate in the fall of Atlanta. When Sherman swung his army to the southwest of the city, to sever the last open rail connections, he left the XX Corps to guard his own railroad supply line. As Hood vacated the city, the Federals pushed into Atlanta, with the 107th among the first to enter. 'Atlanta is ours,' Edgerton crowed to his mother, knowing full well the consequences of that victory.

Throughout the Atlanta campaign, the upcoming presidential election seldom strayed far from the minds of Edgerton and his comrades. Nearly all of them supported Lincoln's re-election bid, even if they were too young to vote, as was Edgerton. 'Our army is full of animation, patriotism &c. [etc.],' he assessed to his mother in early July. '[We] Have a determination to settle this war before next Presidential election for fear of copperhead being elected.' He predicted, 'if Lincoln is reelected next fall the War will end.' Several weeks later, he announced, 'I am for the administration as it is & for an unconditional surrender or extermination of the rebles.' The fall of Atlanta virtually assured that re-election. Still, he pledged his commitment to the Union and all for which it stood. 'I would die far sooner than have it destroyed,' he wrote.

By mid-November 1864, Edgerton and the other 65,000 men in Sherman's two armies had begun their lengthy trek to Savannah. The 107th passed through Milledgeville, the capital of Georgia, where some men held mock proceedings and left the capitol building a mess. Foraging parties gathered food and fodder from the countryside, while soldiers wrecked railroads and anything else of military value. By Christmas time, they had seized Savannah.

Throughout the Georgia campaign and the occupation duty in Savannah, Edgerton expanded his contacts with Southern women. Generally, he had few problems. Their penchant for chewing tobacco disgusted him, and he felt they lacked the intellectual snap of Northern women, but if Union soldiers behaved properly, they responded with respect. In Savannah, they sold meals and other items to soldiers, and the interactions were quite informative. Most Southern white women supported the rebellion, Edgerton thought, because they believed the Federal army would take away their slaves, which of course was true. 'Now that they are going to lose their niggers they dont know what to do,' he explained.

In late January 1865, after a much-needed rest, the army set out once again, this time northward for North Carolina, a campaign that proved much more demanding than the march to Savannah. In addition to stronger Confederate opposition, the topography, winter rains, and scarcity of food took a greater toll on Edgerton and his comrades. After a few days in South Carolina, he announced, 'This

country is nothing but swamps, swamps, swamps.' Along the way, he saw old, worn-out plantations overgrown by woods and underbrush. Although his regiment marched around Columbia, he passed through Fayetteville, North Carolina, which housed a major Confederate arsenal. There, he assessed the campaign as 'the hardest of the war.' Throughout South Carolina, the troops had to forage for their food in a land of scattered farms and plantations. 'Some have went hungry for a long time,' he commented to his mother, 'but *Will* has had plenty to eat.' At Averasborough, North Carolina, the 107th exchanged shots with the Rebels, suffering 27 men wounded.

This is the scene of the Battle of New Hope Church, or Dallas, in late May 1864 during the Atlanta campaign. Private Wilbur Edgerton, a veteran of Antietam, Chancellorsville, and Gettysburg, declared it 'the hottest plase I was ever in.' (Library of Congress)

The only other men the regiment lost in the Carolinas campaign were 19 foragers whom Confederate cavalry and guerrillas captured.

Several days after the army reached Goldsboro, North Carolina, Edgerton announced to his mother, 'I am so sick of soldering that my patriotism is below par.' Fortunately, the war did not last much longer. In April, Sherman's army advanced, and just as quickly it halted for negotiations. By the end of the month, the Confederates had surrendered, and the 107th New York began its march for Washington, DC. On 24 May, it proudly participated in the Grand Review along Pennsylvania Avenue, with the President, Grant, Sherman, and others in attendance. Three and a half weeks later, Wilbur Edgerton had purchased a new suit of civilian clothes and began work in a store. He received an honorable discharge on 18 June 1865.

In the years after the war, Edgerton tried his hand at a variety of occupations. He graduated from medical school and practiced in Kansas and Missouri. Eventually, he gave that up for jobs as a merchant and a banker in Wheeling, Missouri. The father of three children, he became a prominent member of the community, even serving as mayor of the town. Fittingly, he died on Armistice Day (now called Veteran's Day), 11 November 1931.

# The home fronts

## The Northern home front

Opposition to the war gained a big boost from the Emancipation Proclamation and the employment of black soldiers. Peace Democrats, nicknamed 'Copperheads,' hated the notion of fighting a war against Southern whites over slavery. Better to let them leave the Union, they argued, than spill white men's blood over the status of black people. Not only did Copperheads rail against the Lincoln administration and its war policy, some also encouraged individuals to desert the armed forces or resist enforcement of wartime measures. Many Union supporters blamed the Copperheads for the 200,000 men who deserted the Federal blue during the war.

Along with emancipation, the administration policy that generated the harshest criticism was conscription. First begun in 1862 as a kind of quota system, it became necessary to strengthen the recruitment process when enlistment fell off in 1862 and 1863. Although the procedure changed slightly during the war, essentially all males from 20 to 45 had to enroll. If a congressional district failed to reach its manpower quota when the government called for new troops, lots would be drawn to determine who would report. Once the individual selected passed a physical, he could serve, purchase a commutation for $300, or hire a substitute. Rather than suffer through a draft, communities raised money as enlistment bounties to entice volunteers, who would count against the quota. Others joined in insurance programs that purchased a commutation.

Conscription generated only 46,000 draftees who entered the army, and it caused considerable disaffection among Northerners. The commutation and substitute process led to charges of a rich man's war and a poor man's fight, and in several cities draft resistance evolved into riots. Yet the administration saw conscription as a carrot and stick approach, hoping to spur enlistment. From that perspective, it succeeded, since the Lincoln administration assembled enough troops to win the war.

Throughout the war, close to two and a quarter million served in Federal blue, and at peak, the Union had over one million men in uniform at one time. These military personnel had to be clothed, fed, equipped, and paid. As civilians, they were both producers and consumers; as soldiers and sailors, they grew or manufactured nothing, yet consumed massively.

Somehow, the North had to compensate for the manpower losses to the armed forces. Immigrants arrived, but in general the movement of people from Europe slowed down during the war. To fill the void, the Union relied heavily on two sources: women and mechanization. Females took to the fields, factories, and shops to produce the enormous amounts of food and other products to meet the needs of the domestic and the military market. The North also depended on labor-saving equipment to offset the loss of workers. Despite rising prices and income, a huge increase in the production of farm machinery kept the price low, making reapers and other farm implements more affordable. In various industries, too, owners adopted machinery to replace skilled or semi-skilled laborers whom they could no longer find. By the end of the war, the North had actually increased the amount of foodstuffs it grew – so much so that it fed its armies and the folks at home and exported large amounts to Europe – and was producing a sufficient amount of clothing, consumer goods, and war material to meet domestic needs and fuel the war machine.

Still, the absence of husbands and sons placed an enormous strain on families. Without the labor of a valued son or the family's father, parents and especially women had to fill unusual roles and take on added work. Often, neighbors helped each other, and communal organizations tried to soften the burden. Yet primarily, family members had to rely on each other. They picked up the slack and rallied in support of their loved ones in military service, working their way through tough times and encouraging those in uniform to do their duty.

While soldiers and sailors battled their Confederate counterparts, people on the home front warred as best they could against rising prices. The Lincoln government taxed its citizens heavily, but it financed much of the war through the sale of war bonds and the printing of paper notes. The flood of money and limitation on supplies of labor, raw materials, and finished goods drove prices up to double their prewar level, and in some instances even higher. Farmers, at least, produced their own food; inflation placed a huge burden on workers with fixed wages.

Despite the magnitude of the war, it did not suck all traditional impulses from society. Children still attended school, colleges remained open, individuals sought comfort in places of worship, and people fulfilled all sorts of needs in their communities. But the war also promoted a kind of voluntarism that did focus on the war and its consequences. Women sewed clothing for loved ones and strangers, people at home wrote millions of letters to maintain the bond between war front and home front, and tens of thousands flocked to sanitary fairs to raise money for the care and physical and spiritual well-being of the troops. In short, victory required a military and a civilian effort.

## The Southern home front

Most of the men in Rebel service in 1861 had enlisted for a solitary year, and as the term neared a close, the Confederacy confronted the prospect of its army melting away. In desperation, it passed the first Conscription Act in American history in April 1862. The law applied to men from 18 to 35 and allowed for occupational exemptions and the hiring of substitutes. The object was to spur enlistment with the conscription whip. By September 1862, the Rebel Congress had raised the upper limit to 45 years of age. It also yielded to pressure from wealthy slave owners to keep home white males who could control the slave population. The Twenty-Negro Law permitted one exemption per 20 slaves whom the master owned, and it fueled the contention in the seceded states of a rich man's war and a poor man's fight, as in the North. Like the Federal law, conscription stirred opposition, but it also helped to fill the ranks. From a total white population of approximately 5.5 million, perhaps 900,000 men served in the Confederate army, and at peak the Confederacy had about 450,000 men in uniform.

With such an extraordinary percentage of white males in service, comparatively few able-bodied white men remained at home to run farms, fabricate goods, and supervise the slaves, whose productive labors were more important than ever. In many instances, women had to rise to the occasion and take over for loved ones. Yet discipline and force were the principal means of controlling the 3.5 million slave laborers, and without many adult white males around, bondsmen regularly tested the resolve of women and elderly or youthful male owners and overseers.

It did not take slaves long to learn about the war and emancipation. They realized that any work slowdown or disruption on the plantation impaired productivity, thereby hurting the Rebel cause and enhancing the possibility of freedom becoming a reality. Slave-owning wives wrote to soldiers, complaining of slave insolence, resistant attitudes, or flight to Union lines. From hundreds of miles away, soldiers could only advise. Nevertheless, that frustration, and the ever-present fear of servile insurrection,

lingered in their minds throughout the war, and worries distracted them from the business at hand, war making.

Since a majority of Southerners were farmers or planters before the war, their absence cut deeply into agricultural productivity. The Confederacy had to feed the same number of mouths, but with fewer workers, and as the Union army advanced, the Confederacy had to do so on less and less tillable acreage. The Confederate government encouraged individuals to grow more food crops and less cotton, but shortages in the army and in numerous areas of the Confederacy still occurred, leading to protests and even riots.

Refugees from the war flooded cities, seeking protection, jobs, and nourishment. The population of Richmond soared almost out of control; in other cities, it increased astronomically as well. Columbia, South Carolina, for instance, tripled in size over the four years. The local infrastructure lacked the capacity to care for the huge influx, and prices began to skyrocket. Nor did the paper currency, which the Davis administration printed to finance much of the war, help inflation. By the late stages of the war, these paper notes were more valuable as keepsakes than as a medium of exchange.

While prices rose substantially everywhere in the Confederacy, urban areas suffered the greatest escalation. In 1864, corn sold at $20 a bushel in Charleston. By early the next year, it cost $40 per bushel in nearby Columbia, and $25 per bushel in Athens, Georgia. Bacon, a Southern staple, normally sold for 12 cents per pound (0.45kg). By 1865, the prices ranged from $2 to $4 per pound, and were even higher in some areas. Emma LeConte, a 17-year-old South Carolinian, reported that homespun cloth cost $8–10 per yard (0.91m) and calico between $20 and $30. Her parents bought her shoes for $150. A load of firewood, she recorded, went for $100. How poor people survived is a virtual mystery.

Because prices escalated on an almost daily basis, and currency lacked any real value, farmers declined to sell to the government, which would only pay anywhere from one-third to one-eighth of the market price. In order to feed the troops, commissaries confiscated food and livestock, which again alienated farmers. Even then, the Commissary Department procured so little food, and the transportation network had fallen into such decline, that the Confederacy provided less than a third of the standard authorized ration for its troops.

The consequences of war on the Confederacy's home soil, too, took their toll. As Union armies penetrated deeper into the seceded states, they disrupted more and more lives. Soldiers on either side took food wherever they found it, leaving civilians in dire straits. And when Sherman, Sheridan, and others launched raiding marches, seizing food from the countryside and destroying anything of military value, they left those civilians in their wake in horrible circumstances.

Ultimately, this raiding strategy forced Confederates onto a spiral of defeat. Civilians wrote to soldiers, explaining their plight and compelling these men in uniform to choose between their family and their country. Many deserted to care for loved ones. On the way back, they had to take food from farms, which burdened other civilians, and their collective absence dramatically weakened the Rebel armies in the field. With insufficient manpower, Confederates could not check Yankee advances, which in turn exposed more Rebel families to the ravages of Union troops. That prompted more Confederates to leave the ranks to care for family members in need.

Once the spiral began, the Confederates could not halt it. The experiences of the Confederate States of America powerfully illustrate the intricate link between armies in the field and civilians on the home front.

# Emma LeConte

'Reunion! Good Heavens!' exclaimed 17-year-old Emma LeConte about the prospects of peace with those vandals, the Yankees. 'How we hate with the whole strength and depth of our souls.'

Born in Georgia and raised in Columbia, South Carolina, Emma was the daughter of a science professor at the College of South Carolina, later renamed the University of South Carolina. From this privileged background, she received a world-class education for a young woman in her day. Her upbringing bound her intricately to the cultural trappings of Southern society, and her youthful and unyielding passion for the Confederacy reflected broad sentiments among the well-to-do people in South Carolina.

Just a handful of blocks away from her home on campus grounds, South Carolinians celebrated secession from the Union. Emma recalled with delight the moment she and her neighbors learned that Fort Sumter had capitulated. They were seated in her father's library when the bell at the marketplace clanged, announcing a momentous event. Everyone rushed outside, where they heard the news. 'The whole town was in joyful tumult,' she described. Men ushered off to war. Women filled the void in all sorts of ways and contributed to the war effort by supporting the cause, caring for the ill and injured, and enduring any sacrifice necessary for victory.

Emma never doubted the justice of the Confederate cause. Despite her exceptional education in mathematics, science, French, German, philosophy, literature, and history, she did not challenge the notions that blacks were inferior beings and that slavery benefited the African race. The Northern states threatened to undermine the institution of slavery and impose themselves and their ideas on the Southern people. No self-respecting individual, no free person, could justly endure such a humiliation. The North attempted to enslave them, and Southern whites dissolved their connection to the Union. God and justice – inseparably intertwined in her mind and those of fellow secessionists – were on their side.

But by the end of 1864, the prospects looked bleak. Lee and his valiant army had locked in a life-and-death struggle outside Petersburg and Richmond. Sherman's army had swept through Georgia, leaving desolation in its wake. Savannah had capitulated. And 'Sherman the brute avows his intention of converting South Carolina into a wilderness,' she feared.

Even before the Federal army turned northward, it threatened Emma's family. Her 15-year-old sister Sallie, her aunt, and two cousins resided on a plantation 25 miles (40km) south of Savannah. In December, Emma's father, who worked during much of the war for the Nitre and Mining Bureau, embarked on a lengthy trek to find and bring them back to Columbia. While she waited, reports reached her ears on the conditions in Georgia. How would they survive without provisions, she wondered. In her diary, she worried over 'how dreadfully they must have been frightened.' With her father traveling into harm's way, the thought of his death instilled a sense of terror in her. By 7 February 1865, he had brought them all back to Columbia, but in doing so, he had unwittingly moved from an area beyond Sherman's swath to a primary target.

The war had taken its toll on the LeConte family's quality of life, too. Although they were well off financially, skyrocketing inflation, a relatively tight Union blockade, and limited supplies forced them to cut back drastically. The family ate two meals a day.

They had two plates of bread for breakfast, usually made from corn meal. Dinner consisted of a small piece of beef, some corn bread, potatoes, and hominy. Fortunately, they had two cows that furnished milk and butter. 'We have no reason to Complain,' Emma noted, 'so many families are so much worse off.'

Her clothing, too, had declined in quality and quantity. She wore homespun undergarments, more coarse than they gave to slaves in prewar times. She knitted her own stockings, and a pair of heavy calfskin shoes covered her feet. Emma owned two calico dresses and a black and white plaid homespun for everyday use. She also had a few old silk outfits from prewar days which were wearing out rapidly. Those she saved for special occasions.

Each January, the community women held a bazaar at the state house to raise money for the care of soldiers. Emma helped arrange the booths. Despite the wartime shortages, the decorations looked elegant and the tables were loaded with niceties that slipped through the blockade. Cakes, sweets, and other items sold at exorbitant prices. One large doll went for $2,000. Her astonished uncle commented, 'Why one could buy a live negro baby for that!' In the three previous years, the bazaar lasted two weeks. Within four days, though, it closed because of Sherman's advance into South Carolina.

Since early January, Emma had feared for the loss of Columbia. 'The horrible picture is constantly before my mind,' she confessed in her diary, yet she refused to evacuate the city. By the time they closed the bazaar, everyone felt the city was doomed. The Confederacy had no viable force to oppose the Yankee march. Mounting anxiety reached such a peak that Emma, who always found great solace in her books, could no longer concentrate when she tried to read. The War Department ordered her father to pack up the Nitre Laboratory and move it out of danger, which left Emma, her two younger sisters, her mother, and the household slaves to brave it together.

Distant cannon booms alerted locals to the approaching bluecoats. People panicked throughout the city. Crowds, trying to flee from Sherman's path, tangled in traffic snarls. Others, like Emma, awaited the onslaught with no clear picture of how awful it would be. All those tales of brutality and destruction by Sherman's troops played on their imagination. Two days before they reached the city, Emma's sister sobbed hysterically all morning. The next day, they presented a composed front, but 'our souls are sick with anxiety.' When Union shells fell into the city, the family hunkered down in the basement. Emma felt nauseous and faint. Her mother, who had held together all that time, broke down in utter terror when she heard gunfire in the streets.

Once the Rebel cavalrymen evacuated, the shooting died down. There was a calm, and then Emma could hear shouts and finally, some Yankee troops raised the Stars and Stripes over the state capitol. 'Oh, what a horrid sight,' she wrote, that 'hateful symbol of despotism.' Emma could not look upon the Yankees without 'horror and hatred, loathing and disgust.'

That evening, the wind picked up, and by nightfall fires had begun to spread throughout the city. Smoldering cotton bales ignited by rebel cavalrymen and fanned by the high winds initiated the blaze, but Union troops, drunk on alcohol or intoxicated by their success, and fueled by their hatred of South Carolina, the hotbed of secession and in their minds the cause of this unholy rebellion, spread the flames. 'Imagine night turned into noonday,' described Emma in her journal, so bright and extensive were the fires. With hospitals that housed Union and Confederate soldiers nearby, the LeConte home escaped the ravages. Others – men and women, elderly and infant alike – did not. Except for a handful of clothing and a few morsels of food, they escaped with only their lives. The flames consumed everything else.

The inferno destroyed one-third of the city, including much of the heart of old Columbia. Charred brick walls and scorched

chimney stacks were all that remained of entire city blocks. Several days after the Federal army left, Emma wandered about the town. Only a foundation and chimney remained from the old state house, where just a month earlier she had witnessed such gaiety at the bazaar. At the market, she saw the old bell, nicknamed 'secessia,' which had chimed as South Carolina and each succeeding state seceded. Now it lay half buried amid the ashes.

Emma's father escaped. He and another officer narrowly avoided capture and, after enduring considerable hardships, worked their way back home. His appearance lifted her spirits tremendously.

To feed the people, Sherman left 500 scraggly head of cattle. While many slaves took off with the Federals, quite a number stayed behind, and refugees from outlying areas flocked to the city for sustenance. Government officials, Emma's father among them, traveled far and wide in search of food to supplement the beeves. Each day, Emma drew some rancid salt pork or stringy beef and a pint of corn meal as rations.

Even though Federal troops had marched right through her state, and were at least partially responsible for the destruction of much of their city (Emma, like most locals, blamed Sherman exclusively), Emma remained defiant. She so detested the Yankees, and believed so strongly in the righteousness of the cause, that she could not imagine a just God would allow the Federals to win. She had no confidence in Johnston, who was restored to command. When she

This is a photograph taken by George N. Barnard of the ruins of Columbia, South Carolina, from the capitol. Emma LeConte walked past this place regularly and described the destruction all around it. (National Archives)

learned he had fallen back to Raleigh, North Carolina, Emma predicted that he would retreat all the way to Lee, who 'may put a stop to his retrograde movement.' All her faith rested in Lee and his army, 'an army that has never suffered defeat, a contrast to the Western army.' When word of Lee's surrender arrived, she was so overwhelmed that 'there seemed no ground under my feet.' She resisted to the last, but Jefferson Davis's capture and the surrender of all western troops brought an end to her dreams. Her only consolation was the assassination of Abraham Lincoln, which elicited cheers from her and her family and friends.

In the immediate aftermath of the war, occupation soldiers irritated Emma, and the prospect of black soldiers overseeing them outraged her. Dreams of emigration to a different land or hopes that the next generation could wage a more successful war nourished her spirit.

Emma's father moved the family to California, where he taught at the University of California. Emma remained east. She married a Citadel cadet who entered the army with his classmates. They settled on a 1,000 acre (400ha) farm. Emma bore two girls. When the older daughter was 12, Emma's husband died. Not surprisingly, Emma ran the farm on her own and still managed to raise and educate her daughters.

# Peace is declared

On 27 and 28 March 1865, Sherman visited Lincoln, Grant, and Porter at City Point. After his long travels, Sherman regaled them with tales of the trek. But this was not all fun. Grant and Sherman discussed the closing campaign, and Lincoln instructed both officers on the terms of surrender they could offer.

Before Sherman had reached North Carolina, Grant had turned Lee out of his defenses around Petersburg. Both Union generals were wary that Lee would somehow unite with Johnston and attack Sherman. With 100,000 troops, Sherman felt confident he could withstand any onslaught, but he accelerated the pace of replenishing his supplies to get his army into the field as soon as possible. The march against Johnston began on 10 April, and within two days, he learned that Lee had surrendered to Grant on the 9th. His army celebrated wildly.

Johnston had hoped that Lee could elude Grant and unite with him. While his army waited to see the results of Lee's desperate move, Johnston gathered with President Davis and other cabinet members at Greensboro, North Carolina. During the meeting, they received confirmation of the rumors that Lee had surrendered. Davis urged them to keep fighting, but Johnston announced his opposition. The people were whipped and his army was deserting in large numbers. The war was over.

With Davis's reluctant consent, Johnston contacted Sherman to open negotiations for peace. On 17 April, the two generals who had opposed each other in Mississippi, in Georgia, and again in North Carolina, assembled at the home of James and Nancy Bennett, not far from Durham Station. Sherman, forceful in war and soft in peace, offered Johnston mild terms that clearly overstepped his bounds. He permitted Confederate soldiers to take their arms home and deposit them at state capitals; he recognized state governments, restored the franchise, and said nothing of emancipation.

Had Lincoln been president, he no doubt would have corrected his general's excessive generosity. By then, however, an assassin named John Wilkes Booth had shot and killed him. At the moment when Sherman's terms arrived, Washington officials were in near hysteria. The new President, Andrew Johnson, and the cabinet unanimously rejected the terms, and Secretary of War Stanton intimated in a letter published in the *New York Times* that Sherman was a traitor.

Grant volunteered to resolve the problem. President Johnson directed Grant to supersede Sherman, but Grant refused to insult his friend that way. He traveled down to North Carolina with little fanfare and instructed Sherman to offer the same terms as he gave Lee, that they would stack arms and sign paroles, and as long as they behaved themselves and obeyed the laws, the Rebels could live undisturbed by Federal authorities. The two wrangled a bit, but Johnston, confronted with the reality of a collapsed war effort, signed on 26 April.

On 12 April, Union forces under Major-General E. R. S. Canby battled their way into Mobile. For two years, Grant had sought its capture, and as Grant ruefully noted, it finally happened when its fall meant nothing. Two weeks after Sherman and Johnston concluded the surrender agreement, Union cavalrymen captured Confederate President Jefferson Davis in Georgia. By 26 May, General Edward Kirby Smith had surrendered the Rebel forces in the trans-Mississippi west. The war was over.

On 23 May 1865, the Army of the Potomac paraded
down Pennsylvania Avenue before government officials
and huge crowds. The next day, Sherman's army, fresh
from its lengthy campaigns, marched. Sherman feared
that the dilapidated condition of his soldiers' clothing and
equipment and their broad campaign stride would prove
embarrassing in the parade. Instead, they delighted the
crowds and made their commander proud once more.
(Library of Congress)

# United States

The Union army demobilized in rapid order, from one million strong at the end of the war to 80,000 men a year later. Yankee soldiers returned to their rendezvous point, received back pay, signed documents, and were officially mustered out of service. Others viewed the delay as another ridiculous government policy and simply walked home. Several decades later, when they applied for veterans' pensions, that decision proved nettlesome.

Confederate soldiers simply headed home. Men who owned their horses were allowed to take them. Some received railroad transportation as far it would take them, which in the aftermath of Sherman's marches was not usually very far. For the men from Texas, it took up to two months to make it back home.

Scholars and military experts have posited a host of reasons why the Confederacy lost. Immediately after the war, a prominent Virginia journalist and numerous military leaders blamed Southern defeat on Jefferson Davis's incapacity as commander-in-chief. Hatred of Davis motivated most of these early critics. Later scholars who attributed Rebel defeat to Davis lacked the hatred of that earlier generation. They derived their criticism of Davis largely by comparing him with Lincoln. Yet all American presidents pale whenever they are juxtaposed with Lincoln, and recent military historians and biographers of Davis have demonstrated clearly that, despite some weaknesses, Davis was certainly a competent commander-in-chief. Other students of the Civil War have argued that internal dissension undid the Confederacy, or that Southern whites lost the will to resist. But by comparison, dissension in the North was at least as powerful, and every nation that

suffers a defeat ultimately loses the will to continue the fight.

In more recent years, some scholars have embraced the idea that the Confederacy should have adopted a guerrilla war. Brigadier-General Edward Porter Alexander, perhaps the most thoughtful young officer in the Confederacy, proposed the idea to Robert E. Lee in the waning days of the war. At the time, Lee rejected it, insisting that the Confederacy had borne the battle for four long years, and a guerrilla war would only extend and increase the suffering on both sides, with no real benefit. Nonetheless, a handful of historians have challenged Lee's assessment as faulty. They draw on the partisan success of the Rebels in the American Revolution, and the triumph of North Vietnam against the United States in the 1960s and 1970s. These scholars point out how vexing the guerrilla war was in Missouri, and how much difficulty the Federal army encountered in trying to protect Unionists in Tennessee and Kentucky.

Each of these views, however, suffers from serious flaws. During the American Revolution, partisans in the South performed successfully because they served in conjunction with traditional armies. Nathanael Greene and his Continentals fought alongside the guerrillas, and George Washington in New York and later Virginia commanded a standing army. By contrast with the American Revolution, which was fought in a pre-industrial era, warfare in an industrial age requires mass production, either by the nations at war or by sponsor nations that provide it to them. When a nation adopts guerrilla warfare, it exposes its people and land to enemy invasion, thereby endangering its ability to produce munitions and other materiel that are necessary for war. Vietnam received massive support from the

Soviet Union and the People's Republic of China; the Southern Confederacy had no such patron. In Vietnam, moreover, the United States imposed restrictions on where its ground troops could advance. No massive ground invasion took place in North Vietnam, and the United States only blocked supply shipments by water in the late stages of the war. During the Civil War, the Confederacy was the primary battleground, and an ever-tightening blockade, working in conjunction with land troops, had choked off imports to the Confederacy almost completely by 1865.

Selected scholars have argued that the difficulty of quelling the guerrilla war in Missouri and Tennessee demonstrates just how effective it could have been on a larger scale. But two factors undercut that assertion. First, Missouri remained in the Union, and an overwhelming percentage of its people opposed the Confederacy. Three of every four men from Missouri who entered the army donned the Union blue. Federal authorities had to deal with the people of Missouri respectfully, because so many supported the Union. Tennessee also had a strong pro-Union contingent, especially in the eastern part of the state. In other seceding states, Federals had no reason to protect the people, except for pockets of hill-country Unionists.

Second, by the late stages of the war, the Union had begun to adopt the raiding strategy, which targeted civilians and property, along with soldiers in the field, as the enemy. This was ideally suited to crushing guerrilla activities by destroying or confiscating property and making life a hell for Confederate civilians and soldiers alike. As Emma LeConte recorded in her diary, when her Uncle John, a prisoner of war, discussed the possibility of guerrilla fighting with a soldier in Sherman's army, the Yankee replied, 'Well, I hope the South won't do anything of *that* kind, for of course in that event we would not spare or respect your women.' Beneath his bluster, the soldier's comments suggested both the hardened nature of Union troops and their growing callousness toward

Southern civilians. They possessed just the right attitude to combat guerrillas.

National approaches to war are products of social structure, economy, technology, and culture. Confederate whites were a propertied people, who seceded from the Union in order to protect what Mississippi called 'the greatest material interest of the world.' Their constitution attempted to secure two elements of that society, white persons and property, and they entered military service to defend both of those elements. A guerrilla war policy would have exposed their families and that property to Federal destruction or abuse, a strategy that would have undercut the very reasons for a Southern Confederacy. And by drawing food and supplies from the Southern people, while at the same time exposing their homes and property to Union destruction, Confederate guerrillas would have alienated them from the cause as well.

In organizing for war, Confederates drew on what they perceived as the Southern military tradition. They aspired to build armies along Washington's model, which would exploit martial aspects of Southern character and establish for the Confederacy a credibility with other nations of the world that guerrilla forces would not. Their heritage, secessionists believed, would more than compensate for any manpower advantages that the Union possessed.

When asked some years afterwards why the Confederates lost at Gettysburg, George Pickett replied, 'I think the Yankees had something to do it with.' That same argument best explains why the Confederacy lost the war. For all the sacrifices, for all the losses, for all the hardships, for all the narrow defeats, the Confederacy simply could not overcome the Union. Internal strife, patchy leadership, and many other factors hindered its war effort. The same, of course, could be argued for the Yankees. But in the end, the Union defeated the Confederacy; the Confederacy did not defeat itself.

Many scholars believe that the Union won because of overwhelming numbers, what one scholar has called 'the heaviest battalions.' There is truth to the North's preponderance of strength. Federals employed over two million soldiers, while the Confederacy mustered close to 900,000. Despite having one million men in uniform at once, the Northern states grew enough food to feed civilians and soldiers and still market huge amounts overseas. By the end of the war, the Union had over 700 navy vessels, many of them ironclads; the Confederacy had almost none. From November 1862 to late October 1863, the Union army purchased from Northern factories as many field artillery guns as the Confederacy's principal producer, Tredegar Iron Works, manufactured in the entire war. That same year, the Federal Ordnance Department bought over 1.4 million artillery rounds and 260 million small-arms cartridges from Northern munitions makers. For the entire war, the Confederacy produced only 150 million small-arms cartridges, and the Richmond Arsenal, the Confederacy's largest manufacturer, made 921,000 artillery rounds. Nor were these lopsided statistics simply anomalies. The same overwhelming advantages existed in weapons, clothing, and other military accouterments. But as the Vietnam experience demonstrated, overwhelming superiority in equipment, population, and even technology do not assure victory.

Ultimately, three critical factors enabled the Union to win the war. First, it possessed overwhelming resources in population, industrialization, agriculture, and transportation, and a slight edge in technology. Second, the Union benefited from political and military leaders who harnessed those resources, transforming them into military might and focusing that power on the critical aspects of the Confederacy. Finally, the Federals had a home front that remained committed enough to the war to see it through to its conclusion, despite all the losses, hardships, and sacrifices.

What were the consequences of the war? Several were obvious. More than 260,000 Confederate soldiers and over 360,000 Federals died in the war. The preponderance

lost their lives to disease. An additional 500,000 suffered wounds, and hundreds of thousands more endured ailments and disabilities from their days in the service. According to the best estimate, the total cost of the Civil War exceeded $20 billion, a figure 31 times larger than the federal government's budget in 1860. In fact, so devastating was the war to the Confederacy that it took some six decades for the Southern states to reach their 1860 level in agricultural productivity.

Once and for all time, the war removed the scourge of slavery from the American landscape. Well over four million African-Americans had been held, sold, and controlled as chattel. The war destroyed that institution. Hundreds of thousands entered Federal lines on their own. Others followed the Union armies to freedom. Still many more waited until the fighting ceased before securing their liberty. Passage and ratification of the Thirteenth Amendment to the US Constitution, abolishing slavery forever, made certain that wartime measures freeing slaves could not be overturned in peacetime.

While the achievement of freedom was a wondrous thing for blacks, white society prevented them from exploiting its benefits fully. The Fourteenth Amendment secured citizenship and equal protection and due process of law. The Fifteenth Amendment granted black males the right to vote. But in time, Southern whites resurrected their power and stripped African-Americans of many of their rights. Northerners, tired of war and struggles over power in the South, yielded Southern control to Southern whites. Although African-Americans in the South and the North were better off after the destruction of slavery, it took more than a century for them to achieve their Civil War goal of basic civil rights.

By winning the war, too, the Northern vision of the United States took precedence over the more local, states' rights, agriculturally oriented version of the South. No longer were they states united, but a United States. The federal government established its preponderance over the state governments, a trend that has continued ever since. The nation moved on an accelerated course of industrialization and urbanization. And finally, the Northern version of freedom, with aspirations of egalitarianism and economic opportunity for all, prevailed for white Americans.

Although Southern whites howled over Reconstruction policies, they were under the circumstances quite mild. There were no wholesale land confiscations, no widespread imprisonments, no mass executions for treason. Only Major Henry Wirz, Commandant of Andersonville Prison, was put to death. Among Rebel leaders, Jefferson Davis alone was held in jail for two years, but Northerners never had the stomach for a trial. After his release, Davis lived a long life in the United States. By 1877, the US government had removed all soldiers from the former Confederacy, and the last of the secessionist states had returned as full and equal partners in the Union.

After the war, word circulated that the great Prussian general Helmuth von Moltke had said of Sherman's army that there was nothing one could learn from 'an armed mob.' When asked about it, Sherman replied that he knew Moltke but never questioned him on the story, 'because I did not presume that he was such an ass as to say that.'

From a military standpoint, the Civil War offered an extremely valuable legacy for thoughtful analysts. American military leaders realized that rifles, artillery, and field fortifications weighed heavily on the side of defenders. Over the next few decades, US army officers sought to restore the tactical offensive to warfare through single-line formations with greater dispersion and mobility, to reduce the impact of defensive weapons.

Most European analysts dismissed the war as one conducted by bumbling amateurs. They insisted that breech-loading small arms of the late 1860s made lessons from all previous wars obsolete. In the minds of most foreign experts, the lightning offensives and decisive campaigns of the Austro-Prussian and Franco-Prussian Wars readily cast a dark shadow over any insights into future conflicts from the American Civil War. Yet the Civil War proved more prophetic of the First World War than either of those clashes between European powers. Analysts failed to grasp the enhanced power of the defensive and the value of good field works. They also missed valuable lessons from cavalry serving as mounted infantry, a combination of mobility and firepower that proved so decisive in the Second World War.

Lieutenant-General Philip Sheridan, the hard-charging general who had arrested a corps commander for arriving with his men 12 hours late, observed the Franco-Prussian War from the Prussian side. In a letter to Grant in 1870, he thought that the battles were actually not that distinct from the Civil War, and 'that difference is to the credit of our own country.' Sheridan believed, 'There is nothing to be learned here professionally, but it is a satisfaction to learn that such is the case.' He insisted that Europeans could benefit from studying Americans' more effective use of cavalry and rifle pits, better protection of their lines of communication, and more efficient staff departments. By the end of the century, some European officers had extracted valuable lessons from studying the Civil War, particularly tactics, but not enough to anticipate the unparalleled bloodshed in the First World War.

Little more than a month before his death, Lincoln had called for the nation to complete its undertaking and then bind its wounds. Several decades later, survivors on both sides attempted to do just that, to set aside old grudges and to shake hands at several battlefield commemorations. In their youth, they had been touched by fire. By middle and old age, that passion and animus had largely flickered out. And while veterans retained many fond memories, and preferred to emphasize those aspects in their letters and conversations, they never forgot the harsh side of war.

In 1864, an Illinois officer assessed, 'There is no God in war. It is merciless, cruel, vindictive, un-christian savage, relentless. It is all that devils could wish for.' Few veterans would have disagreed.

# Further reading

## Primary sources

Basler, Roy F., ed., *Collected Works of Abraham Lincoln*, 8 vols, New Brunswick, New Jersey, 1953.

Davis, Keith F., *George N. Barnard: Photographer of Sherman's Campaigns*, Kansas City, Missouri, 1990.

William W. Edgerton Papers, University of Houston.

Grant, U. S., *Personal Memoirs*, 2 vols, 1885.

LeConte, Joseph, *'Ware Sherman: A Journal of Three Months' Personal Experience in the Last Days of the Confederacy*, Berkeley, California, 1938.

Miers, Earl Schenck, ed., *When the World Ended: The Diary of Emma LeConte*, New York, 1957.

Record Group 94, National Archives.

Sherman, William T., *Memoirs of W. T. Sherman By Himself*, 2 vols, New York, 1891.

*War of the Rebellion: Official Records of the Union and Confederate Armies*, 128 vols, Washington, DC, 1880–1901.


## Secondary sources

Bailey, Anne J., *The Chessboard of War: Sherman and Hood in the Autumn Campaigns of 1864*, Lincoln, Nebraska, 2000.

Ballard, Michael B., *Pemberton: A Biography*, Jackson, Mississippi, 1991.

Bearss, Edwin C., *The Vicksburg Campaign*, 2 vols, Dayton, Ohio, 1985–86.

Boatner, Mark M., III, *The Civil War Dictionary*, New York, 1959.

Bradley, Mark L., *Last Stand in the Carolinas: The Battle of Bentonville*, Campbell, California, 1996.

Castel, Albert, *Decision in the West: The Atlanta Campaign of 1864*, Lawrence, Kansas, 1991.

Castel, Albert, *William Clarke Quantrill: His Life and Times*, New York, 1962.

Connelly, Thomas L., *Army of the Heartland: The Army of Tennessee, 1861–1862*, Baton Rouge, Louisiana, 1967.

Connelly, Thomas L., *Autumn of Glory: The Army of Tennessee, 1862–1865*, Baton Rouge, Louisiana, 1971.

Cooper, William J., Jr, *Jefferson Davis, American*, New York, 2000.

Coulter, E. Merton, *The Confederate States of America, 1861–1865*, Baton Rouge, Louisiana, 1950.

Cozzens, Peter, *This Terrible Sound: The Battle of Chickamauga*, Urbana, Illinois, 1992.

Daniel, Larry J., *Soldiering in the Army of Tennessee: A Portrait of Life in a Confederate Army*, Chapel Hill, North Carolina, 1991.

Davis, William C., *Jefferson Davis: The Man and His Hour*, New York, 1991.

Fellman, Michael, *Inside War: The Guerrilla Conflict in Missouri During the American Civil War*, New York, 1989.

Gallagher, Gary W., *The Confederate War*, Cambridge, Massachusetts, 1997.

Glatthaar, Joseph T., *Forged in Battle: The Civil War Alliance of Black Soldiers and White Officers*, New York, 1990.

Glatthaar, Joseph T., 'Lord High Admiral of the US Navy,' *Military History Quarterly*, vol. 6, no. 4 (summer 1994), pp. 6–26.

Glatthaar, Joseph T., *The March to the Sea and Beyond: Sherman's Troops in the Savannah and Carolinas Campaigns*, New York, 1985.

Glatthaar, Joseph T., *Partners in Command: Relationships Between Leaders in the Civil War*, New York, 1994.

Hattaway, Herman, and Jones, Archer, *How the North Won: A Military History of the Civil War*, Urbana, Illinois, 1983.

Lamers, William M., *The Edge of Glory: A Biography of General William S. Rosecrans, USA*, Baton Rouge, Louisiana, 1999.

McMurry, Richard M., *Atlanta 1864: Last Chance for the Confederacy*, Lincoln, Nebraska, 2000.

McPherson, James M., *Battlecry of Freedom: The Civil War Era*, New York, 1988.

Marszalek, John F., *Sherman: A Soldier's Passion for Order*, New York, 1993.

Marvel, William, *Andersonville: The Last Depot*, Chapel Hill, North Carolina, 1994.

Roland, Charles P., *The American Iliad: The Story of the Civil War*, Lexington, Kentucky, 1991.

Simpson, Brooks D., *Ulysses S. Grant: Triumph Over Adversity, 1822–1865*, Boston, Massachusetts, 2000.

Sword, Wiley, *Embrace an Angry Wind: The Confederacy's Last Hurrah: Spring Hill, Franklin and Nashville*, New York, 1992.

Symonds, Craig L., *Joseph E. Johnston: A Civil War Biography*, New York, 1992.

Symonds, Craig L., *Stonewall of the West: Patrick Cleburne and the Civil War*, Lawrence, Kansas, 1997.

Wiley, Bell I., *The Life of Billy Yank: The Common Soldier of the Union*, Indianapolis, Indiana, 1952.

Wiley, Bell I., *The Life of Johnny Reb: The Common Soldier of the Confederacy*, Indianapolis, Indiana, 1943.

Woodworth, Steven E., *Jefferson Davis and His Generals: The Failure of Confederate High Command*, Lawrence, Kansas, 1990.

# Index